First World War
and Army of Occupation
War Diary
France, Belgium and Germany

19 DIVISION
58 Infantry Brigade
Royal Welsh Fusiliers
9th Battalion
18 July 1915 - 31 March 1919

WO95/2092/1

The Naval & Military Press Ltd
www.nmarchive.com
Published in association with The National Archives

Published by

The Naval & Military Press Ltd

Unit 10 Ridgewood Industrial Park,

Uckfield, East Sussex,

TN22 5QE England

Tel: +44 (0) 1825 749494

www.naval-military-press.com

www.nmarchive.com

This diary has been reprinted in facsimile from the original. Any imperfections are inevitably reproduced and the quality may fall short of modern type and cartographic standards.

© Crown Copyright
Images reproduced by permission of The National Archives, London, England, 2015.

Contents

Document type	Place/Title	Date From	Date To
Miscellaneous	This item has been conserved as part of the WO95 Digitisation Project Please Keep this sheet at the front of the box		
Heading	2092/1 9th Bn Royal Welsh Fusiliers		
Heading	18th Division 58th Infy Bde 9th Bn Roy. Welsh Fus. Jly 1915-Mar 1919		
Heading	War Diary 9th Battn. The Royal Welch Fusiliers. July (18.7.15-31.7.15) 1915 to May 19		
War Diary	Judgeshall	18/07/1915	19/07/1915
War Diary	Enroute	20/07/1915	20/07/1915
War Diary	Near Audruick	21/07/1915	23/07/1915
War Diary	Arques	24/07/1915	24/07/1915
War Diary	Cottes St Hilaire	25/07/1915	31/07/1915
Heading	58th Inf. Bde. 19th Div War Diary 9th Battn. The Royal Welch Fusiliers. August 1915		
War Diary	Havers Kerke	01/08/1915	05/08/1915
War Diary	Regnier Le Clerc	06/08/1915	20/08/1915
War Diary	Vieille Chapelle	21/08/1915	21/08/1915
War Diary	Company in Trenches E of Riche-Bourg	22/08/1915	23/08/1915
War Diary	St Vast	23/08/1915	26/08/1915
War Diary	Regnier Leclerc	27/08/1915	31/08/1915
Heading	58th Inf. Bde. 19th Div. War Diary 9th Battn. The Royal Welch Fusiliers. September 1915		
War Diary	Trenches Ind I (R) Near Festubert	01/09/1915	09/09/1915
War Diary	Ind I (f) Near Festubert In Brigade Reserve at Estaminet Corner	10/09/1915	19/09/1915
War Diary	Ind I (R)	20/09/1915	30/09/1915
Miscellaneous	Appendix I		
Map	Intermediate Line		
Heading	58th Inf. Bde. 19th Div. War Diary 9th Battn. The Royal Welch Fusiliers. October 1915		
War Diary	Cambrin	01/10/1915	03/10/1915
War Diary	Le Preol	04/10/1915	06/10/1915
War Diary	Pa Radis	07/10/1915	13/10/1915
War Diary	Vieille Chapelle	14/10/1915	17/10/1915
War Diary	Paradis	18/10/1915	19/10/1915
War Diary	Le Casen	20/10/1915	31/10/1915
Heading	58th Inf. Bde. 19th Div. War Diary 9th Battn. The Royal Welch Fusiliers November 1915		
War Diary	Rue Depi-Nette Near Festubert	31/10/1915	07/11/1915
War Diary	Rue D'Epinette near Festubert and Trenches Ind. II Subsection (a)	07/11/1915	07/11/1915
War Diary	Trenches Ind II Subsection (a) E of Festubert	02/11/1915	08/11/1915
War Diary	Trenches Ind II Sub Sect (a)	09/11/1915	09/11/1915
War Diary	Ind II Sub Sec (a)	10/11/1915	11/11/1915
War Diary	Brigade Reserve From Ind II Sub-sec (a)	12/11/1915	12/11/1915
War Diary	Rue De L'Epinette in Brigade Reserve	13/11/1915	13/11/1915
War Diary	Litts	13/11/1915	13/11/1915
War Diary	Brigade Reserve at Rue De L'Epinette	14/11/1915	16/11/1915
War Diary	Les Choquaux Near Locon	17/11/1915	23/11/1915

War Diary	Corbie	24/11/1915	30/11/1915
Miscellaneous	Appendix II		
Map	Sketch of Ind II Sub Sec (a)		
Heading	58th Inf. Bde. 19th Div. War Diary 9th Battn. The Royal Welch Fusiliers. December 1915		
War Diary	Corbie	01/12/1915	03/12/1915
War Diary	Trenches Right Sub Sect S. Division between Festubert & Richeburg	03/12/1915	03/12/1915
War Diary	Trenches Right Sub Sect S Divn	03/12/1915	07/12/1915
War Diary	Brigade Reserve Rue Des Chavattes	08/12/1915	10/12/1915
War Diary	La Crea Marmuse Eprinette	11/12/1915	18/12/1915
War Diary	Of Left Sub Sect S Divn	19/12/1915	19/12/1915
War Diary	Trenches Left Sub Sect Cent S Divn	19/12/1915	20/12/1915
War Diary	Trenches Capt Battn Left Sub Sec S Divn	21/12/1915	23/12/1915
War Diary	Croix-Barbee	24/12/1915	26/12/1915
War Diary	Croix-Barbe & Left Sub Sect S Divn	27/12/1915	27/12/1915
War Diary	Left Shbsut S Divn	28/12/1915	31/12/1915
Heading	Appendices III & IV		
Map	Appendix IV		
Heading	9th R.W. Fus. Vol 7 Jan 1916		
War Diary	Croix Barbee	01/01/1916	04/01/1916
War Diary	Croix Marmeuse	05/01/1916	14/01/1916
War Diary	Ricy Bourg L'Avoue	15/01/1916	18/01/1916
War Diary	Ricy Bourg St Vaast	19/01/1916	23/01/1916
War Diary	Lies Laurier Area	24/01/1916	31/01/1916
Miscellaneous	D.A.G. 3rd Echelon	11/03/1916	11/03/1916
War Diary	Les Lauriers Area	01/02/1916	14/02/1916
War Diary	La Gorgue	15/02/1916	16/02/1916
War Diary	Laventie Section	17/02/1916	23/02/1916
War Diary	Merville	24/02/1916	29/02/1916
Miscellaneous	D.A.G. 3rd Echelon	29/04/1916	29/04/1916
War Diary	Richbourg St Vaast	01/03/1916	07/03/1916
War Diary	Croix Marmeuse	08/03/1916	31/03/1916
Miscellaneous	D.A.G. 3rd Echelon Base	03/05/1916	03/05/1916
War Diary		01/04/1916	20/04/1916
War Diary	Robecq	21/04/1916	22/04/1916
War Diary	Serny	23/04/1916	07/05/1916
War Diary	Monton Villers	08/05/1916	28/05/1916
War Diary	Brucamps	29/05/1916	29/05/1916
War Diary	Neuf Moulin	30/05/1916	10/06/1916
War Diary	Bruchamps	11/06/1916	11/06/1916
War Diary	La Chussee	12/06/1916	16/06/1916
War Diary	St Gratien	17/06/1916	27/06/1916
War Diary	Bresle	28/06/1916	30/06/1916
Heading	58th Inf. Bde. 19th Div. War Diary 9th Battn. The Royal Welch Fusiliers. July 1916		
War Diary	Bresle	30/06/1916	31/07/1916
Miscellaneous	Special Order of The Day by Major-General T. Bridges C.M.G., D.S.O. Commanding 19th Division.	04/07/1916	04/07/1916
Miscellaneous	Special Order of The Day by Major-General T. Bridges C.M.G., D.S.O. Commanding 19th Division.	11/07/1916	11/07/1916
Heading	58th Brigade. 19th Division. 1/9th Battalion Royal Welch Fusiliers. August 1916		
War Diary		01/08/1916	31/10/1916
Miscellaneous	App No.		
Miscellaneous	9 RWF Vol 17 Nov 1916		

Type	Description	Start	End
Miscellaneous	On His Majesty's Service.		
War Diary	Aveluy	01/11/1916	25/11/1916
War Diary	Le Meillard	26/11/1916	30/11/1916
Operation(al) Order(s)	58th Brigade Order No. 89 App XXXIa	01/11/1916	01/11/1916
Miscellaneous	Administrative Orders	01/11/1916	01/11/1916
Miscellaneous	Relief Table.		
Miscellaneous	App XXXI	02/11/1916	02/11/1916
Miscellaneous	App XXXIC	03/11/1916	03/11/1916
Miscellaneous	58th Bde App XXXII	03/11/1916	03/11/1916
Miscellaneous	App XXXII		
Miscellaneous	Relief Table		
Operation(al) Order(s)	App XXXIII a 58th Brigade Order No. 90	00/11/1916	00/11/1916
Miscellaneous	Administrative Arrangements for move	04/11/1916	04/11/1916
Miscellaneous	App XXXIIa		
Miscellaneous	App XXXIII6	04/11/1916	04/11/1916
Miscellaneous			
Miscellaneous	Transport Officer	04/11/1916	04/11/1916
Miscellaneous	XXXIIIG		
Miscellaneous	A Form. Messages And Signals.		
Miscellaneous	XXXIIIc		
Miscellaneous	A Form. Messages And Signals.		
Miscellaneous	XXXIIId		
Miscellaneous	Messages And Signals.		
Miscellaneous	XXXIV		
Miscellaneous	All Units.	14/11/1916	14/11/1916
Operation(al) Order(s)	58th Brigade Order No. 94	13/11/1916	13/11/1916
Miscellaneous	A, B, C, D		
Miscellaneous	A Form. Messages And Signals.		
Operation(al) Order(s)	58th Brigade Order No. 98	17/11/1916	17/11/1916
Miscellaneous	Relief Table		
Miscellaneous	War Diary		
Miscellaneous	A Form. Messages And Signals.		
Operation(al) Order(s)	58th Brigade Order No. 96	15/11/1916	15/11/1916
Miscellaneous	WD		
Miscellaneous	A Form. Messages And Signals.		
Miscellaneous	O.C. 9/Cheshire Regt	19/11/1916	19/11/1916
Miscellaneous	To Lt Col Worgan Comm'd 9th Cheshire	19/11/1916	19/11/1916
Miscellaneous	A Form. Messages And Signals.		
Operation(al) Order(s)	58th Brigade Order No. 100	21/09/1916	21/09/1916
Miscellaneous	Relief Table		
Operation(al) Order(s)	58th Brigade Order No. 101	22/11/1916	22/11/1916
Miscellaneous	March Table		
Miscellaneous	A Form. Messages And Signals.		
Miscellaneous	B Form. Messages And Signals.		
War Diary		01/12/1916	31/12/1916
Miscellaneous	Preliminary Instructions for The Offensive		
War Diary		01/06/1917	30/06/1917
Miscellaneous	9th (S) Bn. Royal Welch Fusiliers. Instructions for The Offensive.	04/06/1917	04/06/1917
Miscellaneous	Operation Orders by Lieut-Colonel L.F. Smeathman, M.C. Commanding 9th (S) Bn. Royal Welch Fusiliers.	04/06/1917	04/06/1917
Miscellaneous	Report on Raid	05/06/1917	05/06/1917
Miscellaneous	Awards Granted for The Raid on 5th June 1917		
Miscellaneous	O.C. 9th R.W. Fusiliers.		
Miscellaneous	To all Units.		
War Diary		01/07/1917	01/08/1917

Type	Description	Date From	Date To
Miscellaneous	Operation Orders by Lieut.-Colonel L.F. Smeathman M.C. Commanding 9th (S) Bn. Royal Welch Fusiliers.	29/07/1917	29/07/1917
War Diary		01/08/1917	27/08/1917
War Diary		13/08/1917	31/08/1917
War Diary		25/08/1917	25/08/1917
Miscellaneous	9th (S) Bn. Royal Welch Fusiliers. Instructions for The Offensive		
Miscellaneous	Instructions for The Offensive		
War Diary		01/09/1917	30/09/1917
Miscellaneous			
Miscellaneous	9th (S) Bn. Royal Welch Fusillers Instructions for The Offensive		
Miscellaneous	Appendix I Contact Patrols		
Miscellaneous	9th Royal Welch Fusiliers. Instructions for The Offensive Part I		
Miscellaneous	9th (S) Bn. Royal Welch Fusiliers Instructions for The Offensive Part I Operations.		
Miscellaneous	9th (S) Bn. Royal Welch Fusiliers Instructions for The Offensive Part II Administrative		
Miscellaneous	Instructions for The Offensive-Part II.		
War Diary		01/10/1917	30/11/1917
War Diary	Field	01/12/1917	28/02/1918
Heading	19th Division. 58th Infantry Brigade War Diary 9th Battalion Royal Welch Fusiliers March 1918		
War Diary		01/03/1918	31/03/1918
Miscellaneous	9th (S) Bn Royal Welch Fusiliers	01/04/1918	01/04/1918
Heading	58th Brigade. 19th Division. 1/9th Battalion Royal Welch Fusiliers April 1918		
War Diary		01/04/1918	30/04/1918
Miscellaneous	9th (S) Bn. Royal Welch Fusiliers	19/04/1918	19/04/1918
War Diary	Trenches	01/05/1918	12/05/1918
War Diary	Herzeele	13/05/1918	31/05/1918
Miscellaneous	9th (S) Bn Royal Welch Fusiliers.		
War Diary	Chambrecy	01/06/1918	30/06/1918
War Diary	Haussimont	01/07/1918	03/07/1918
War Diary	Happe	04/07/1918	11/07/1918
War Diary	Ligny Les Aire	12/07/1918	16/07/1918
War Diary	Ligny Les Aire (Sheet 36a)	16/07/1918	31/07/1918
War Diary	Ligny Les Aire	01/08/1918	06/08/1918
War Diary	Chocques	07/08/1918	10/08/1918
War Diary	Hinques	11/08/1918	14/08/1918
War Diary	Trenches	15/08/1918	18/08/1918
War Diary	Chocques	19/08/1918	25/08/1918
War Diary	Trenches	24/08/1918	30/09/1918
War Diary	In The Field	01/10/1918	30/11/1918
Miscellaneous	Short Account of Operation Undertaken by The 9th (S) Bn Royal Welch Fusiliers from Nov: 3rd to Novr: 9th 1918		
War Diary	Canaples	01/12/1918	12/12/1918
War Diary	Berteaucourt	13/12/1918	23/02/1919
War Diary	Villers L'Hopital	24/02/1919	31/03/1919
Map			
Miscellaneous	Map A War Diary		
Map	Trenches Corrected		
Miscellaneous			
Map	Puisieux		

Miscellaneous
Map
Map   Belgium And Part Of France
Map   Edition 2

This item has been conserved as part of the WO95 Digitisation Project

Please keep this sheet at the front of the box

2092/1

9TH Bn

Royal Welsh Fusiliers

58TH INFY BDE

9TH BN ROY. WELSH FUS.
JLY 1915-MAR 1919

58th Inf.Bde.
19th Div.

Battn. disembarked
Boulogne from
England 19.7.15.

```
┌──────────┐
│   WAR    │
│  DIARY   │
└──────────┘
```

9th BATTN. THE ROYAL WELCH FUSILIERS.

J U L Y

(18.7.15 - 31.7.15)

1 9 1 5

9th Royal Welch Fusiliers

WAR DIARY
or
INTELLIGENCE SUMMARY

Army Form C. 2118

Instructions regarding War Diaries and Intelligence Summaries are contained in F.S. Regs., Part II and the Staff Manual respectively. Title Pages will be prepared in manuscript.

(Erase heading not required.)

Place	Date 1915	Hour	Summary of Events and Information	Remarks and references to Appendices
Ludgershall	July 18th	9 a.m.	Major C. Burrard, 2nd in command, Lt. W.G. Thomas M.G. Officer & Lt. Stephens T.O. + R.B. Winan Esqre (Chaplain) left with Transport & machine gun section for HAVRE via SOUTHAMPTON	
	- 19th	3:30 p.m.	The following Officers travelled from LUDGERSHALL to BOULOGNE via FOLKESTONE:— Major H.J. Madocks, acting (Commandant); Captains C.A. Acton, K.J. Nicholl, E.B. Payne, B.W.E. Hoyle, F.M. Jones, L.S. Hogg (Adjutant); Lieutenants M.M. Lewis, M.H. Davies, H.J. Williams, C. Heald, C.F.S. Symons, A.T. Orr, G.H. Charlton, L.G. Meade, 2nd Lt R.J. Williams, C.V. Fawcett, R.H. Higham, C.G.G. Roberts, Y.E. Owen, R.E. Ruck-Keene, H.C. Wancke (Sig.O.) R.N. Thomas, T.W. Karran, Lt + 2nd Master Lowry, Lt A.G. Gilchrist M.O. Both parties had a very good crossing. The party under Major C. Burrard passed the 19th in a camp just outside HAVRE. The above party left HAVRE in the early morning + picked up the remainder of the battalion at a station just outside BOULOGNE. Travelled on to AUDRUICK arriving about 2 a.m. on 21st.	
En route	- 20th			
near AUDRUICK	21st		AT OSTOVE and ZULKERKE. Good billets. Weather — fine + hot.	
"	22nd		Battalion concentration parade 2:30 p.m. Very wet night.	
"	23rd	9:30 a.m.	Marched to ARQUES beyond ST. OMER. A 15 mile march.	
ARQUES	24th	8:30 a.m.	Marched through AIRE to COTTES – ST. HILAIRE. A very interesting village but a few comfortable billets. We discovered our first battalion had been there 10 days before.	
COTTES – ST. HILAIRE	25th		Rested.	
"	26th		8 Sergeants Court-martialed for desertion prior to battalion proceeding on active service. Sentenced to varying terms of imprisonment but sentences suspended during war.	

9th ROYAL WELCH FUSILIERS

WAR DIARY or INTELLIGENCE SUMMARY

Army Form C. 2118

(Erase heading not required.)

Instructions regarding War Diaries and Intelligence Summaries are contained in F. S. Regs., Part II. and the Staff Manual respectively. Title Pages will be prepared in manuscript.

Place	Date 1915	Hour	Summary of Events and Information	Remarks and references to Appendices
COTTES ST. HILAIRE	July 27th		Company parades	
"	28th		Battalion route march	
"	29th		Company parades	
"	30th		Brigade route march	
"	31st		Weather hot. Left at 10.45 a.m. Marched to HAVERSKERQUE via ST. VENANT. Billets very bad, excepting those occupied by C company. Throughout our stay at COTTES - ST. HILAIRE and other subsequent places we received unfailing courtesy from the inhabitants, who also showed no disposition to make money out of us.	

Burnard Major
Comdg 9 R. W. Fus.

58th Inf.Bde.
19th Div.

WAR DIARY

9th BATTN. THE ROYAL WELCH FUSILIERS.

A U G U S T

1 9 1 5

August 1915

9th R.W. Fus.

Army Form C. 2118

WAR DIARY
or
INTELLIGENCE SUMMARY
(Erase heading not required.)

Place	Date 1915	Hour	Summary of Events and Information	Remarks and references to Appendices
HAVERS-KERKE	Aug 1st/2nd/3rd		Company parades	as
"	4th		Route march to meet 1st Battalion R.W. Fusiliers	as
"	5th		Inspection by General WILLCOCKS, Com'dg Indian Corps. At 2.30 p.m. marched to new billets at REGNIER LE CLERC near MERVILLE.	as
REGNIER LECLERC	6th		Company parades	as
"	7th		Brigade route march. Very hot.	as
"	8th-9th		Company parades. Very hot.	as
"	10th		Brigade route march. Very hot.	as
"	11th-12th		Company parades.	as
"	13th		Night march 10.30 p.m. to 2 a.m.	as
"	14th		Company parade	as
"	15th		Church parade.	as

9th R.W. Fus.

August 1915

WAR DIARY or INTELLIGENCE SUMMARY

Army Form C. 2118

Place	Date 1915	Hour	Summary of Events and Information	Remarks and references to Appendices
REGNIER LECLERQ	Aug. 16th		Occupied as a Brigade a line of redoubts in scheme of defence. Marched back & encamped near Guesville. A terrific thunder-storm. Some poplar trees on the canal were struck just before A Company reached them.	es
"	17th		Lecture by Lt. MEADE, R.A.M.C. on methods of defence against Chlorine gas. Scouts disbanded.	es
"	18th		Gas lecture for Senior Officers by gas expert.	es
"	19th		1st LT THOMAS and 3 men wounded by a bomb, whilst undergoing a course of instruction.	es
"	20th		MAJOR MADOCKS appointed to command the battalion. Paraded at 6.30 p.m. & marched to Vieille CHAPELLE. D Company went into trenches with the SUFFOLK & MANCHESTER regiments for instruction.	es

"August 1915"

9th R.W. FUSILIERS

WAR DIARY or INTELLIGENCE SUMMARY
(Erase heading not required.)

Army Form C. 2118

Instructions regarding War Diaries and Intelligence Summaries are contained in F.S. Regs., Part II. and the Staff Manual respectively. Title Pages will be prepared in manuscript.

Place	Date	Hour	Summary of Events and Information	Remarks and references to Appendices
Vieille Chapelle	Aug 21st		Company parades	
1 Company in trenches E of RICHE-BOURG ST.VAST	22nd		Church parade. 2nd Lt. R.N. THOMAS died in hospital at MERVILLE from wounds received in accident with bombs. A Company to trenches in place of D.	
	23rd		Company parades	
	24th		Very hot. 2nd Lt. R.N. THOMAS buried at MERVILLE B Company to trenches in place of A.	
	25th		Company parades	
	26th		Marched at 7.40 a.m. arriving at VIEILLE CHAPELLE at 10.20 a.m. During our stay at REGNIER LECLERQ three companies did an instructional course, each of 2 days, in the trenches; they acquitted themselves very well and there were no casualties.	

WAR DIARY or INTELLIGENCE SUMMARY

9th R.W. FUSILIERS

August 1915

Army Form C. 2118

Place	Date	Hour	Summary of Events and Information	Remarks and references to Appendices
REGNIER LECLERC	Aug 27th & 28th		Company parades	etc.
	29th		Marched to RUE DELANNOY preparatory to taking over a section of the trenches	ditto
	30th		Marched to GORRE at 9.30 a.m. and in the evening took over IND(b). 9th Cheshires were on our right and the 6th Welsh on our left. The 9th Welch in Divisional Reserve.	do
	31st		A quiet day with no unusual occurrence.	do

Burrard Major
Comdg 9 R.W. Fus.

58th Inf.Bde.
19th Div.

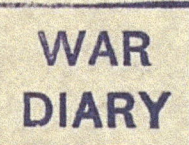

9th BATTN. THE ROYAL WELCH FUSILIERS.

S E P T E M B E R

1 9 1 5

Attached:

Appendix I.

9th R.W. Fus.

WAR DIARY
or
INTELLIGENCE SUMMARY
(Erase heading not required.)

Army Form C. 2118

September 1915

Instructions regarding War Diaries and Intelligence Summaries are contained in F.S. Regs., Part II. and the Staff Manual respectively. Title Pages will be prepared in manuscript.

Place	Date	Hour	Summary of Events and Information	Remarks and references to Appendices
Trenches	Sept 1st		A & B companies in firing line, D in support, C in reserve.	
Ind T (R) near	2nd		Hostile working parties were dispersed by our machine gun fire. A few shells fell near GOLDNEY'S KEEP	
FESTUBERT	3rd		Enemy opened fire on a working party of B company near ROTHESAY BAY. 1 man wounded.	
	4th		Weather very bad.	
	5th		Work was continued on dug outs & communication trenches	
	6th		1 man killed.	
	7th		Enemy working hard at the end of the old German trench running from BARNTON ROAD to their line. 2 wounded.	
	8th		Nothing to record — work continued as before — all ranks working exceptionally well & hard.	
	9th		Desultory sniping & some shell fire. Work continued and good progress made. 1 wounded	

Army Form C. 2118

9th R.W. Fus.

September 1915

WAR DIARY
or
INTELLIGENCE SUMMARY

(Erase heading not required.)

Instructions regarding War Diaries and Intelligence Summaries are contained in F. S. Regs., Part II. and the Staff Manual respectively. Title Pages will be prepared in manuscript.

Place	Date	Hour	Summary of Events and Information	Remarks and references to Appendices
Ind I (b) near #FESTUBERT in Brigade Reserve at ESTAMINET CORNER	10th		Artillery and machine guns active on both sides. Relieved by 9th Cheshires. Relief completed by 10.30 p.m.	c/s
	11th		A hostile aeroplane was brought down on our left.	c/s
	12th		Nothing of interest to record	c/s
	13th to 19th		Employed occasionally in working parties. 1 man wounded.	c/s
Ind I (b)	20th		The 9th R.W. Fus. moved into IND I (b) occupying the trenches from BARNTON ROAD to FIFE ROAD, 9th Welch on our right, the 9th Cheshires & the 6th Wilts being in Brigade Reserve.	c/s
	21st		Our artillery very active	c/s
	22nd		4 wounded. Our artillery bombarding.	c/s

September 1915

WAR DIARY
or
INTELLIGENCE SUMMARY

Army Form C. 2118

9th K.R.W. Fus.

Place	Date	Hour	Summary of Events and Information	Remarks and references to Appendices
Ind T(8)	23rd		1 killed, 2 wounded. Bombardment still continuing.	(3)
	24th		Brigade H.Q. moved to Advanced Report Centre. Very wet & muddy. Our Artillery continued to bombard. We had been in the trenches since Augt. 30th & our total casualties up to the evening of the 24th had been 2 men killed and 11 wounded. On the evening of the 24th Lt Col MADOCKS and his battalion H.Q. Quarters moved up to A company men in the firing-line. He asked me (Major C. BURRARD) to meet him there at 4.15 a.m. the next morning. I retired for the night to a disused dug-out I found in one of the old support trenches. It was then drizzling.	(4)
	25th		I met the C.O. in A company men's at 4.15 a.m. & had some coffee. I then went back to my dug-out. It was drizzling & what breeze there was seemed to be unfavourable for the use of gas; I began to think the attack would be postponed.	(3)

Army Form C. 2118

9th R.W. Fus.

September (Battle of Loos)

WAR DIARY
or
INTELLIGENCE SUMMARY

(Erase heading not required.)

Place	Date	Hour	Summary of Events and Information	Remarks and references to Appendices
Ind I (b.)	Sept 25th (cont.) (2)	5.50 a.m.	Our artillery started a furious bombardment. I hurried down to the firing line & found the smoke candles at work. On my way there, I observed a mile to the south, a thin cloud floating slowly toward the German lines; this I took as asphyxiating gas. The breeze was still very slight but seemed to have veered temporarily in our favour. It was not to be depended on however & too weak & I am of opinion that the pall of smoke in front of our lines did more harm than good as it brought on inactivity on the part of our Artillery. The smoke was intended to supplement the gas & mislead the them into believing that there was an immense amount of that commodity coming towards them. None of our men were injured by our own gas, though I believe a few of the 6th Wilts suffered	

Army Form C. 2118

September (Battle of LOOS) 9ᵗʰ R. W. Fus.

WAR DIARY
or
INTELLIGENCE SUMMARY

(Erase heading not required.)

Instructions regarding War Diaries and Intelligence Summaries are contained in F. S. Regs., Part II. and the Staff Manual respectively. Title Pages will be prepared in manuscript.

Place	Date	Hour	Summary of Events and Information	Remarks and references to Appendices
Ind I(b)	Sept 25th (Cont.) 3	6.30 a.m.	About this time I was informed that a sheaf of rockets had been sent up by the Brigade, intimating the commencement of the attack. I personally did not see it. From subsequent inquiring I learnt the following which bore out to some extent the message sent by the Artillery Observation Officer at 6.25 that the Royal Welch were already attacking. Col. Madocks remained at A company lines till the sheaf of rockets went up, he then told Captain HOYLE, commanding A company to commence the attack (A company was to be directing). Captain HOYLE proceeded to No 10 sap but he had already at 6.15 a.m. had men out in the sap & I think it is probable that his leading platoon was already extended, lying down, in line with the head of the sap, ready to advance	Vide Appendix I

WAR DIARY or INTELLIGENCE SUMMARY

9th R.W. Fus.

September 1915 (Battle of LOOS)

Army Form C. 2118

Place	Date	Hour	Summary of Events and Information	Remarks and references to Appendices
Tr I(A)	Sept 25th (Cont) 4		The order had been issued to be ready to commence the attack at 6.30 a.m. This order might be differently interpreted. It should have been made clear whether troops were to enter the sap or remain behind the parapet till 6.30 a.m. The leading platoon of A company being extended in front of the sap it is possible an advance was made before Capt HOYLE returned from H⁴ Q⁵. As any rate an Officer of B company on the left where company was keeping in touch with A looked at his watch when the advance commenced and it was 6.20 a.m. The pall of smoke was very thick; Capt HOYLE had orders for his directing flank to march on a certain willow tree but this was now hidden from view & it is believed he diverged to the right in front of the 9th Welsh. The Artillery Observation Officer who had wired down that	

Army Form C. 2118

September 1915 (Battle of LOOS)   9 F R. W. Fus.

WAR DIARY
or
INTELLIGENCE SUMMARY.
(Erase heading not required.)

Instructions regarding War Diaries and Intelligence Summaries are contained in F. S. Regs., Part II. and the Staff Manual respectively. Title Pages will be prepared in manuscript.

Place	Date	Hour	Summary of Events and Information	Remarks and references to Appendices
In I (b)	Sept 25th (contd)	5	the attack had commenced, about this time surprised himself by ploring that the 9 R.W. Fus. had taken the first line of trenches. This must have been an effort of the imagination on his part as owing to the smoke, nothing could be seen. messages like this led to evil rumours after the action of spies having tapped the wires. At about 6.50 I met Lt. Col. MADDOCKS & his Adjutant in one of the centre bays. He seemed very optimistic & asked me if D company was out yet; if so, we would follow. The arrangements for attack were as under :- B Coy ——— A Coy ——— D Coy ——— D Coy ——— 50 yds distance between platoons	

Army Form C. 2118

September 1915 (Battle of LOOS)

9th R.W. Fus

WAR DIARY
or
INTELLIGENCE SUMMARY
(Erase heading not required.)

Place	Date	Hour	Summary of Events and Information	Remarks and references to Appendices
Ind I(b)	Sept 25th (contd)		I reported that D company was not yet out. A quarter of an hour later Captain HOGG the Adjutant again went to enquire & in the meantime Col. MADDOCKS who was observing over the parapet was struck by a shot in the temple & fell dead at my feet. It was evident by this time that things were not going well; not much could be seen on account of the smoke but there were rumours of the sepoys being & encumbered with wounded which accounted for the delay with D company. — I had seen Capt ACTON, O.C. D company a few minutes before just outside our wire entanglement & I suggested to Capt HOGG to get into communication with him & obtain his opinion; Capt HOGG had been gone about 10 minutes when I received information that both he & Capt ACTON had been shot. The 6th Wilts were now beginning to arrive; to avoid a useless sacrifice of life I gave orders for a retirement. Col. JEFFREYS, Com of 6th Wilts.	

September 1915 (Battle of LOOS)

9th R.W. Fus.

WAR DIARY
or
INTELLIGENCE SUMMARY

Army Form C. 2118

Place	Date	Hour	Summary of Events and Information	Remarks and references to Appendices
Int(6)	Sept 25th (Cont) 7		who arrived shortly afterwards concurred with me. Our action north of the LA BASSÉE canal was intended as a demonstration. The principle attack being carried out south of the canal; our energetic action was the means of withdrawing several battalions of reserve to our front, which the Germans could otherwise have utilised further south. But would not this advantage have been gained without such loss of life? Undoubtedly both the G.O.C. 58th Brigade & Col. MADOCKS had been misled as to the damage our Artillery had effected on the enemy's wire after several day's bombardment also the effect it had had on the enemy's morale; the effect on the wire was, as a matter of fact, negligible & the crews of not reporting this, of not making a more thorough reconnaissance rests on the companies who were in the front line; it was unduly optimistic to suppose that the enemy's morale had gone, as during a bombardment the	

September 1915 (Battle of LOOS)

9th R.W. Fus.

Army Form C. 2118

WAR DIARY
or
INTELLIGENCE SUMMARY

(Erase heading not required.)

Place	Date	Hour	Summary of Events and Information	Remarks and references to Appendices
Ind I(b)	Sept 25th (Cont.)	8	Germans are adepts at burrowing themselves into specially deep dug-outs on keeping out of the way. It was confidently believed that we should have no difficulty in rushing across the intervening space & capturing the German front & support trenches. — When the time came to to carry this out- we found ourselves up against a row of impenetrable wire and the intervening ground swept by half-a-dozen machine guns. C Company under Capt K. NICHOLL had been detailed to act as a flanking party & moved up FIFE ROAD. They suffered severely from the enemy's artillery which was most accurate. The remainder of the morning was taken up in moving the remnants of the battalion to the Reserve Line. During the hours of darkness many of the wounded were brought in.	

Army Form C. 2118

September 1915 (Battle of LOOS) 9. R. W. Fus.

WAR DIARY
or
INTELLIGENCE SUMMARY
(Erase heading not required.)

Instructions regarding War Diaries and Intelligence Summaries are contained in F.S. Regs., Part II. and the Staff Manual respectively. Title Pages will be prepared in manuscript.

Place	Date	Hour	Summary of Events and Information	Remarks and references to Appendices
Ind I(b)	Sept 25th (cont.)	9	The following is a list of the casualties on Sept 25th :— Killed (Officers) — LT. COL. H. J. MADOCKS, CAPT. C. A. ACTON, CAPT. E. E. PAYNE, CAPT. L. S. HOGG, CAPT. B. W. E. HOYLE, LIEUT. F. J. SYMONS, 2nd LT. R. J. WILLIAMS. Officers wounded — LIEUT. H. J. WILLIAMS, LT. G. H. CHARLTON, 2nd LT. R. H. HIGHAM, 2nd LT. C. FAWCETT Rank + file H.Qrs killed wounded missing A Coy 10 45 28 B " 2 23 44 C " 5 28 3 (believed buried) D " 7 31 7 Total 24 129 85 (Total casualties Officers & men 249) It is believed a few of the missing are prisoners of war. The numbers that went into action were :— 25 Officers, 781 rank + file	My

September 1915
9th R.W. Fus.

Army Form C. 2118

WAR DIARY
or
INTELLIGENCE SUMMARY

Place	Date	Hour	Summary of Events and Information	Remarks and references to Appendices
Ind I (b)	Sept 26th		Weather very bad. During the course of the day we were withdrawn to the intermediate line, a mile back.	MS
	27th & 28th		In great discomfort owing to mud. On a parade I held, I complimented the men on their heroism in recovering the wounded.	MS
	29th		Relieved by 57th Brigade. Moved to LO CON; went into billets.	MS
	30th		Orders were received during the course of the morning to march at 3.30 p.m., and take over trenches near CAMBRIN south of the canal. This was a very trying march as the weather was cold & it started raining before we arrived. There were very long waits owing to the congestion of traffic. We arrived at about 10 p.m. & took over BRADDELL and CAMBRIN POSTS in Brigade Reserve.	MS

Bourard Major
Comdg 9th R.W. Fus.

A P P E N D I X I.

APPENDIX I

(rough sketch to illustrate action of Sept 25th 1915)

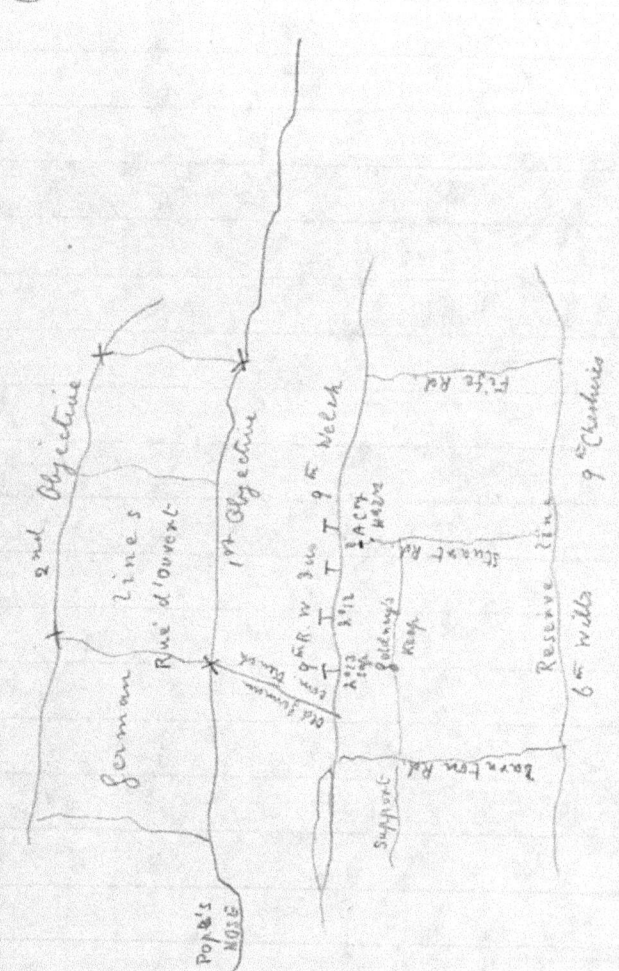

Festubert

Intermediate line

Brassard Major
(Comdg 9th R.W. Fus.)

58th Inf.Bde.
19th Div.

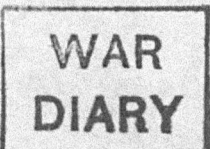

9th BATTN. THE ROYAL WELCH FUSILIERS.

O C T O B E R

1 9 1 5

9th R.W. Fus.

October 1915

WAR DIARY
INTELLIGENCE SUMMARY

Army Form C. 2118

Place	Date	Hour	Summary of Events and Information	Remarks and references to Appendices
CAMBRIN	Oct. 1st		Settled down in billets. Dried clothes. Companies are billeted at BRADDELL & CAMBRIN posts and in the village. — Owing to the rising ground near GIVENCHY this village has partially escaped destruction. — It is an extremely annoying place as our batteries are in the immediate neighbourhood.	as.
"	2nd & 3rd		Working parties were employed in carrying gas cylinders to the front trenches. This was a very tedious job. The roads were bad & the cylinders weigh 150 lbs. A mine was exploded during the night of the 2nd & buried one of our grenadiers & some of the Wilts.	as.
LE PREOL	4th		Relieved by the 2nd Bn R. Scots Fusiliers. Moved into billets at LE PREOL, two miles back. Extremely bad billets.	as.
"	5th & 6th		Company parades.	as.
PARADIS	7th		The Brigade was relieved by the 22nd. We moved into billets at EGLISE & PARADIS.	as.
"	8th		Battalion had the use of the baths.	as.

October 1915

9th R.W. Fus

WAR DIARY
INTELLIGENCE SUMMARY

Army Form C 2118

Place	Date	Hour	Summary of Events and Information	Remarks and references to Appendices
PARADIS	Oct 9th to 11th		Engaged in refitting, washing & getting new clothes. Route-marching, bomb-throwing, physical training etc.	as.
"	12th		The G.O.C. 19th Division (Maj. Gen FASKEN) inspected us and congratulated us on the work done in the action of Sept 25th.	as.
"	13th		Company parades	as.
VIEILLE CHAPELLE	14th		Moved into billets at VIEILLE CHAPELLE in the afternoon in order to furnish working parties to the forward area	as
"	15th to 17th		Furnishing working parties	as.
PARADIS	18th		Were relieved by the 6th Wilts. Moved back to PARADIS & PACAUT.	as.
	19th		Received orders that 19th Divn had been allotted a new front extending from junction of GRENADIER ROAD to PIPE communication trench. 58th Infy Brigade to move into billets at LOCON.	as.
LE CASAN	20th		Moved to billets at LE CASAN, a mile E of LOCON.	as.

October 1915

9th R.W. Fus.

WAR DIARY or INTELLIGENCE SUMMARY

Army Form C 2118

Place	Date	Hour	Summary of Events and Information	Remarks and references to Appendices
LE CASAN	Oct. 21st		A Brigade bombing class was started	Ms.
"	22nd		Company parades.	"
"	23rd		All C.O.'s of 58th Brigade went over the trenches to be taken over.	"
"	24th		We took over Ind. II (a) from the N. Lancashires (Major Montagu-Moore Esq. in command)	"
"	25th		A very quiet day	"
"	26th		Enemy threw rifle grenades into Salient. They also shelled the reserve trenches near the Brewery and Indian Village.	" Vide App. III
"	27th		Enemy's Artillery active. Weather very bad & trenches filling with water. Working parties sent from Reserve batt. to make gas recesses.	"
"	28th		ORCHARD SALIENT again bombarded with rifle grenades & bombs but without causing loss of life. Work on repairs.	"
"	29th		Many dug-outs collapsed owing to wet weather. A good deal of sniping. Our artillery retaliated on the German trench mortars. Some of our shots fell short, narrowly missing some of our Grenadiers in the APEX. On warning being given, the artillery range was rectified.	"
"	30th		Perfect injured by bombs. We replied effectively with rifle grenades & the night before silenced a machine gun.	"
"	31st		Were relieved by 9th Cheshires. Relief completed by 10p.m.	

(N.B. Up to this date The War Diary had not been kept up, back work had to be written up by me.) R.W. Fus.
Bernard Magor, 9 R.W. Fus.
58th Brigade, 19th Div.

1875. Wt. W593/826 1,000,000 4/15 J.B.C. & A. A.D.S.S./Forms/C. 2118.

58th Inf.Bde.
19th Div.

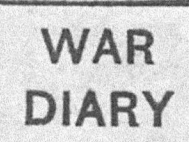

9th BATTN. THE ROYAL WELCH FUSILIERS.

N O V E M B E R

1 9 1 5

Attached:

Appendix II.

November 1915 · 9th R.W. Fusiliers · Volume 5, Page 1

Army Form C. 2118

WAR DIARY or INTELLIGENCE SUMMARY
(Erase heading not required.)

Instructions regarding War Diaries and Intelligence Summaries are contained in F.S. Regs., Part II. and the Staff Manual respectively. Title Pages will be prepared in manuscript.

Place	Date 1915	Hour	Summary of Events and Information	Remarks and references to Appendices
RUE D'EPI-NETTE near FESTUBERT	Oct 31st to Nov 7th		In Brigade Reserve. Head Quarters, C & D companies in billets. A & B companies occupying posts. A company's post — RUE DE CAILLOUX Post. B company's posts — EPINETTE N(H&D₂₀), EPINETTE W, CHAVATTE POST and some smaller ones. Nearly all available men were employed daily + sometimes by night in the trenches, repairing parapets, digging and carrying up materials. A great deal of rain fell during this week — The estimated fall was about 4 in. The trenches towards the end of the week were in a terrible condition — in some places in the communication trenches the water was well above the knee. Our dug-outs were constantly leaking + there was a great want of repairing material. The RUE DE CAILLOUX post were nearly as bad as the trenches. The temperature was also below the normal with a NE'ly breeze. Average number reporting sick per day about 40, of which perhaps 2 would be sent to the Ambulance, 15 excused duties + the remainder given medicine. Only 6 cases of trench foot have up to the end of the period been sent to Hospital.	

November 1915   9th R.W. FUSILIERS   Vol. 5, page 2.

Army Form C. 2118

WAR DIARY
or
INTELLIGENCE SUMMARY
(Erase heading not required.)

Place	Date 1915	Hour	Summary of Events and Information	Remarks and references to Appendices
RUE d'EPI- NETTE near FESTUBERT and Trenches Ind. II subsection	Nov. 7th cont.		Took over Ind. II subsection A from 9th Cheshires. The relief was arranged to take place during the day but owing to disagreements between myself and Lt Col. DAUNTESEY, com. of the 9th Cheshires as to the times and manner of relief, things did not work as smoothly as I might have wished. There had been a thick mist for some mornings back and on the morning of the 7th it appeared as if the same conditions would prevail. C & D Companies were to start at 10 & 10.30 a.m. respectively but owing to orders having been carried late there were some delay. Before D company (which started very late) had reached the fire trenches, the mist had lifted. Two platoons, divided by a wide interval, filed up PIONEER communication trench as this led to the right of the line which D company was in orders to take over. I had not been informed however of the impassable condition of the upper portion of this trench, have it would have been better to send by the more circuitous route by SHETLAND street.	

November 1915 9th R.W. FUSILIERS Vol.5/page 3 Army Form C. 2118

WAR DIARY or INTELLIGENCE SUMMARY

Place	Date 1915	Hour	Summary of Events and Information	Remarks and references to Appendices
RUE D'EPI- NETTE near FESTUBERT and 'trenches Incl. II Sub-sec (a)	Nov 7th continued (2)	Between 2 & 3 p.m. Lieut V.E. OWEN who was at the head of the leading platoon finding they could advance no further and that some of his men were bogged and couldn't move, climbed over the small parapet to see if he could proceed outside the communication trench under cover. Many of the men followed his example but fortunately were not hit. LIEUT OWEN got a bullet wound in his thigh, which broke the bone. This unfortunate incident does not prove that it is wrong to attempt reliefs by day, it was rather the terribly boggy state of the trenches that led to it. Undoubtedly it was an error of judgment going outside because the Officer not only risked his own life but those of his men; at the same time it must be said, that if the relief had been carried out at night, the advance would have been chiefly across the open and might have led to a number of casualties from stray bullets or a haphazard burst of machine gun fire.	A3

November 1915

9th R.W. FUSILIERS
WAR DIARY
or
INTELLIGENCE SUMMARY
(Erase heading not required.)

Vol. 5 / page 4
Army Form C. 2118

Instructions regarding War Diaries and Intelligence Summaries are contained in F.S. Regs., Part II. and the Staff Manual respectively. Title Pages will be prepared in manuscript.

Place	Date 1915	Hour	Summary of Events and Information	Remarks and references to Appendices
Trenches 2nd W. Subsection E of FESTUBERT	Nov 1st Oct (3)		Relief was completed by 6 p.m. A man was blown to pieces by a shell from a Minenwerfer shortly after arrival in trenches. Casualties for the day 1 Officer wounded, 1 man killed	A3
	Nov 2nd		A company occupies centre of line i.e. right of ORCHARD SUPPORT and salient, B company left of line and D company the right as far as BOMB LANE. — Between 11 a.m. & 2 p.m. the extreme left of our line was treated as our heavy batteries were bombarding the German "Cupola" over our heads. General FASKEN passed through about 11 a.m. & informed me it was past our battalion head Quarters to hold the front line very additional his intention during the winter months to accommodated in our Reserve line if the dug-outs were improved. Trinity. — I reported to Brigade Hd Quarters that any men could be accommodated in our Reserve line if the dug-outs were improved. Also a water pipe has been laid one as far as the RICHMOND Tribunal. This was available for use today.	A4

1875 Wt. W593/826 1,000,000 4/15 J.B.C. & A. A.D.S.S./Forms/C. 2118.

November 1915   Vol 5/page 5

Army Form C. 2118

WAR DIARY
or
INTELLIGENCE SUMMARY
(Erase heading not required.)

Instructions regarding War Diaries and Intelligence Summaries are contained in F. S. Regs., Part II. and the Staff Manual respectively. Title Pages will be prepared in manuscript.

Place	Date 1915	Hour	Summary of Events and Information	Remarks and references to Appendices
Trenches Ind. II. sub-sec.(a)	Nov. 9th		During the morning a great improvement in the trenches was noticeable but about 4 with a freshening southerly wind and an overcast sky, little doubt was left that we were in for a dirty night. It poured steadily the whole evening making everyone most uncomfortable. If the rain had only held off 3 days we should have gone a long way to carrying out a scheme which has been maturing at Corps H.Q. — to hold the front line by a series of posts & to withdraw the bulk of the troops to the reserve. In this however a large number of dug-outs would be required in the Reserve line & the difficulty is the want of the right transport to the railhead material, also when material is forthcoming to Company Commanders to exercise careful Orders have been issued supervision to prevent the men opening what is known as "trench feet". In this purpose whale oil is issued. The feet are well massaged when applying this oil.	

9ᵗʰ R.W. FUS.

Vol. 5/page 6

Army Form C. 2118

November 1915

WAR DIARY
or
INTELLIGENCE SUMMARY
(Erase heading not required.)

Place	Date	Hour	Summary of Events and Information	Remarks and references to Appendices
Ind. II. sub.sect. (a)	Nov. 10ᵗʰ (1)		Fine after a wet night. Rain ceased early. General Stuart, commanding the 50ᵗʰ Brigade inspected the trenches. Enemy was very active with whizz-bangs & trench mortars; a good deal of damage was done ✗ in BOMB LANE, the right of our line. The trenches were in a horrible condition, in many places knee-deep in water; in one part of COLMAN STREET the water was up to the hips. The worst parts of the trenches however in wet weather are not those under water, but those where the water has oozed off and the mud remaining is of the consistency of glue mixed with porridge. Napoleon I. when he invaded Poland is supposed to have said, he had discovered a fourth element viz: mud; a similar remark might	1/15

November 1915

G.R.W. Ins.

Vol. 5, page 7
Army Form C. 2118

WAR DIARY
or
INTELLIGENCE SUMMARY
(Erase heading not required.)

Place	Date	Hour	Summary of Events and Information	Remarks and references to Appendices
2nd II. Sub Sec. (a) (b)	Nov 10th		be made by anyone visiting the trenches in this part of the world today. — In this kind of mud, it is not rare to have to be dug-out, eventually leaving one's waders behind and in any case progression of any sort is slow and most tedious. On the tour of inspection many rifles were noticed in a dirty and rather rusty condition and Company Commanders had to be reminded, that making all allowances for the dreadful conditions in which they were living, the cleaning of rifles, as well as the condition of the men's feet, required constant supervision. Work was carried on chiefly on the Reserve Line; it was difficult however to make much progress on account of the floods	

November 1915 9 F.R.M. Jun. Vol. 5 / page 8

Army Form C. 2118

WAR DIARY
or
INTELLIGENCE SUMMARY
(Erase heading not required.)

Instructions regarding War Diaries and Intelligence Summaries are contained in F.S. Regs., Part II. and the Staff Manual respectively. Title Pages will be prepared in manuscript.

Place	Date	Hour	Summary of Events and Information	Remarks and references to Appendices
Trel D. Sub. sect. (u)	Nov. 10th (13)		and the want of material. There has hitherto been a want of system in the supply of Engineer stores; in time, if Commanding Officers, taking over the trenches, work on a uniform plan, this may be overcome. The first thing to establish is an Infantry store-room with a surplus stock of such things as sand-bags, beams, corrugated sheets already for an emergency, and the next a permanent uniform supply of these articles based on probable requirements. Hitherto, when anything has been required of this nature, the R.E. Storekeeper has been consulted and his invariable reply is that nothing can be issued without the signature of an R.E. Officer; the R.E. Officer has been searched, but being in the front trenches, has	

1875 Wt. W593/826 1,000,000 4/15 J.B.C. & A. A.D.S.S./Forms/C.2118.

November 1915
9 "R.W. Fus.
Vol. 5/page 9
Army Form C. 2118

WAR DIARY
or
INTELLIGENCE SUMMARY
(Erase heading not required.)

Place	Date	Hour	Summary of Events and Information	Remarks and references to Appendices
Ind. II. Pol.Sec.(a)	Nov. 10		not been easily found. When at last discovered, after much talking, he sends out an indent for a totally inadequate supply because he has none in stock. Then nothing can be done till next day. The Quartermaster at the Depôt has to be asked to send a limber to the R.E. Depôt to draw the stores & convey them to the railhead. The train cannot be worked by day, so the material is not brought up till night. - In this way two days are lost. This might be termed "want of organisation". Our German critic says "organisation is hardly more than industry and faithfulness to duty; as the English are deficient in organising power, they have ceased to consider the legal fulfilment of duty to be a necessity." There is much in this definition of "organisation" but I think our defects arise chiefly from an archaic & hide-bound system generally depicted by the word "red-tape".	

Army Form C. 2118

9th R.W. Inx.   Vol. 5/ page 10

WAR DIARY
or
INTELLIGENCE SUMMARY
(Erase heading not required.)

Instructions regarding War Diaries and Intelligence Summaries are contained in F. S. Regs., Part II. and the Staff Manual respectively. Title Pages will be prepared in manuscript.

Place	Date	Hour	Summary of Events and Information	Remarks and references to Appendices
2nd I. Sub. Sec. (a)	Nov. 10th (5)		There has been a noticeable increase of German artillery fire since the battle of Sept 25th. Some of this fire is singularly ineffective. For instance, their favourite targets are INDIAN VILLAGE and the BREWERY behind our Reserve line where they suspect & quite rightly artillery observation posts, but they seldom do any damage & have not yet after many weeks obliged the posts to remove elsewhere. On the other hand their accuracy in searching out our communicating trenches on the morning of Sept 25th was extraordinary. Everything tends to show that our SHETLAND ROAD which we now use so constantly is well marked on their maps and it is receiving, we notice, ever increasing attention. There must only be casualty observing procedure. (1 man wounded.)	vide Appendix II

November 1915

9ᵗʰ R.W. FUSILIERS

Vol. 5 page 11

Army Form C. 2118

WAR DIARY
or
INTELLIGENCE SUMMARY
(Erase heading not required.)

Instructions regarding War Diaries and Intelligence Summaries are contained in F.S. Regs., Part II. and the Staff Manual respectively. Title Pages will be prepared in manuscript.

Place	Date	Hour	Summary of Events and Information	Remarks and references to Appendices
Ind. II sub.sec.(a).	Nov. 11ᵗʰ (1)		Weather fine morning & afternoon, then steady rain with strong south-westerly wind. Issued orders for relief by 9ᵗʰ Cheshires today (Nov. 12ᵗʰ). A memo was lately circulated by the G.O.C., that orders for the relief of battalions in the trenches were to be always formulated by the O.C. outgoing battalion. I arranged in my orders that the posts CHILLOUX and EPINETTE (with its outlying ones) should be relieved by day; two whole companies were to be relieved by driblets leaving the remaining two till after dark. But when this the O.C. 9ᵗʰ Cheshires thought too much; he pointed out that the Brigade orders said that no movement was to be made E. of the RUE DE L'EPINETTE till 5 p.m. and that as to the relief of the posts, though this was sanctioned by day, only the skeleton garrisons were meant, not whole companies. — It is a great pity these reliefs cannot be carried out in the early morning; it is doubtful too if the risks are greater when carried out in the day-light, judiciously, in small bodies, than when there by night; when the tendency is to move across the open; exposed to stray shot or hap-hazard	As

9th R.W. FUS.

November 1915

Vol. 5, page 12

Army Form C. 2118

WAR DIARY
or
INTELLIGENCE SUMMARY

(Erase heading not required.)

Place	Date	Hour	Summary of Events and Information	Remarks and references to Appendices
2nd D. Sub. Sec. (a)	Nov. 11th (B)		bursts of machine gun fire. The last time we came in, we relieved the 9th Cheshires by day; there was only one casualty and that was due to carelessness. — But if there is more risk relieving by day, there is another question viz. the health of the men, which should be taken into account when the trenches are — in their present horrible state. If the men could be put into their new huts or billets fairly early, there would be a chance of drying their clothes before they turned in for the night. And there would be far less standing about, confusion & consequent loss of kit. As today (Nov. 13th) has turned out a drenching, wet day, with no clear view, it is little less than criminal that the relief is not in full swing at this moment (10 a.m.). Casualties on the 11th — nil but the number of trench feet are on the increase. 8 cases were reported today.	a3

November 1915

9th R.W. Fus.

Vol. 5 page 13

WAR DIARY
or
INTELLIGENCE SUMMARY

Army Form C. 2118

Place	Date	Hour	Summary of Events and Information	Remarks and references to Appendices
Brigade Reserve "from II" sub-sec.(a)	Nov. 12th		Reliefs carried out under great difficulties. Two companies did not reach the RUE DE L'EPINETTE where our forward billets are till past midnight. Men extremely tired & wet — with no change of clothing. Enemy shelled a platoon of B Company moving by a gateway to the RUE DE L'EPINETTE between 3 & 4 p.m. There were no casualties. There was one casualty in D Company	

9th R.W. Fus.

November 1915

Vol. 5 page 14 Army Form C. 2118

WAR DIARY
or
INTELLIGENCE SUMMARY
(Erase heading not required.)

Instructions regarding War Diaries and Intelligence Summaries are contained in F. S. Regs., Part II. and the Staff Manual respectively. Title Pages will be prepared in manuscript.

Place	Date	Hour	Summary of Events and Information	Remarks and references to Appendices
RUE DE L'ÉPINETTE in Brigade Reserve	Nov 13th		N.W. gale with rain. Enemy fires salvo. Working parties supplied to the trenches. The most we can supply is about 210 men a day. We are very low in strength and there are a large number of sick. The men are sticking it remarkably well. — Some of them were up to their hips in water last night on their way to work. On return most of them have dry socks & drawers to change into, but not all; but none of them have day to a change of boots or trousers. The Quartermaster is buying up with the rations tonight 100 prs. of trousers — This will do something towards their comfort. It seems advisable that Quartermasters should make it their business to accumulate Service socks and boots for occasions like the present and then store them when no longer required. The soldier is not really allowed by the F.S. Regulations a second pr. of trousers or boots. — When working parties return	no

WAR DIARY or INTELLIGENCE SUMMARY

November 1915

9 R.W. Fus.

Vol. 5 pay 15 Army Form C. 2118

Place	Date	Hour	Summary of Events and Information	Remarks and references to Appendices
Lille	Nov 15th cont. (2)		at night, they are provided with tea at the Brigade Club, but my men generally prefer tea. The Club is located in a mined house in the RUE DE L'EPINETTE and consists of a bar where refreshments are served (non-alcoholic) and a reading & writing room. A Brigade hospital has also been lately established in the same road. This is for men suffering from minor ailments, not bad enough to send to the Ambulance. Both these houses are unfortunately liable to be hit by a shell any day; not many houses have been hit, recently in this area for some time, but of late the enemy's artillery has been increasingly active. Strength of the battalion this date — 26 Officers, 745 R.& F. & more i.e. about 250 rank & file short Of these about 53 are in hospital & 43 suffering from minor ailments (including jaws abcessed)	Cas.

9th R.W.Fus
November 1915   Vol. 5 page 16

WAR DIARY or INTELLIGENCE SUMMARY

Place	Date	Hour	Summary of Events and Information	Remarks and references to Appendices
Brigade Reserve at RUE DE L'EPINETTE	Nov. 14th		Nothing of importance to report. One of our men was wounded in the evening when on a working-party. — Weather fine & cold. A certain number of men went to Brigade Head Quarters to have baths; there is a barn fitted out for this. The F.O.O. is very insistent that only a few men at a time should approach Brigade Head Quarters, so as not to draw the enemy's artillery fire. The enemy have a captive balloon, some miles behind their trenches, from which they observe very accurately movements of troops. Men going to these baths, or to any baths under divisional or brigade arrangements, can have a change of underclothing in exchange for their own; unfortunately it is often a bad exchange; some of the underclothing we got yesterday was damp & decidedly "lousy".	Nil

November 1915.

9th R.W.Fus.

Vol. 5 page 17

Army Form C. 2118

WAR DIARY or INTELLIGENCE SUMMARY

(Erase heading not required.)

Instructions regarding War Diaries and Intelligence Summaries are contained in F. S. Regs., Part II. and the Staff Manual respectively. Title Pages will be prepared in manuscript.

Place	Date	Hour	Summary of Events and Information	Remarks and references to Appendices
Brigade Reserve at RUE DE L'EPINETTE	Nov. 15th		We provided working parties morning & evening as usual for the trenches. Capt. Miller reported this morning that one of our parties had a narrow escape last night; they were working on the new supports in the Cheshire lines (right section) lately vacated by our D company. Some of the above regiment heard us and sent a couple of very lights in our direction, shouting out "Who are you?" They might have known it was a friendly working party, as one goes up every night. However three minutes after a machine gun was turned on to our party and three bombs from a minenwerfer fell in our direction; by a miracle there were no casualties. Received orders that we would be relieved by the 8th N. Stafford on the 17th & proceed to the neighbourhood of LOCON.	As.

9th R. W. Fus.

November

Vol. 5 pages Army Form C. 2118

WAR DIARY
or
INTELLIGENCE SUMMARY
(Erase heading not required.)

Instructions regarding War Diaries and Intelligence Summaries are contained in F. S. Regs., Part II. and the Staff Manual respectively. Title Pages will be prepared in manuscript.

Place	Date	Hour	Summary of Events and Information	Remarks and references to Appendices
Brigade Reserve at RUE DE L'EPINETTE	Nov. 16th		Supplied working parties morning & evening.	
LES CHOQUAUX near LOCON	17th		Relieved by 8th North Staffords. Relief completed by 4.30 p.m. Reached new billets at 6 p.m. Squally & rainy, at one time hail & snow, wind N.W., cold.	
	18th		Company parades. Drizzling rain. Cold. I sent during night. I saw some of the men on parade. They were still plastered with mud. I bought 16 clothes brushes, one for each platoon. A great deal of brushing will be required before their clothes are fit to be seen. My aim is to have two suits per man; one for dirty work, such as in the trenches, the other for walking out when they are resting. Close order drill, guards & inspections. I have given orders that no old suits are to be thrown away.	

9 R.W. Fus.

WAR DIARY
or
INTELLIGENCE SUMMARY
(Erase heading not required.)

Army Form C. 2118

Vol. 3 page 19

November 1915

Instructions regarding War Diaries and Intelligence Summaries are contained in F. S. Regs., Part II. and the Staff Manual respectively. Title Pages will be prepared in manuscript.

Place	Date	Hour	Summary of Events and Information	Remarks and references to Appendices
LES CHO- -QUAUX near LOCON	Nov. 19th		N.E'ly breeze. Temperature varying between 37° & 30°. We were informed that a move would shortly be made to billets further back for a month's "rest". A programme of work to be carried out was also issued — "winter training." It has been suggested it might be called, a preparation for a future offensive. A very well worded memorandum was circulated by the C.in C. to Commanding Officers, asking them to devote special attention to discipline & training personally, + the inculcation of an offensive spirit in their men. The following is a summary of our late experiences in the trenches: — The battalion was 23 days in the trenches. Our total casualties were 2 men killed, 1 Officer (2nd LT. V.E. OWEN) & 13 men wounded. We were extraordinarily lucky in losing so few; the men had a very trying time, as the trenches were in a horrible condition, but they stuck it manfully. There were several cases of "trench foot", but only a dozen of these were bad enough to send to the Ambulance. In regard to "trench foot" we had the fewest cases in the Brigade, the two Welsh battalions had far fewer cases than the two English battalions. — In all we sent about 50 men to hospital (viz from all causes, excepting wounds)	as

- J.B.C. & A. A.D.S.S./Forms/C. 2118.

November 1915

J.R.W. Ins

WAR DIARY
or
INTELLIGENCE SUMMARY

Army Form C. 2118

Vol. 5 page 20

(Erase heading not required.)

Instructions regarding War Diaries and Intelligence Summaries are contained in F. S. Regs., Part II. and the Staff Manual respectively. Title Pages will be prepared in manuscript.

Place	Date	Hour	Summary of Events and Information	Remarks and references to Appendices
LES CHOQUAUX near LOCON	Nov. 20th		Cold. Company parades. Number of braziers quite insufficient for men's comfort. S.S.O. reduced our ration of coal as he found we had been giving us too much. The method of weighing out the coal is most unsatisfactory & I reported the matter to the General. As regards supplies, we are entirely in the hands of the A.S.C.; if they are done & draw too little coal from the pit-head, they make us suffer. The parade state today shows our strength as 25 Officers — 684 rank&file (including attached). Men who have been admitted to the Field Ambulance & remained there 5 days have been struck off the strength. Temperature between 30° & 37°.	Aps.
"	21st		Church parades. Working party to SHETLAND RD.	A3.
"	22nd		Company parades	A3
"	23rd		Marched to new billets in neighbourhood of LE CORBIE between HAVERSKERQUE & MERVILLE. A trying march of 10 miles. Arrived at 7.45 p.m.	A3

November 1915

9th R.W. Fus.

Vol. 5 page 21   Army Form C. 2118

WAR DIARY
or
INTELLIGENCE SUMMARY
(Erase heading not required.)

Place	Date	Hour	Summary of Events and Information	Remarks and references to Appendices
CORBIE	Nov. 24th		Comfortable billets. Shortage of fuel, but weather mercifully mild with rain. A very serious bomb accident took place on the 23rd inst. during the Brigade course of instruction. 2 men are said to have been killed & 9 wounded (including 1 Officer). Of our men 1 was killed & 2 were wounded. One was also wounded the day before (22nd inst.)	us.
"	25th to 27th		Company parades. Weather cold. A good deal of rain & some snow.	as.
"	28th		Hard frost. Divine service. Men utilised baths at Merville.	as.
"	29th		17 motor buses arrived at 11 a.m. to take 300 of our men to the neighbourhood of LAVENTIE to work on drainage system. Milder with rain & southerly breeze.	as.
"	30th		Rain. Men working on drainage system.	as.

C. Burrard Major
Comdg 9/R.W. Fus.

A P P E N D I X   II.

APPENDIX (II)

SKETCH OF IND II Sub-sec. (a) at beginning of November 1915

GERMAN LINE

APEX

SALIENT

CANADIAN ORCHARD

ORCHARD SUPPORT

Support

NEW SUPPORT

BOMB LANE

COLEMAN STREET

SHETLAND TRENCH (in ROAD)

RICHMOND SUPPORT TRENCH (incomplete)

ROYLE ROAD

PIONEER ROAD

OLD GERMAN LINE (reversed) (not in use)

RESERVE TRENCH (OLD BRITISH LINE)

TUBE STATION

INDIAN VILLAGE

tram line

BREWERY

Rue de Cailloux

Scale of Yards 0 100 200 300 400 500

C. Burrard Major
Comdg 1/4th R.W. Fus.

58th Inf.Bde.
19th Div.

WAR
DIARY

9th BATTN. THE ROYAL WELCH FUSILIERS.

DECEMBER

1915

Attached:

Appendices III & IV.

December 1915

9th R.W.Fus.

WAR DIARY or INTELLIGENCE SUMMARY

Army Form C. 2118
Vol 6, page 1.

Place	Date	Hour	Summary of Events and Information	Remarks and references to Appendices
Corbie	Dec. 1st		Men returned to billets. They did good work at LAVENTIE on the drainage system, but as usual there was want of organisation on the part of the Engineers which led to loss of time.	Cos.
"	2nd		Company parades morning. Lecture & demonstration by O.C. Grenadier Platoon.	Cos.
"	3rd		At 1 a.m. we received orders to march at 9 a.m. & take over a section of trenches during the evening. This knocks on the head battalion, brigade & Divl. training. We marched at 9.30 a.m., as the transport was not ready & followed the route ST. VENANT, ROBECQ, LES CHOQAUX, LE TOURET arriving at RUE DE CHAVATTE near the RUE DU BOIS at 3 p.m., a march of about 16 miles.	Cos.

9 R.W.Jus.

December, 1915.   Vol. 6, page 2.

Army Form C. 2118

WAR DIARY
or
INTELLIGENCE SUMMARY
(Erase heading not required.)

Instructions regarding War Diaries and Intelligence Summaries are contained in F. S. Regs., Part II. and the Staff Manual respectively. Title Pages will be prepared in manuscript.

Place	Date	Hour	Summary of Events and Information	Remarks and references to Appendices
Trenches Right sub-sect S. Division (between Festubert & Richebourg l'Avoué)	Dec. 3rd (2)		Here there was an hours halt to allow the men to have their dinners. C company's cooker was under repairs & the dinners of this company should have been brought in a G.S. wagon but it had lagged behind. They did not get anything to eat till 11 p.m. We took over the section held by the 1st Leicesters & part of that held by the 5th. The guides provided by these two battalions were of no use & led the two companies in the firing line viz A & C hopelessly astray. A company had not taken up its position on the left till midnight, C company on the right with its right flank resting on QUINQUE ROE did not extend sufficiently to the	

9th R.W. Jus
WAR DIARY
or
INTELLIGENCE SUMMARY

Army Form C. 2118
Vol. 6, page 3

December 1915

Place	Date	Hour	Summary of Events and Information	Remarks and references to Appendices

Trenches
Richebourg St
S. Dir

Dec. 3rd (3) — left, in consequence one company of the 4th Leicesters remained unrelieved. This company was relieved next morning at 7.15 a.m. but the Officer in command was of opinion, that it was already too light to take his company back overland, the trenches being in places quite impassable; he therefore deferred his departure till dusk. — Owing to A company going astray, they got no rations. At 9 a.m. on the 4th, I got a letter from A company by an orderly saying they were standing in water, without proper dug-outs & without food. L⁴ ORR & WANKE volunteered to take up food to them with 12 men of D company. These arrived in A company's front-line at about noon; they were discovered & shelled on their way up.

4th

WAR DIARY

9th R.W. Fus.

Vol. 6, page 4

December 1915

Place	Date	Hour	Summary of Events and Information	Remarks and references to Appendices
Festubert S. Sect	4th		but suffered no casualties. The night previous, during the relief, there had been two; of these Sergt Daniels was shot through the lung & Pte Rumpley hit in the back with shrapnel. The conditions of both are rather serious. Whilst this food was being distributed to A company, Pte Parry was struck behind the ear & fell groaning into the water. He died in the advanced dressing station the same night. A & C occupying the firing line, a length of about 1000 yds. with 3 machine guns. B & D occupy the Reserve trench. B on the left; this trench is a continuation of the O.B.L. Battalion H.Q. D.H. is ½ a mile N of TUBE STATION on the RUE DU BOIS. In addition to other casualties during the day, one grenadier was wounded.	

WAR DIARY or INTELLIGENCE SUMMARY

9th R.W. Fus.
December 1915
Vol. 6 page 5
Army Form C. 2118

Place	Date	Hour	Summary of Events and Information	Remarks and references to Appendices
Trenches	5th		The weather has been again bad & the trenches are full of water.	AB.
Right Sub-sect S. Div?			We have two companies in the firing-line and two in reserve. The right company in the firing-line holds from FERME COUR QUINQUE RUE to a point directly opposite FERME COUR D'AVOUÉ, the left company from here to FARM CORNER. We have the 9 Welch on our left. The length of front is about 1000 yards; as we have only 200 men in the firing line, it is only possible to hold it with groups at 50 yds. interval. — The left company in Reserve hold also the following posts behind the line — Z ORCHARD, CHOCOLATE POST, DITCH POST, DEAD COW POST, HAYSTACK. I accompanied the Brigade Major to the firing-line during the evening. The communication trenches are of no good.	Vide App. III.

WAR DIARY
or
INTELLIGENCE SUMMARY

(Erase heading not required.)

December 1915

Vol. 6, page 6

Place	Date	Hour	Summary of Events and Information	Remarks and references to Appendices
Trenches	5th (2)		in places they are breast-high in water. We started from where FRY TRENCH meets the Reserve Line, moved diagonally along a path towards CADBURY TRENCH and then kept this trench till we struck the firing line. B company had 2 platoons on either side of CADBURY. Owing to the crumbling of the parapet & the level of the ground being raised there is no longer shelter for men standing up. By night the men walk along the top of the parapets + hitherto without casualties. There are very few dug-outs or shelters. No-one could stand the fatigue + discomfort & involved for more than 48 hours. Companies are therefore being frequently relieved. - There have been suggestions of friendly relations between ourselves & the Germans + talk of a truce at Christmas; strict orders have	

December 1915

J.R.W. Ino.

WAR DIARY
or
INTELLIGENCE SUMMARY

Army Form C. 2118

Vol 6, page 7

Place	Date	Hour	Summary of Events and Information	Remarks and references to Appendices
Trenches Right sub sect. S. div.	5th (3)		been warned against anything of the kind. Officers who countenance groups meeting & exchanging cigars, engaging in friendly talk etc. will be severely dealt with. The white flag has been waved several times during the day from the German parapet but it is not taken seriously.	
do	6th		The BOAR'S HEAD was bombarded by our artillery between 11 & 12 a.m. B company's dug-out was hit by a whizz-bang about 2:30 p.m. — it was about the only dug-out in their part of the firing-line fit to sit in. Two Officers were there at the time, but no-one was hurt.	as.
do	7th		We were relieved during the course of the evening by the 6th Wilts & went into Brigade Reserve at the RUE DES CHAVATTES. Relief completed by 9.30 p.m.	as.

December 1915.

1/5 R. W. Jus.

WAR DIARY or INTELLIGENCE SUMMARY

Army Form C. 2118

Vol. 6 page 8

Place	Date	Hour	Summary of Events and Information	Remarks and references to Appendices
Brigade Reserve	8th		Fairly comfortable billets though still nominally "in trenches". Furnished working parties evening to build breastwork behind Reserve Line.	an.
RUE DES CHAVATTES	9th		Furnished working parties to R.E. evening. Very wet.	as
"	10th		Ditto. Fine	
La Croix Marmuse / Epinette	11th		Relieved by 1/N. Staffords. Moved into Divisional Reserve between LA CROIX MARMUSE & EPINETTE. Billets stretch along road for distance of 2 miles. A part of this road is under water. Owing to the heavy rain today, the floods are increasing. The billets are good & comfortable.	as
do	12th		Rain morning, clearing later with northerly wind. Colder. During our late spell in the trenches viz 8 days from Dec. 3rd to 11th (of which the latter 4 days were in Brigade Reserve) our casualties were (rank & file) 2 killed, 5 wounded. 32 men were sent to hospital, of which only 3 were cases of "trench foot".	as.

9th R.W. 9ns

WAR DIARY
or
INTELLIGENCE SUMMARY

Army Form C. 2118

Vol. 6, page 9

December, 1915

Place	Date	Hour	Summary of Events and Information	Remarks and references to Appendices.
La Croix Marmuse	13th		Company parades.	as
Epinette	14th		ditto	as
"	15th		G.O.C. Brigade inspected companies moving in marching order. Weather cold & raw. Received information that Lt. Col. R.A. BERNERS was appointed to the command of the battalion.	as
"	16th / 17th		Company parades. Inspected companies in marching order.	as
"	18th		I accompanied by Company Commanders visited new line of trenches at NEUVE CHAPELLE which we take over from the 7 S. Lancashires tomorrow. A draft of 50 men joined us. Our previous drafts since arrival in the country have been 70 rank & file on Oct. 8th, 11 on Oct. 22nd (sick & wounded returned), 62 rank & file on Oct. 15th. In addition several officers.	as

9TH R.W. Fus.

WAR DIARY
or
INTELLIGENCE SUMMARY
(Erase heading not required.)

Army Form C. 2118

December, 1915

Place	Date	Hour	Summary of Events and Information	Remarks and references to Appendices
Left sub-sect. S. Div.	19th		Relieved the 7th S. Lancashires. Relief completed by 7/p.m. 1200 yds of front are occupied by A & C companies, A on the right. B & D companies are in support, B on the right. A's front extends from LIVERPOOL STREET to CHURCH ROAD & C's from here to SIGNPOST LANE. A company of the 10th Welsh are in with us for instruction. B company has 2 platoons at CHURCH POST, 1 platoon at HILL'S REDOUBT and 1 platoon in the support line behind the right of A (occupied by 1 company of the 1st King's Liverpool Regt, attached to the 50th Brigade). The 9th Welsh occupy the line further to our right extending to the south of the LA BASSÉE road. — D company has 3 platoons at the railhead (MOGG'S HOLE) and 1 platoon at the CHATEAU POST.	Vide Appendix IV. Vol. 6, page 10 M3.

Army Form C. 2118

WAR DIARY
or
INTELLIGENCE SUMMARY
(Erase heading not required.)

December, 1915

Vol. 6, page 11

Place	Date	Hour	Summary of Events and Information	Remarks and references to Appendices
Trenches left sub sec(tion) S. Div.	19"		We arrived in the trenches to find they had been heavily shelled that afternoon. There had been a great deal of damage done to the parapets & several casualties. We busied ourselves 2 casualties from four of their men. — We had ourselves 2 casualties from stray shots among men putting up returns. The front parapet is a breastwork. The men are far more comfortable in every way than during our late experience. One of the communication trenches (CHATEAU ROAD) is well provided with trench boards & it is only a quarter of an hours walk from the front trench to the rail head. The dug-outs are insufficient in number, but good; more are being built. The men in the front trench can keep comparatively dry.	

December, 1915

9th R.W. Fus.

WAR DIARY
or
INTELLIGENCE SUMMARY
(Erase heading not required.)

Army Form C. 2118

Vol. 6, page 12

Place	Date	Hour	Summary of Events and Information	Remarks and references to Appendices
Trenches left sub sect.(cont) S. Div.	19th		Battⁿ Headquarters is in a ruined house, 300 yds behind the firing-line. The Guards Division are on our left, to the north of SIGNPOST LANE.	
	20th		Hostile snying very active, especially to the north of the N.E.B. Three men of A company were hit there between 11 a.m. & 1 p.m. In the evening we received a message that an attack was to made at 2 a.m. (the 21st) by the 9th Welsh on our right, to be preceded by gas. The wind however was unfavorable & at 1 to 2 we heard it was cancelled. All our men had been held ready with their smoke helmets. Two more casualties were reported from A company.	us

1875. Wt. W593/826 1,000,000 4/15 J.B.C. & A. A.D.S.S./Forms/C. 2118.

WAR DIARY or INTELLIGENCE SUMMARY

2nd Bn. W. Regs.

Vol. 6 page 13

Army Form C. 2118

December 1915

Place	Date	Hour	Summary of Events and Information	Remarks and references to Appendices
Trenches, left half, left sub sec., S. Div'n	21st		Our snipers were active during the day, otherwise quiet.	
	22nd		Our artillery kept up a heavy bombardment during the night. Hostile working parties were dispersed by our fire. Our snipers did a lot of firing. Sniping was carried on from loopholes.	
	23rd		A few shell hit our parapet making small breaches. Very good work was done in mending parapet & making traverses, especially on the north of the line. We were relieved in the course of the evening by the 9th Cheshires & went back to CROIX-BARBÉE.	
CROIX-BARBÉE	24		Provided small working parties morning & evening. Lt Col. R.O. BERNERS took over command of the battalion.	
"	25		Our losses in the trenches (Dec 19th to 23rd) were 2 men killed & 5 wounded. 5 of these casualties are supposed to have been due to a machine gun of the Grenadier Guards on our left, enfilading us.	

9th Bn. Royal Welsh Fusiliers
WAR DIARY
or
INTELLIGENCE SUMMARY

December 1915

Army Form C. 2118
Vol: 6. Page 14.

Place	Date	Hour	Summary of Events and Information	Remarks and references to Appendices
CROIX-BARBÉE	26th		In Brigade Reserve. Working parties furnished for work on the trenches, wiring and revetting.	R.C.
CROIX-BARBÉE & Supports and S. Bn.	27th		In Brigade Reserve. Relieved the 9th Bn. Cheshire Regt. in the line passing overnight — B and D Coy occupying the Right — left of the Front lines respectively. A Coy 2 platoons in CUDNEY POST and fire REDOUBT and 1 platoon in the support line S. of the OXFORD ROAD. C. Coy 1 platoon in CHATEAU POST. and 3 platoons in MOGGS HOLE — (Reinforce). 1 Coy 13th Welsh Regt. attached — 2 platoons with each Coy in the front line.	R.C.
Supports 28th S. Bn.	28th		Incorporation of trenches. Hostile artillery active.	R.S.
"	29th		Incorporation of trenches. Hostile artillery active.	R.S.

December 1915

9/3 Royal Scots Fusiliers
WAR DIARY
or
INTELLIGENCE SUMMARY
Army Form C. 2118
Vol. 6. Page. 15.

Place	Date	Hour	Summary of Events and Information	Remarks and references to Appendices
Left sub-section S.Br.	30th		Incorporation of trenches - Hostile artillery active over trenches.	R.S.
"	31st		The Coy 13/Welsh Regt: attacked left 16th B?: numerous snipers from 16th/Welsh Regt: Relieved by the 9/Cheshires: - Relief completed 7 to 10 p.m. Communication holes dug two as the rear lost left the line - and the Rue Bessa Road shelled between 8.11.15 p.m. 11.45 p.m. Battn: crossing. The B?: bivouacked in billets in Bois Grenier - Croix Barbée. Casualties during tour were - 8 wounded of whom 1 has since died.	R.S.

L.S. Danver
do/do
Commandg 9/Royal Scots Fusiliers

1.1.16

A P P E N D I C E S

III & IV

(Note: Appendix III is MISSING)

Appendix IV

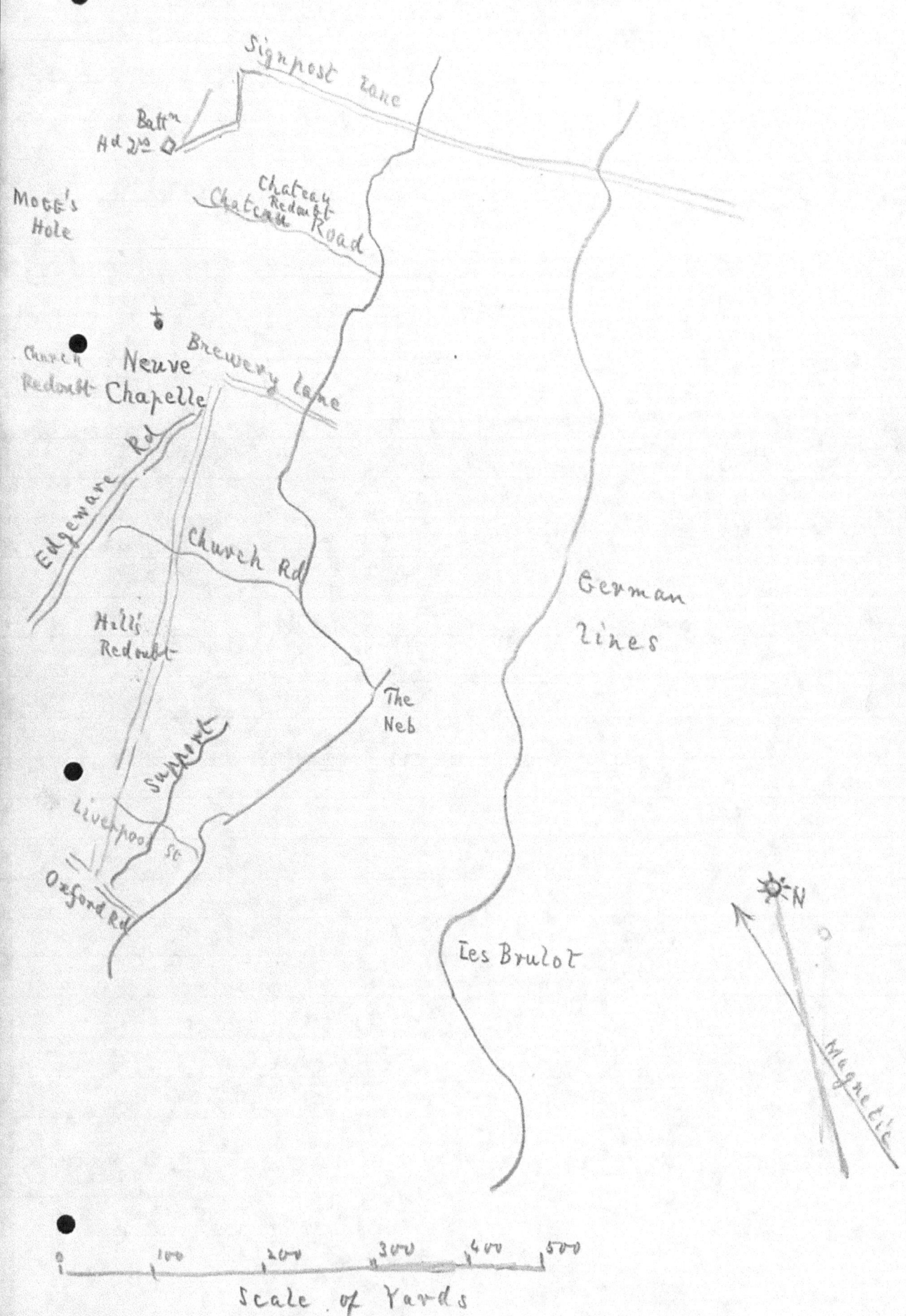

9th R.W. Fus:
1st: 7

19
Jan 1916

January 1916

9th Regt Bel[ge] f[usi]li[er]s

Vol: 7. Page

WAR DIARY
or
INTELLIGENCE SUMMARY

Army Form C. 2118

Place	Date	Hour	Summary of Events and Information	Remarks and references to Appendices
CROIX-BARBÉE	1st		Jubilate et Beigue Reserve. Fatigue parties for work on the front tranches & wiring and cleaning.	R.S.
"	2d		In Brigade Reserve "	R.S.
"	3.		In Brigade Reserve "	R.S.
"	4th		In Brigade Reserve. Relieved 8.10 p.m. 5th by Cornwall Rgt and proceeded billets at CROIX MARMEUSE in Divisional Reserve.	R.S.
CROIX-MARMEUSE	5th		Jubilete in Divisional Reserve " CROIX MARMEUSE	R.S.
"	6th		In Divisional Reserve " CROIX MARMEUSE	R.S.
"	7th		In Divisional Reserve " CROIX MARMEUSE	R.S.
"	8th		"	
	9th		"	
	10th		"	
	11th		"	
	12th		"	
	13			

WAR DIARY
9/K Royal Scot Fusiliers Vol: 7 pages 2
INTELLIGENCE SUMMARY

January 1916.

Army Form C. 2118

Place	Date	Hour	Summary of Events and Information	Remarks and references to Appendices
CROIX MARMEUSE	14th		In Divisional Reserve.	RSF
		9.30pm	Relieved 15/Royal Scots Fusiliers in front line trenches in front Liverpstein RICHBOURG L'AVOUÉ.	2.3
RICHBOURG L'AVOUÉ	15th 16th 17th		In front line trenches, front Liverpstein.	2.3
"	18th	8.15pm	Relieved 8 9/Cheshires in reserve, & front Liverpstein and returned to billets in RICHBOURG ST VAAST in Brigade Reserve.	2.3
RICHBOURG ST VAAST	19th 20th 21st 22		In Brigade Reserve.	2.3
"	23rd	2.0pm	Relieved in Brigade Reserve by 15/Royal Scots Fusiliers and withdrew to billets on the LES LAURIER area. N of MERVILLE in Divisional Reserve.	2.3
LES LAURIER area	24th to 31st		In Divisional Reserve.	La Beuvier Suis Cie Ceased 9/Royal Scots Fus 4 1.2.16 — 2.3

Secret

D.A.G. 3rd Echelon.

I beg to forward herewith War Diary for February 1916, of the battalion under my command.

R.A. Berners
Lt-Col,
Commandg 9th Royal Welch Fus.

11/3/16.

Army Form C. 2118

February 1916

WAR DIARY
9/Battn (or Intelligence Summary)
Vol. 8 page 3.

INTELLIGENCE SUMMARY
(Erase heading not required.)

Instructions regarding War Diaries and Intelligence
Summaries are contained in F. S. Regs., Part II.
and the Staff Manual respectively. Title Pages
will be prepared in manuscript.

Place	Date	Hour	Summary of Events and Information	Remarks and references to Appendices
LES LAURIERS AREA	1st		In Army Reserve.	S/
	2nd		"	S/
	3rd		"	S/
	4th		"	S/
	5th		"	S/
	6th		"	S/:
	7th		In Army Reserve. Seven specimens received. 4 men killed.	S/
	8th		1 Officer 2 men wounded.	S/:
	9th		In Army Reserve.	S/:
	10th		"	S/:
	11th		"	S/:
	12th		"	S/:
	13th		"	S/
	14th	8.0am	Bn. B all moved to billets in - LA GORGUE	
LA GORGUE	15th		The Bn. began Reserve at LA GORGUE.	
	16th		The Bn. att. moved into occupation of trenches north of NEUVE CHAPELLE from SIGNPOST LANE to MOATED GRANGE TRENCH, in relief of 8/3rd Bn. Seaforth Queens —	

Army Form C. 2118

WAR DIARY
9/Royal Welsh Fusiliers
INTELLIGENCE SUMMARY

(Erase heading not required.)

Vol: 8. (page 4)

Instructions regarding War Diaries and Intelligence Summaries are contained in F. S. Regs., Part II. and the Staff Manual respectively. Title Pages will be prepared in manuscript.

February 1916

Place	Date	Hour	Summary of Events and Information	Remarks and references to Appendices
LAVENTIE Section	Feb: 16" 17" 18"		Reoccupation of trenches.	2.C.
	19"		The B.N. was relieved in the trenches by 5th of Cheshire Regt: and proceeded to billets about RIEZ BAILLEUL.	
	20"		In billets near RIEZ BAILLEUL	
	21st		The B.N. relieved the 5th of Cheshire Regt in occupation of the trenches.	
	22nd		In occupation of trenches.	
	23rd		The B.N. was relieved in the trenches by 5th of Cheshire Regt & in Brigade Reserve.	
MERVILLE	24"		The B.N. moved into Divisional Reserve at MERVILLE.	
	25" 26" 27" 28" 29"		In Divisional Reserve.	

R.A. Berners
Lieut Col.
Comdg. 9/ Royal Welsh Fusiliers
1.3.16

D.A.G.

3rd Echelon.

War Diary for March is sent herewith.

[signature] Major.

Comanding 9th Royal Welch Fusiliers.

29/4/16.

Army Form C. 2118

V of J.B. pages
9 Welsh Fus

Vol 9

WAR DIARY
2/Royal Welsh Fusiliers
INTELLIGENCE SUMMARY
(Erase heading not required.)

Instructions regarding War Diaries and Intelligence Summaries are contained in F.S. Regs., Part II. and the Staff Manual respectively. Title Pages will be prepared in manuscript.

March 1916

Place	Date	Hour	Summary of Events and Information	Remarks and references to Appendices
RICHBOURG ST VAAST.	1st		The Battn. marched from MERVILLE to RICHBOURG ST VAAST, into Brigade Reserve.	
	2nd		In Brigade Reserve.	
	3rd		In Brigade Reserve. Cold weather with snow.	
	4th		The Battn. relieved the 9/Cheshire Regt. in occupation of the Keep at RICHBOURG L'AVOUÉ – Snowy weather.	
	5th		Inoccupation of Keep. – Snowy weather	
	6th		Inoccupation of Keep. – Snowy weather	
	7th 4.47pm		The Battn. was relieved at 7.47pm & the Bn. took place in the trenches to billets at CROIX MARMEUSE and marched there down to billets at CROIX MARMEUSE in Divisional Reserve.	
CROIX MARMEUSE	8th		In Divisional Reserve. Snowy weather	
	9th		"	
	10th		"	
	11th		" – A draft of 104 other ranks joined the Battn. from D-Base.	
	12th		The Battn. moved into Bde. Reserve at CROIX BARBEE.	
	13th		The Battn. relieved the 7th Lord Nott. Lancaster Regt. in NEUVE CHAPELLE Section.	

WAR DIARY

or INTELLIGENCE SUMMARY

9th R. Welsh Fus. Vol 9 Page 2.

Army Form C. 2118

March 1916.

Place	Date	Hour	Summary of Events and Information	Remarks and references to Appendices
	14th		In occupation of trenches.	
	15th		do.	
	16th		do. Major E. H. Pott, 1st Lancers reported his arrival on appointment to B.W. Coldstream Gds, joined on up in opps to the Bathn. 2Lt. S.G. Manders from 2nd in command and to Com and of 2nd	
	17th		In occupation of trenches. The Battn was relieved in the evening by the 9th Cheshire Regt.	
	18th		In Brigade Reserve at CROIX BARBÉE. 7 Lt. May joined from 18th R. Welsh Fus.	
	19th		do. Capt Williams took over command of D	
	20th		do. Capt Williams sick to hospital.	
	21st		Con from Capt Jones sick. The Battn relieved the 9th Cheshire Regt in occupation of trenches in NEUVE CHAPELLE sector	
	22nd		In trenches.	

WAR DIARY of 9th R. Welch Fus.

March 1916

Vol 9 Page 3.

Place	Date	Hour	Summary of Events and Information	Remarks and references to Appendices
	23rd		The Battn was relieved by the 7th South Lancashire Regt and moved into billets at LA GORGUE in Divisional Reserve.	
	24th		Battn at LA GORGUE. Capt Jones from 8th R.W.F. & Lt BARTLE from 18th R.W.F. reported their arrival on appointment to 9th R. Welch Fus.	
	25th		Battn relieved the 20th Lancashire Fus. Bn in rec reputation of trenches in Fme du Bois section. Lt Col Benzie went into hospital at MERVILLE sick. Maj Griffiths was wounded. Lt. ORR rejoined from En Hqrs.	
	26th		In trenches. 7th Cheshire Regt & moved into the 9th Cheshire Regt. A draft of 28 men arrived.	
	27th		The Battn was relieved by 9th Cheshire Regt. VARST.	
	28th		Bn Reserve at RICHEBOURG St. VAAST.	
	29th		In Bde Reserve. do	
	30th		In Bde Reserve. do	

Army Form C. 2118

WAR DIARY of 9th R. Welsh Fus.

INTELLIGENCE SUMMARY

March 1916.

Vol 9 Page 4

Place	Date	Hour	Summary of Events and Information	Remarks and references to Appendices
	31st		The Battn relieved the 9th Cheshire Regt in occupation of the trenches in the Ferme du Bois section. S/MPGt. Malm. Comdg 9th R. Welch Fus.	

D.A.G.

   3rd Echelon,

      Base.

Herewith War Diary, Volume 10 for the month of

April. 4/6.

                              Lieut.- Colonel.

3/5/16.   Commanding 9th Royal Welch Fusiliers.

Army Form C. 2118

WAR DIARY
or
INTELLIGENCE SUMMARY
of 9th R. Welch Fus. Vol. 10 Page 1.

(Erase heading not required.)

Instructions regarding War Diaries and Intelligence Summaries are contained in F. S. Regs., Part II. and the Staff Manual respectively. Title Pages will be prepared in manuscript.

Place: April 1916

Date	Hour	Summary of Events and Information	Remarks and references to Appendices
1st		In trenches in FERME du BOIS section.	
2nd		do.	
3rd		do. 2Lt. L. W. Jones was wounded Whilst on patrol.	
4th		The Battn was relieved by the 9th Battn Cheshire Regt & moved into Bde Reserve at RICHEBOURG ST VAAST.	
5th		In Bde Reserve at RICHEBOURG ST VAAST.	
6th		do.	
7th		do.	
8th		The Battn relieved the 9th Cheshire Regt in occupation of the trenches in FERME du BOIS section.	
9th		In trenches. do. 2Lt. _____	
10th		In trenches. 2Lt. Evans was wounded Whilst on patrol.	
11th		In trenches.	

Army Form C. 2118

WAR DIARY of R. Welch Fus
INTELLIGENCE SUMMARY

April 1916   Vol 10. Page 2

(Erase heading not required.)

Place	Date	Hour	Summary of Events and Information	Remarks and references to Appendices
	12.		The Battn was relieved by the 5/6 Battn Cheshire Regt and moved into Bn Reserve at RICHEBOURG St VAAST.	
	13.		In Bde Reserve at do.	
	14.		do. Br Gen. J.D. JEFFREYS was wounded and 2/Lt R.A BERNERS assumed command of the 58th Bde. Capt. M.M. LEWIS assumed command of the Battn.	
	15.		do	
	16.		The Battn relieved the 5/6 Battn Cheshire Regt in reserve trenches in FERME du BOIS section.	17
	17.		In trenches	
	18.		do.	
	19.		The Battn was relieved by the 15th Battn Cheshire Regt & moved to billets at FOSSE near LESTREM. Capt. S.H. Pott rejoined from leave and took over the command of the Battn from Capt. M.M. LEWIS.	

WAR DIARY

INTELLIGENCE SUMMARY

April 1916. Vol 10 Page 3   Army Form C. 2118

9th R<u>n</u> Welch Fus.

Place	Date	Hour	Summary of Events and Information	Remarks and references to Appendices
	20<u>th</u>		The Batt<u>n</u> marched at 10 a.m. to ROBECQ a distance of 12½ miles.	
ROBECQ	21<u>st</u>		The Batt<u>n</u> in billets at ROBECQ.	
	22<u>nd</u>		The Batt<u>n</u> marched in B<u>de</u> to SERNY a distance of 15 miles, a very hot day.	
SERNY.	23<u>rd</u>		In FIRST ARMY training area.	
SERNY.	24<u>th</u>		The Batt<u>n</u> commenced Company & platoon training. Lt. R.H. HIGHAM rejoined from England. A draft of 15 men arrived	
SERNY	25<u>th</u>		Company training. Sir Charles MONRO G.O.C. 1<u>st</u> ARMY visited the training area and saw the Companies at work.	
do	26<u>th</u>		Company training.	
do	27<u>th</u>		Company training.	
do	28<u>th</u>		Batt<u>n</u> training commenced	
do	29<u>th</u>		Batt<u>n</u> training	

April 1916 Vol: 10 Page 4 Army Form C. 2118
9th Bn. Royal Welsh Fusiliers

WAR DIARY
or
INTELLIGENCE SUMMARY

(Erase heading not required.)

Place	Date	Hour	Summary of Events and Information	Remarks and references to Appendices
SERNY.	April 30		Battalion training.	
			R. D. ennes	
			Lieut Colonel	
			Commanding 9th Bn. Royal Welsh Fusiliers	

May 1916   9th Welch
G.R.B.&tt ?? ???
Vol II Feb
XIX

WAR DIARY
INTELLIGENCE SUMMARY

Place	Date	Hour	Summary of Events and Information	Remarks and references to Appendices
SERNY	1st		} Battalion Brigade training.	
"	2nd		}	
"	3rd		}	
"	4th		} Divisional training.	
"	5th		}	
"	6th		}	
"	7th	12 noon	The Batt. marched to BERGUETTE station, and entrained, leaving that station at 6.15 pm. —	
MONTONVILLERS	8th		The Batt. reached LONGEAU station at 2.30 am and marched 12 miles to billets at MONTONVILLERS.	
"	9th–20		} Company and Platoon training.	
"	28th		On the 23rd inst, a draft of 65 N.C.Os and men joined the Bn. from the IIIrd Corps Cyclists and were posted to "B"Coy.	
BRUCAMPS	29th	6.15 am	The Bn. moved & marched to BRUCAMPS. (12 miles)	
NEUF MOULIN	30th	6.15 am	The Bn. moved & marched to NEUF MOULIN. (10 miles)	
"	31st		In billets.	

R. Devereux Lieut Col.
Comdg 9th Bn. Regt Welsh Territorials.

9th Welsh Regt
Army Form C.2118/2
Vol 12

XIV

WAR DIARY
9th Batt'n. 1st or Welsh Division
INTELLIGENCE SUMMARY
(Erase heading not required.)

Volume 12. Page 1.

Dec 1916

Place	Date	Hour	Summary of Events and Information	Remarks and references to Appendices
NEUF MOULIN	1st to 8th		In billets – for Brigade and Divisional Training.	
"	9th			
BUCHAMPS	10th 11th	8.0 a.m.	The Bn moved (over own route) to BUCHAMPS – (12 miles)	
LA CHAUSSÉE	12th	8.0 a.m.	The Bn moved (over own route) to LA CHAUSSÉE – (9 miles)	
"	13th to 15th		In billets.	
LA CHAUSSÉE	16th	8.0 a.m.	The Bde moved & marched to ST GRATIEN. (14 miles)	
ST GRATIEN	17th to 26th		In billets.	
"	27th	7.30 p.m.	The Bn. moved (over own route) to BRESLE (9½ miles) – 2nd Lieut Z.A. Neal, 2nd Lieut L. Hughes, J.P. Lloyd, H.H.L Griffiths, P.H. Williams joined on appointment	
BRESLE	28th		In billets.	
"	29th		In billets	Re Benson Lieut Col Crew 9th/13th Royal Welsh Fusiliers
"	30th		In billets	

58th Inf. Bde.
19th Div.

VOL 13

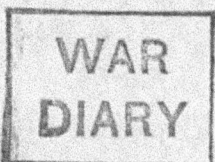

9th BATTN. THE ROYAL WELCH FUSILIERS.

J U L Y

1 9 1 6

WAR DIARY
9th Royal Welch Fusiliers
INTELLIGENCE SUMMARY

Vol. 13 Page 1.

Army Form C. 2118

Place	Date	Hour	Summary of Events and Information	Remarks and references to Appendices
BRESLE	30/6/16	10.0 pm	At 10.0 pm the Battalion left its billets and proceeded to a preliminary position of assembly in a hollow immediately West of the railway South of the main AMIENS - ALBERT Road at the latter town. Here the Battalion bivouaced for the night.	
	1/7/16		June 30th, July 1st and at 10.30 a.m proceeded in its turn to the trenches on the TARA - USNA line some 1,000 yards East of ALBERT, where the remainder of the 58th Brigade, of whom all day in readiness to join in the battle it remained all day in readiness to join in the battle which after an Artillery bombardment since the 24th June had been commenced by the Infantry that morning. The 19th Division to which the 58th Brigade belonged, was in Corps Reserve to the South of ALBERT. The 34th Division to the South of ALBERT. The latter Division had been called upon on the morning of the 1st July to capture the village of LA BOISSELLE, some 2000 yards to the N.E. of ALBERT on the BAPAUNE Road. The attack against the enemy's quick line trenches but was brought to a standstill, when owing to the heavy casualties caused by the Machine guns mounted in the enemy's line, the 58th Brigade was then ordered to seize and make good the enemy's second line from LA BOISSELLE R.2.D

Place	Date	Hour	Summary of Events and Information	Remarks and references to Appendices
	2/7/16		Some 600 yards eastwards - and the 9th Batt. Cheshire Regiment was directed to make good by bombing attacks, the trenches leading up to this line with the 9th Batt. Royal Welch Fusiliers in support - the 6th Wiltshire Regt. being ordered to consolidate the line when captured and the 9th Batt. Welch Regt. held in reserve. This attack was ordered for but owing to the congestion of the communication trenches, and to the fact that the front line system of our trenches had been greatly injured by the enemy's artillery barrage during the assault. By the 3rd Sussex that morning, the assaulting Battalion was not able to reach its starting off position till daybreak of the 2nd by which time the Artillery programme had been completed - this Batt. therefore only reached the German trenches - which had been turned in the German trenches the previous morning - at day break of the 2nd, less one Company which rendered in our front and support lines, and did not proceed further. Orders were issued on the afternoon of the 2nd for the attack to be carried out, as per Genl's orders	

WAR DIARY

1st Royal Welch Fusiliers

INTELLIGENCE SUMMARY Vol. 13 Cape 3

Army Form C. 2118

Place	Date	Hour	Summary of Events and Information	Remarks and references to Appendices
			At 4.0am that day, the assault to be delivered and the objective gained, regardless of loss, and this was done, the remainder of the 6th Cheshires with the 9th Royal Welch Fusiliers and the 6th Wiltshire Regt gaining considerable ground towards their objective before daybreak set in. Owing to the congestion of troops in our front line system of trenches and to the havoc wrought by the hostile artillery the previous morning it was found impossible to launch the attack on a regular montage and it was entirely due to the handling by their leaders of the various Companies of the 9th Royal Welch Fusiliers that the advance to the German line was effected so few casualties. On reaching this German attack were immediately initiated along the trenches which had been severely molested and considerable progress was made, in at some cost, owing to bombing counter attacks delivered by the enemy in co-operation with his snipers, who showed to be very deadly. The following officer casualties occurred on this day. July 2nd :- Captain E. K. Jones } Killed Lieut W. J. Jones 2/Lieut E.S. McCammon } 2/Lieut F.A. Neave } wounded	25

Army Form C. 2118

WAR DIARY of Royal Welch Fusiliers

INTELLIGENCE SUMMARY

(Erase heading not required.)

Vol 13
Cape 4

Instructions regarding War Diaries and Intelligence Summaries are contained in F.S. Regs., Part II. and the Staff Manual respectively. Title Pages will be prepared in manuscript.

Place	Date	Hour	Summary of Events and Information	Remarks and references to Appendices
	2/7/16		The advance ceased with darkness. Companies leaving their position in the night, dying which orders were received for the advance to be continued at 2.45 a.m. on the 3rd instant.	
	3/7/16		The orders for the renewal of the advance required the 9th Royal Welch Fusiliers to make good the intervening Trenches between itself and the S.E. edge of LA BOISSELLE Village, where it was to join hands with the 57th Infy Brigade, and then turning E.N.E. gain the line in which to consolidate with the widths and Churches in sight. The direction of this plan was corner B and B-La C Company bombing along the Souchez trench and B-la next on to the Y Sick, till these forward some 100 yards East of the village, while D & A Coys advanced in Support. On reaching the edge of the village the leading Company found touch with troops of the 57th Brigade, and the advance in an E.N.E. direction was commenced. The Royal Welch Fusiliers moving with its left outside the edge of the village - which the leading troops of the 57th Brigade appeared to have cleared. On reaching the N.E. corner of the village, however, the enemy counter-attacked these troops which fell back through	S.S.

WAR DIARY
9th Welch Fusiliers
INTELLIGENCE SUMMARY
Vol/3. Page 5.

Place	Date	Hour	Summary of Events and Information	Remarks and references to Appendices
	3/7/16		The village while Snipers who had evidently remained in the ruined houses caused severe casualties amongst the leading Company of the 9 Batn. Royal Welch Fusiliers which had passed them. Here 2 Lieut. Wauchope R. Signal Officer was wounded and Capt. B.G. Roberts the Adjutant was killed by a bullet from apparently some direction while running to his assistance. The enemy continued his advance developing a strong attack into the centre and along the S. W. edge of the village, the troops falling back before it leaving the left of the 9 Royal Welch Fusiliers unsupported. This necessitated its retirement to the German trench 300 yards to its rear, where it was joined by elements of the 57th Bde... Here a stand was made and the enemy checked from advancing along the S.E. edge of the village, but his snipers and snipers penetrated into the centre of the village and the fire of the latter, taking the men in enfilade, and intense, caused a considerable number of casualties amongst our men. The enemy then developed a strong bomb attack along the N.E. edge of the village which was vigorously sustained for some time 3SS	

WAR DIARY
or Intelligence Summary

Army Form C. 2118

(Erase heading not required.)

Place	Date	Hour	Summary of Events and Information	Remarks and references to Appendices
	3/7/16		but was eventually beaten off successfully, and Glock's having been established with the Communication trenches leading into the village, the enemy bombers were kept at a distance. Later, the troops of the 5th Bde. which were then holding a line further South through the village advanced to a line running to with the left of the Battn. and secluded from further annoyance throughout the day - but at night fire the enemy made several bomb attacks, and his Snipers became quite a nuisance through the section of parados and traverses during the day prevented their fire causing any number of casualties.	
	4/7/16		The Battn. was relieved at 2.0 am on the 4th July and during the relief the enemy's bombers and snipers were particularly active, thus indicating that he was well aware of our intended movement. On relief by the 7th Battn. the Kings Own Regiment the Battalion returned to Bivouac in the TARA — USNA Redoubts line - to refit and rest till the 7th July the following casualties were sustained by	29

WAR DIARY

G.H.Q. Troops or Welsh Frontiers Vol. 13. Page 7.

INTELLIGENCE SUMMARY
(Erase heading not required.)

Army Form C. 2118

Place	Date	Hour	Summary of Events and Information	Remarks and references to Appendices
	4.7.16		8th Batt: casualties on the 3rd July: Killed. Lieut: Col. C. E. Roberts. Wounded. 2 Lieut: H. C. Walker. " H. T. Jones. " J. L. Hughes. The casualties to the Periods 1st to 4th July being — Killed. 3 Officers. 32 men Wounded 5 " 128 " Missing. — " 48 " _____ Total. 8 Officers. 208 men. Reinforcement Draft of 85 men. 	
	4.7.16		The following officers joined the Bn. for duty. 2 Lieut C. D. Jones – H. S. Humphreys – F. S. K. Lewis J. E. Bowen-Lloyd –	

WAR DIARY

9th Royal Welsh Fusiliers
INTELLIGENCE SUMMARY

Vol 13 page 8

Army Form C. 2118

Place	Date	Hour	Summary of Events and Information	Remarks and references to Appendices
July	4 & 5th		In bivouac in the TARA - USNA line.	
	6th		In bivouac on the TARA - USNA line. A draft of 20 other ranks joined the Battn. from the Base. During the afternoon and again in the evening of the 6th the German Artillery shelled the bivouacs of the 9th Royal Welsh Fusiliers and 9th Cheshire Regiment which had been erected S.E. of BECOURT WOOD, and it was considered necessary to move the men back into the line of trenches in the TARA - USNA line for the time. On the afternoon of this day orders were received for the 58th Infantry Brigade, to take Contl- in a further advance and in cooperation with the 56th Brigade on it's left and the 68th Brigade on it's right, to gain roughly the line of the road leading from the N.W. corner of CONTALMAISON through the Centre of LA BOISSELLE, and for this purpose the 9th Battn. Welsh Regiment was sent in to hold our front line, during the night of 6th July, in a part of some 600 yards it's left at the junction of the track running up the SAUSAGE VALLEY with the road leading S.E.	2.B

WAR DIARY
9th Royal Welsh Fusiliers
INTELLIGENCE SUMMARY

Army Form C. 2118
Vol 13 Page 9

Place	Date	Hour	Summary of Events and Information	Remarks and references to Appendices
	July 6th		The Eastern corner of LA BOISSELLE. The 6th Battn Wiltshire Regt. was ordered to be in position, in support, some 500 yards to the South of this line by 7.0 a.m on the 7th inst. where the 9th Royal Welsh Fusiliers were to be in the old German front line trenches at HELEGOLAND at that hour, ready to take the place of the 6th Battn Wiltshire Regt. as they moved forward and to assist the attack in any way possible. The 9th Cheshire Regt. were to remain at the commencement of the attack in the TARA- USNA line, to be utilised as circumstances might require in carrying forward stores, etc. and in supporting the advance. Copy of "Special Order of the Day" issued to-day is attached.	
	July 7th		The 9th Battn Royal Welsh Fusiliers was in position at the hour indicated, and moved up the German 6th Wiltshire communication trench to gain touch with the 6th Wiltshire ahead of it, and to form a chain for passing up stores of bombs, S.A.A. etc. Before reaching the WBR however, the attack commenced, and the enemy put down a very heavy barrage on the area through which the Battalion was passing. But their shells, failing to find the communication trenches, out casualties were inconsiderable.	

Army Form C. 2118

WAR DIARY
9th Royal Welch Fusiliers Vol. 13 page 10
INTELLIGENCE SUMMARY
(Erase heading not required.)

Instructions regarding War Diaries and Intelligence Summaries are contained in F.S. Regs., Part II and the Staff Manual respectively. Title Pages will be prepared in manuscript.

Place	Date	Hour	Summary of Events and Information	Remarks and references to Appendices
July	7th		At 8.30 a.m. the 9th Welch advanced over the open and gained its objective, supported by the 6th Wilts who prolonged the line to form the 12th Durham L.I. on their right. The various German communication trenches leading towards the enemy having been made good by forming parties. One of these parties, along a trench leading to point 81 on the right of our objective, had been driven in and a party of 10 Foster Snipers, which returned along it, was able to do some damage to the 9th Welch and 6th Wilts, who were holding the position gained, and caused a number of casualties by being into them on their right rear. The Coun. the caught the leading Company of the 9th Royal Welch Fusiliers, coming up to reinforce the line. This Company took over in the German trench, running immediately in rear of the position taken up. The 3 other Companies coming up later, prolonged this line to the left - 2 of them, A & C Coys. established themselves further to the West along the line of the Sunken road. This proved to be an unfortunate position for them, as the Germans shelled the road.	2S3

1875 Wt. W593/826 1,000,000 4/15 J.B.C.&A. A.D.S.S./Forms/C. 2118.

WAR DIARY
9th Royal Welch Fusiliers
INTELLIGENCE SUMMARY Vol 13. Page 11

Place	Date	Hour	Summary of Events and Information	Remarks and references to Appendices
	July 7.		During the night the East, taking it in English and the Fusiliers occupying the bank, having little protection from their rear, sustained several casualties from this cause - including Capt. Rush - "C" Coy and 2/Lieut. Rees Comdg. "A" Coy wounded; the latter it is feared, dangerously so. During the night of the 7/8th July, the enemy communication trenches were again cleared and kept by Gloucester & harassed our party of German snipers which had accounted for nine of our successfully accounted on the German strong point at Counl. S.I. was occupied by the 12th Durham L.I. in the morning and was later handed over to the 9th Royal Welch Fusiliers who consolidated it and formed a defensive flank facing East, thus securing the right of the Brigade which till then had been in the air, the attack by the 68th Brigade on CONTALMAISON the day previous having failed and left a gap in the line of the British advance.	20
	July 8.		During the afternoon of the 8th July a number of the enemy were observed to be running across the open from the direction of POZIÈRES into CONTALMAISON, and	

WAR DIARY
Royal Welch Fusiliers
INTELLIGENCE SUMMARY Vol 13

Army Form C. 2118
Cope. 12

Place	Date	Hour	Summary of Events and Information	Remarks and references to Appendices
	July 8th		About 4am a continuous stream of Germans were seen hurrying through the communication trenches into the latter village giving the impression that an attack was impending. This suspicion was borne out by heavy Artillery fire which the enemy brought to bear on the Strong Points, S.I. and our front line generally from 5.15 to 7pm while a heavy Artillery barrage was put down right across the SAUSAGE VALLEY and on the German trenches occupied by our outposts 600 yards in rear. On the aerotime our Field and Heavy Artillery fire was directed on CONTAL MAISON, where a fine effect was observed, our Heavy Shells bursting amongst the enemy troops seen to be massing there and scattering them in disorder. The attack was evidently curtailed before it could be launched, but signs being noticed of another attack threatening at 9.0 pm our Artillery again locked any progress. The Germans continued their Artillery fire from 9.0 pm throughout the night, covering our front line with Shrapnel and searching the SAUSAGE VALLEY and trenches in rear, with heavy Shells — this barrage was intense	2.5.

WAR DIARY
9th Welch Fusiliers
INTELLIGENCE SUMMARY
Vol 13 Page 13

Army Form C. 2118

Place	Date	Hour	Summary of Events and Information	Remarks and references to Appendices
July	9th		During the night 8/9th July the Battalion was relieved by the - Warwickshire Regt. and returned to billets in ALBERT the relief being completed at 6.0 a.m. on the 9th. In addition to the 2 Officers mentioned above as wounded, the Medical Officer, Capt. R.H. Miller was struck by a fragment of H.E. Shell during the afternoon of the 8th but continued at duty for some time before going down to Field Ambulance. Total casualties for period 6th to 9th:— Killed 1 Wounded 3 Officers 25 men Missing 10 " At 8.0 a.m. the Battalion moved to bivouac at BAIZIEUX, some 6 miles distance. Passing 19th Division F.G. en route where the G.O.C. was present with his staff and the Divisional Band to welcome the troops as they marched through the village.	
July	10th		In bivouac in BAIZIEUX WOOD.	
July	11th		In bivouac in BAIZIEUX WOOD. Copy of a "Special Order of the Day" issued this day is attached	B.O.

Army Form C. 2118

WAR DIARY or Intelligence Summary

9th Bn. or Welch Fusiliers Vol 13 Page 14

(Erase heading not required.)

Instructions regarding War Diaries and Intelligence Summaries are contained in F. S. Regs., Part II. and the Staff Manual respectively. Title Pages will be prepared in manuscript.

Place	Date	Hour	Summary of Events and Information	Remarks and references to Appendices
July	12		In bivouac in BAIZIEUX WOOD	
	13		In bivouac in BAIZIEUX WOOD. The Battalion was inspected by Lieut-General Sir W.P. Pulteney K.C.B, D.S.O, Commanding 3rd Corps, at BAIZIEUX, who addressed the troops of the 58th Infantry Brigade on the parade, expressing his appreciation of the work done during the fights between the 1st and 9th July, by the 19th Division and the 58th Brigade in particular.	
July	14		In bivouac in BAIZIEUX WOOD	
	15		In bivouac in BAIZIEUX WOOD.	
	16		bivouac in BAIZIEUX WOOD	
	17		bivouac in BAIZIEUX WOOD	
	18		bivouac in BAIZIEUX WOOD	
	19		bivouac in BAIZIEUX WOOD	
July	20	2 pm	The Battalion moved to bivouac in BECOURT WOOD	
	21		The Battalion with the remainder of the 58th Bde moved to bivouac in MAMETZ WOOD in support of the 56 & 57th Brigades which had relieved the 34 Division in the line	2.D

WAR DIARY
9th Battalion Welch Fusiliers
INTELLIGENCE SUMMARY Vol 13 Page 15

Army Form C. 2118

Place	Date	Hour	Summary of Events and Information	Remarks and references to Appendices
	July 21st		In front of BAZENTIN-LE-PETIT village the Grenon's night. On reaching its bivouac in the wood about 7.30 pm the Bn. was subjected to shelling by 5.9 howitzers, which searched the wood but caused few casualties to the Bn. The enemy shelled heavily again during the night, but no casualties resulted in the Bn, though the 9th Cheshire and 9th Welch Regts in the adjoining bivouacs lost a certain number of men in killed and wounded from this cause.	
	July 22nd		In bivouac in MAMETZ WOOD. The Bn remained in bivouac during the day and was 3 times subjected to heavy bombardment by 5.9 howitzers and H.E. Shrapnel fire, but, considering the intensity of fire sustained comparatively few casualties. After the 2nd bombardment arrangements were made to move to a different locality, but this could not be effected before the 3rd bombardment took place – A 4th bombardment, however, found the Bn. gone and a peaceful night's rest was secured for the men.	ES

WAR DIARY

of Welch Fusiliers Vol 13 Coy 6

INTELLIGENCE SUMMARY

Army Form C. 2118

Place	Date	Hour	Summary of Events and Information	Remarks and references to Appendices
	July 22nd		During the night the 56th & 57th Brigades assaulted the German intermediate line in front of BAZENTIN-LE-PETIT but the attack failed and the troops returned to their original lines. The 9th Cheshires being called up into closer support at 3.0 a.m. July 23rd. A draft of 86 Other ranks joined the Battn on this day and remain with the transport.	
	July 23rd		In Bivouac in MAMETZ WOOD. At 6.0 p.m. the Bn moved into the line in relief of the 9th Bn Royal Warwickshire Regt. taking over a line of trenches running for 300 yards N.E. from the Crucifix 5 ways at BAZENTIN-LE-PETIT. These trenches were dug along the line of the road leading directly to HIGH WOOD, part of which was held by the Germans, and immediate steps were taken to render these tenable and secure from the enfilade fire which was directed from the German batteries about FLERS.	
	July 24th		The enemy continued to shell from the direction of	2.S.

WAR DIARY
of 9th Bn. Welsh Fusiliers
INTELLIGENCE SUMMARY

Army Form C. 2118

Vol 13 Page 17.

Place	Date	Hour	Summary of Events and Information	Remarks and references to Appendices
	July 24th		FLERS and also from MARTINPUICH carrying a number of casualties, which however, lessened as the men improved their defences. During the late afternoon, aeroplane scouts reported FLERS to be free of Germans troops and the trenches W. of DELVILLE WOOD to be thick with men while the enemy were reported to be crawling up through the grass in large numbers on either side of HIGH WOOD. A protective artillery barrage was thereupon ordered from H.Q. 19th Division at 8.30 p.m. and was responded to by a barrage of great intensity which was placed by the Germans on our front-line trenches and on that of 3rd Batt. R.W. Fus. in the village itself, the shelling in this being so heavy that it was found impossible to leave the Bn. H.Q. with any chance of safety. At midnight the German barrage was lifted. From 2 to 3.0 a.m., 25th July, was renewed in reply to an artillery bombardment ordered from 1.0 a.m	2.5
	July 25th		The enemy shelled our trenches intermittently during the day with shrapnel and bombarded the H.Q at dug-out with 5.9 how. shells.	

WAR DIARY
1st Royal Welch Fusiliers
INTELLIGENCE SUMMARY Vol 13 Page 18

Army Form C. 2118

(Erase heading not required.)

Place	Date	Hour	Summary of Events and Information	Remarks and references to Appendices
July	25th		During the day orders were received to dig a fresh line of trench some 120 yards in front of the line occupied, in which to subsequently assault the German intermediate line and this was commenced that night and continued during the next day.	
	July 26th		The advanced trench commenced the previous night was continued during the day and completion and occupied the same night. At a good communication trench dug connecting it with the original trench. 2/Lieut. N. L. Ward reported his arrival on this day for duty with the Bn.	
	July 27th	10.0 a.m	The Battn. continued to hold the line and at 10.0 a.m. was ordered to join up with the 9th Welch Regt. on its right. If that Bn. succeeded in seizing a German strong point situated some 300 yards N.E. of the Battn. HQ which had been heavily shelled by our G.2 m² shells during the afternoon. The enemy were found in some strength holding a R.B.	

WAR DIARY or INTELLIGENCE SUMMARY

Army Form C. 2118.

Vol 13 Cap 19

859c
SB

RB

Place	Date	Hour	Summary of Events and Information	Remarks and references to Appendices
July	27th		Line in advance of the Stn. Govt. and a heavy barrage being immediate. Placed on our front line and the village by his Artillery, the enterprise had to be abandoned.	
July	28th		The Battalion continued to hold the line under the same conditions of intermittent heavy shelling.	
July	29th		The enemy shelled our new front heavily during the afternoon, having apparently got the range accurately, and brought up field guns to positions from which he could enfilade it. The men were, however, dug in deep and the casualties sustained were few. During the evening the Bn was relieved by the 10th Batt Worcester Regt, and returned to bivouac in BECOURT WOOD. Companies reporting no casualties during the relief. The casualties sustained during this tour in the line from the 21st to 29th July amounted to 2 Officers — 2 Lieuts Nunnerley and J.R. Roger wounded and 4 other ranks killed and 88 wounded.	

Army Form C. 2118

WAR DIARY
of 9th Royal Welch Fusiliers
INTELLIGENCE SUMMARY

Vol 13   Page 20

(Erase heading not required.)

Instructions regarding War Diaries and Intelligence Summaries are contained in F. S. Regs., Part II. and the Staff Manual respectively. Title Pages will be prepared in manuscript.

Place	Date	Hour	Summary of Events and Information	Remarks and references to Appendices
July	30		In bivouac in BÉCOURT WOOD. The Battalion moved to Grellis at LA HOUSSOYE, 10 miles along the main ALBERT-AMIENS Road. The G.O.C. 19th Division was present with the Bde. and to see the Battn. start on its march and later on expressed to the C.O. his appreciation and thanks for the work done by the Officers and men during its turn in the line.	
July	31		In Grellis at LA HOUSSOYE.	

R.C. Cooper
Lieut Col.
Comdg 9/Royal Welch Fusiliers
1.8.16

SPECIAL ORDER OF THE DAY
by
Major-General T. Bridges, C.M.G., D.S.O.
Commanding 19th Division.   July 4th 1916.

    The Army Commander called at Divisional Headquarters this morning in order to congratulate all ranks concerned in the capture of LA BOISELLE.   He considers this a fine feat of arms, and ordered the Divisional Commander to convey his appreciation to all concerned. He hopes that ground so well won and at such sacrifice will never be allowed to fall again in to the hands of the enemy.

(Sd) P.M. Davies, Lieut.-Colonel.

A.A. & Q.M.G., 19th Division.

SPECIAL ORDER OF THE DAY
by
Brigadier-General A.J. Dowell,
Commanding 58th Infantry Brigade.   July 4th 1916.

    The Brigadier-General Commanding would like to place on record his keen appreciation of the magnificent work done by the Brigade during the last two days in the attack on LA BOISELLE. The village is now practically in our hands, but this result would not have been possible had it not been for the previous good work of the 58th Brigade.
    The success of the operation was due, not only to the fine fighting qualities of the Brigade but also to the excellent work carried out by the carrying parties.
    While regretting the loss of some very valuable lives, the Brigadier feels convinced from the general bearing of all ranks that the fighting value of the Brigade has been in no way diminished and that all ranks are ready to take their place in the line again when required.

(Sd) J.A. Durie, Captain.

Staff Captain, 58th Infantry Brigade.

SPECIAL ORDER OF THE DAY
by
Major-General T. Bridges, C.M.G., D.S.O.
Commanding 19th Division.

11/7/16.

The General Officer Commanding 19th Division congratulates all ranks on the results achieved by the Division in the fighting of the last few days.

The storming of the village of LA BOISSELLE and its surroundings, fortified with every contrivance that an ingenious enemy could devise, almost impervious to artillery fire, and garrisoned by desperate men is a feat which will live in history.

During these first nine days of operations the Division has successfully carried out every task that it has been allotted.

In the course of a victorious advance in which every unit of the Division took part, it has captured over 500 prisoners, some guns and mortars and many machine guns, and has inflicted great loss on the enemy in morale, men, and material. The determination and gallantry shewn by all ranks under conditions of the utmost difficulty and discomfort has been the subject of congratulation from the Commander-in-Chief and the Army Commander.

The G.O.C. is proud to command such a fine Division and though many brave Officers and men have fallen, the loss of whom he greatly deplores, he feels confident that the same fine spirit, the same high standard of gallantry and devotion to duty will continue to be shewn by the men of the 19th Division, until complete victory is finally assured.

PM Davies
Lieut-Colonel,
A.A. & Q.M.G., 19th Division.

58th Brigade.
19th Division.

1/9th BATTALION

ROYAL WELCH FUSILIERS.

AUGUST 1 9 1 6 :

WAR DIARY
1st Royal Welch Fusiliers 5B
INTELLIGENCE SUMMARY

Vol 14
Army Form 2118
5/191 9/Vol 14
Page 1.

Place	Date	Hour	Summary of Events and Information	Remarks and references to Appendices
	Aug 1st/16		In billets at LA HOUSSOYE.	K.J.W.
	2nd		In billets at LA HOUSSOYE. The Corps Commander, III. Corps inspected the 58th Brigade near BEHENCOURT on its departure with the remainder of the 19th Division on transfer to the 5th Corps in the 2nd Army.	K.J.W.
	3rd		The Battn. marched at 12.30 p.m. to FRECHENCOURT where it entrained at 4.30 p.m. for LONGPRÉ - and on arrival there at 6.30 a.m. marched some 7 miles to billets & bivouacs at PONT REMY.	K.J.W.
	4th		In billets & bivouac at PONT REMY. A draft of 40 other ranks joined the Battn. from the Base.	K.J.W.
	5th		In billets at PONT REMY.	K.J.W.
	6th		The Battn. entrained at PONT REMY at 4.0 p.m. and was railed to BAILLIEUL arriving there at 1.35 a.m. 7th Aug.	K.J.W.
	7th		The Battn. detrained at BAILLIEUL at 1.35 a.m. and marched via LOCRE to R.C. FARM, where it relieved the 5th Bn. Yorkshire Regt. (T.F.) in Brigade reserve and at 9.0 p.m. took over the defence of a section of the line from the 5th Battn. Durham Light Infantry with Battn. H.Q. in YORKE HOUSE on the KEMMEL - VIERSTRAAT road.	K.J.W.
	8th		In Gen'l line trenches, YORKE HOUSE Sector.	K.J.W.
	9th		ditto ditto	K.J.W.

WAR DIARY
9th Royal Welch Fusiliers
INTELLIGENCE SUMMARY Vol 14 Page 2

Army Form C. 2118

(Erase heading not required.)

Place	Date	Hour	Summary of Events and Information	Remarks and references to Appendices
	August 9th		In front line trenches, YORKE HOUSE Section.	x x x
	10th			
	11th		ditto	x x x
	12th			
	13th		The Battalion was relieved in the front line trenches at midnight by the 9th Bath. Cheshire Regt, and proceeded to billets in Brigade Reserve at R.C. FARM.	x x x
	14th		In billets at R.C. FARM. H.M. the King inspected recipients of awards of the 19th Division at 5th Corps H.Q. Capt. J. Lloyd Williams (Military Cross) 13573 Sgt Beard B. (Distinguished Conduct Medal) representing the Battalion.	x x x
	15th			
	16th		In Brigade Reserve at R.C. FARM.	x x x
	17th			
	18th			

8625

WAR DIARY
9th (Service) Batn. Welsh Fusiliers
INTELLIGENCE SUMMARY Vol 14 Page 3

Army Form C. 2118

(Erase heading not required.)

Place	Date	Hour	Summary of Events and Information	Remarks and references to Appendices
Aug 19th	1916		The In Bivouac Reserve at P.E. Farm. The Battalion relieved the 9th Battn. Cheshire Regiment in the front line trenches during the evening, relief being completed by 11.0 p.m.	K.S.M.
	20th			
	21st			
	22nd		In front line trenches in YORKE HOUSE Section.	K.S.M.
	23rd			
	24th			
	25th			
	26th		In the evening the Battalion was relieved by the 9th Battn. Cheshire Regt. and proceeded to Divisional Reserve at BUTTERFLY CAMP. (N.19.A.) 2/Lieuts. Q.F.G. Fox, L.F. Thomas and W. Davies joined for duty with the Battalion on this date.	K.S.M.
	27th		In bivouac at BUTTERFLY CAMP	K.S.M.
	28th			
	29th		In bivouac at BUTTERFLY CAMP.	K.S.M.
	30th			
	31st		During the evening the Battalion relieved the 9th Battn. Cheshire Regt. in the front line trenches at YORKE HOUSE Section, relief being completed at 11.30 p.m.	K.S.M.

WAR DIARY
Royal Welsh Fusiliers
INTELLIGENCE SUMMARY

Vol 15 Page 1

Place	Date	Hour	Summary of Events and Information	Remarks and references to Appendices
Sept	1st		In front line Trenches, YORK HOUSE SECTION.	K2xx
	2nd			K2xx
	3rd			K2xx
			During the afternoon, the Battalion was relieved by the 73rd Batt. Canadian Royal Highlanders and proceeded to Bivouac at R.C. FARM, relief being completed at 8.30 p.m.	
	4th		In Bivouac at R.C. FARM. The Battalion moved (to a new billeting area in the evening) at LA RUE DU SAC arriving there at 10.0 p.m.	K2xY
	5th		In Camp at LA RUE DU SAC.	K2Y
	6th		Received draft of 12 other ranks from Base.	K2Y
	7th		The Battalion relieved the 4th Gordon Highlanders as Support Battalion for the Brigade in the PLOEGSTEERT SECTOR, relief being completed at 12 noon.	K2N
	8th		Left Support Batt for Br in PLOEGSTEERT Sector.	K2N

73rd Bn H.Q. Canadian Royal Highlanders attached for instruction

WAR DIARY
1st Royal Welsh Fusiliers Vol 15 page 2
INTELLIGENCE SUMMARY

Army Form C. 2118

(Erase heading not required.)

Place	Date	Hour	Summary of Events and Information	Remarks and references to Appendices
Sept.	9th		Left Support Batt. for Bd's in PLOEGSTEERT Sector. The Corps Commander Gen Sir Ch. Monro Ribbons to review us at NIEPPE Chateau at 3 p.m.	K.D.N.
	10th		Left. Support Batt. for Bd's in PLOEGSTEERT Sector	K.D.N.
	11th			K.D.N.
	12th			
	13th		Lieut. E.J. Hughes and 2/Lieut. E.S. Rees reported for duty with the Battalion. The Battalion relieved the 9th Cheshires in the front trenches during the day, relief being completed at 4.0 p.m.	K.D.N.
	14th		In front trenches in PLOEGSTEERT Sector	K.D.N.
	15th		In the evening the 9th Cheshires attempted a raid on the enemy trenches opposite our Battalion front, but this was unsuccessful owing to heavy hostile M.G. fire.	K.D.N.

WAR DIARY of Royal Welsh Fusiliers
INTELLIGENCE SUMMARY

Army Form C. 2118

Vol 15 Page 3

Place	Date	Hour	Summary of Events and Information	Remarks and references to Appendices
Sept	16th		On Front Trenches, PLOEGSTEERT Sector. 2/Lieut. E.F. Moss was mortally wounded in the evening while attempting to rescue a wounded man of the Cheshires who had been left in No Man's Land during the raid of the previous night. Two stretcher bearers also killed in the attempt.	K.2.N
	17th		In front Trenches, PLOEGSTEERT Sector. 2/Lt. E.F. Moss died of wounds at BAILLEUL at 6.40 AM. Received draft of 13 other ranks from Base.	K.2.N
	18th		In front trenches, PLOEGSTEERT Sector.	
	19th		The Battalion was relieved by the 2nd Border Regiment and marched to Camp at LA RUE DU SAC arriving there at 9.0 pm.	K.2.N
	20th		The Battalion left this area for a new billetting area at 8.0 a.m., arriving in billets near STRAZEELE at 2.0 pm. Received draft of 9 other ranks from Base.	K.2.N

WAR DIARY
4th Royal Welch Fusiliers. Vol. 15 Page 4
INTELLIGENCE SUMMARY

Army Form C. 2118

(Erase heading not required.)

Place	Date	Hour	Summary of Events and Information	Remarks and references to Appendices
Sept.	21st		In billets near STRAZEELE.	K.2.N.
	22nd		"	K.2.N.
	23rd		Received the following drafts this day – 72 other ranks from 9th Entrenching Batt (1/3rd Monmouths) 97 other ranks from Base. In billets near STRAZEELE.	K.2.N.
	24th		"	K.2.N.
	25th		During the afternoon, the Brigade was inspected by the Army Commander – General Sir Herbert P.C. Plumer, G.C.M.G., K.C.B. at STRAZEELE. In billets near STRAZEELE.	K.2.N.
	26th		"	K.2.N.
	27th		"	K.2.N.
	28th		"	K.2.N.
	29th		Received draft of 126 other ranks. In billets near STRAZEELE.	K.2.N.
	30th		"	K.2.N.

K.J. Nicholl. Major
Comg 9th R Welsh Fusiliers.

WAR DIARY / INTELLIGENCE SUMMARY

Army Form C. 2118

1st/6th J^r Royal Welsh Fusiliers   VOL 16

Place	Date	Hour	Summary of Events and Information	Remarks and references to Appendices
6oE	1st		In billets at STRAZEELE.	
	2nd		" " " "	
	3rd		" " " "	
	4th		" " " "	
	5th		The Battalion marched at 9.0. am for BAILLEUL where it entrained for DOULLENS.	
	6th		The Battalion arrived at DOULLENS at 7.0am and marched some 10 miles to huts at WIRNAMONT WOOD.	
	7th		The Battalion moved some 6 miles to and bivouacs West of SAILLY-AU-BOIS. (J.17.)	6 dug. m(l)s
	8th to 15th		The Battalion remained in bivouacs at J.17. and was occupied at fatigue duty in the trenches and in Battalion and Brigade training.	
	16th		The Battalion moved by march route 6 VAUCHELLES — 5 miles	6
	17th		The Battalion moved by march route 6 TOUTENCOURT — 6 miles	6
	18th		The Battalion moved by march route 6 OVILLERS POST. — some 11 miles — and was inspected.	a

October 1916

WAR DIARY
9th Royal Welsh Fusiliers
INTELLIGENCE SUMMARY

Army Form C. 2118
Vol 16
Page 2

Place	Date	Hour	Summary of Events and Information	Remarks and references to Appendices
	Oct. 18th		as it marched on from TOUTENCOURT. by General Sir Herbert Gough K.C.B. Commanding the Reserve Army, who expressed his approval of its workmanlike appearance and of the fitness of the men. The Battalion reached OVILLERS POST at 4.30pm where it bivouaced in hutments for the night.	23
	19th		The Battalion bivouaced at OVILLERS POST. In bivouac furnished a fatigue party of 500 men to cable laying under the orders of the A.D. Signals 2nd Corps - and also proceeded with the erection of huts which had been commenced by the R.E. for its accomodation.	23
	20th to 25th		In bivouac at OVILLERS POST. furnishing fatigue parties for cable laying and for erecting huts. On 25th 2/Lieut. F. E. WOMERSLEY was wounded while in charge of a working party - one other rank Killed.	23
	26th		The Battalion relieved the 10th R Warwick shire	23

WAR DIARY

1st/1st Welsh Fusiliers

INTELLIGENCE SUMMARY

Army Form C. 2118

Vol 16
Page 3

Place	Date	Hour	Summary of Events and Information	Remarks and references to Appendices
Ger.	26		Regiment in the line, occupying parts of the REGINA TRENCH and HESSIAN TRENCH as front and support lines. Kent: J.G. HUGHES wounded (Shell shock) - other ranks, 2 killed, 4 wounded.	25
	27"		In occupation of the line as above. Between 4.0 pm and 5.30 pm the trenches occupied were subjected to heavy and accurate shelling by the enemy with both Shrapnel and high explosive shells. During this bombardment, Lieut. C.G. LAWES was killed and 2/Lieut. F.G. DRIVER wounded - other ranks - 2 killed & wounded.	25
	28"		In occupation of the line as above. The enemy shelled our front and support lines heavily during the day and night. Casualties: Other ranks - 1 killed 10 wounded, 2 missing	25
	29"		In occupation of the line as above. The enemy bombarded our front and support lines	29

WAR DIARY
INTELLIGENCE SUMMARY

Army Form C. 2118

Vol 16
Cape 4

1st Battalion Worcestershire
(Erase heading not required.)

Place	Date	Hour	Summary of Events and Information	Remarks and references to Appendices
Ovillers Post	Oct 30th (Con)		Leaving about 4.30 pm and again about midnight. During the evening Capt. H.L. Williams was slightly wounded, but remained at duty; 4 Other Ranks being killed and 3 wounded.	3/ii 2/i
	30"		In occupation of the line as above:- Our front and Support lines were heavily shelled with H.E. and Shrapnel about	2/i
	31st	2.0 a.m.	The Battalion was relieved by the 10th Worcester Regt, and returned to huts at OVILLERS POST, relief being completed at 12.30 p.m. Casualties - Other Ranks, 1 killed & wounded 1/ii Sum 25 In huts at OVILLERS POST.	1/ii Sum 25

P.O. Bennes
Lieut
Comdg 1st Bn Worcesters

1.11.16

App. Nov 72.

9 RWF
Vol 17

Nov 1916

On His Majesty's Service.

Account 172

Officer i/c of H.S. Office
BASE

WAR DIARY / INTELLIGENCE SUMMARY

9th R.W.F.   November 1916   Vol. 17

Army Form C. 2118

Place	Date	Hour	Summary of Events and Information	Remarks and references to Appendices
AVELUY	1st		In huts at OVILLERS POST.	
	2nd		7th B⁰ relieved the 10th/73rd Worcester Regt in REGINA & HESSIAN Trenches East of STUFFE REDOUBT. Investigation of trenches as above.	
	3rd			
	4th			
	5th		Relieved 5th/7th Reg⁰ Gee Regiment. 7th B⁰ returned to camp at OVILLERS POST.	
	6th			
	6th		In camp at OVILLERS POST. The 9th Bⁿ carrying & working parties.	
	10th			
	11th		7th B⁰ relieved 10th Lancashires in HESSIAN and REGINA trenches in occupation of trenches above.	
	12th			
	13th		7th B⁰ was relieved by the 9th Cheshires at 10.40pm and marched to MARLBOROUGH & "WISSEN" huts	
	14th		7th B⁰ was ordered to hold present to allied the German during the evening and this order was relieved & cancelled, and 7th B⁰ was ordered to return to S. Sefton, and the other reserve dug outs of X.2.a.c.	
	15th		G. 4. Sgn Ste⁰ was received by 7th B⁰ Supper of 7th of Wiltshires, Warwicks	

WAR DIARY / INTELLIGENCE SUMMARY

Vol 17 page 2

Place	Date	Hour	Summary of Events and Information	Remarks and references to Appendices
	15.		J.S. Upson.	
	16.		Inspection in am.	
	17		Division throwing off by Barricks - at 12.15 am. C.O. returned to billets in AVELUY.	
	18		Billets in AVELUY.	
	19		Relieved elements of WARCESTERS + WRCESTERS in Pdlsen and on reduces toi Bn. for Lucky Way to FERGUSSON POST.	
	20		Relieving stews in stores - 2 stretcher bear tive. Lt. Sermon meet the commanding off B 1 B'n. arrangement to 11 September 13 = 4 Division. arrangements to Captain W.S. Thomas who is bn wounded sent to send 4 companions in clearing Major Thistle & Cpl. Davis.	R.S.
	21		Holding line as before.	
	22		Relieved by 8th Northumberland Fus.; to huts in AVELUY	
	23		Marched to WARLOY	
	24		Marched to DOULLENS	

Army Form C. 2118

Vol. 17
Copy 3

WAR DIARY
or
INTELLIGENCE SUMMARY
(Erase heading not required.)

Instructions regarding War Diaries and Intelligence Summaries are contained in F. S. Regs., Part II. and the Staff Manual respectively. Title Pages will be prepared in manuscript.

Place	Date	Hour	Summary of Events and Information	Remarks and references to Appendices
LE MEILLARD	25		March to LE MEILLARD	
	26		In billets at LE MEILLARD	
	27		"	
	28		" : 2nd Lt H. KILVERT joins the Bn.	
	29		As above	
	30		As above	

58th Brigade Order No 89.

App XXXIa

Copy No 8

1st Nov 1916.

1. The Brigade will relieve the 56th and 57th Brigades in the line tomorrow.

2. The relief will be carried out in accordance with attached table.

3. Movement will be by platoons at 100 yards distance.

4. 58th M.G.Company and 58th T.M.Battery will relieve their opposite numbers under arrangements to be made by the O's C concerned.

Acknowledge.

Issued at 11.p.m.

                                               Captain

                            Brigade Major 58th Infantry Brigade

Copy No			Copy No	
1	File		12	58.M.G.Company
2)			13	58.T.M.Battery
3)	War Diary		14	Staff Captain
4	G.O.C.		15	Transport Officer
5	19th Division		16	Signal Section
6	56th Brigade		17	94th Coy R.E.
7	57th Brigade		18	S.S.W.Borderers
8	9.Cheshire		19	A.D.M.S.
9	9.R.W.Fusiliers			
10	9.Welch			
11	6.Wiltshire			

ADMINISTRATIVE ORDERS

GRENADES, PICKS and SHOVELS.

Grenades, Picks and Shovels "to be carried on the man" will be left at Battalions' 1st Line Transport. They will be carried forward to Gravel Pit at a subsequent date under Brigade arrangements.

PACKS, BLANKETS, SURPLUS STORES.

Packs or blankets will be left behind and carried back to dump at BOUZINCOURT as soon as possible by Battalion Transport. This also applies to all surplus stores which are not required at 1st Line Transport.

PETROL TINS.

Petrol tins will be taken over by relieving units. Any shortage of these should be at once reported to the Brigade.

OFFICERS AND OTHER RANKS TO BE LEFT OUT OF THE LINE.

Officers and specialists to be left out of the line in accordance with 19th Division G.54/6/10 para 12. will not proceed to the trenches tomorrow. One Officer from each unit will be at CRUCIFIX CORNER at 9.30 a.m. tomorrow to meet an Officer from 19th Division "Q" Staff who will arrange the billeting of these. Each Officer should bring with him a list showing the exact number of officers and other ranks who will not be going into the line from his own unit.

H. Raymond, Captain,
Staff Captain, 58th Infantry Brigade.

Brigade H.Q.
1st Novr. 1916.

RELIEF TABLE.

Date	Unit	From	To	In relief of	Guides will be at	Time
2nd Novr	9.Cheshire	DONNETS POST	Trenches	7th East Lancs	R.32.b.7.8. where tramway cuts THIEPVAL-MOUQUET FARM Road	8.45.a.m. ※
"	9.Welch	do	do	7th N.Lancs	do	9.30.a.m — 10.15 a.m.
"	9.R.W.Fus	OVILLERS POST	do	"A" Battalion 57th Brigade	GRAVEL PIT R.27.c.central	10.15.a.m. Field C.T. is 9.30 a.m. impassable route will be via STUFF REDOUBT
"	6.Wiltshire	NISSEN Huts CRUCIFIX CORNER	do	"B" Battalion 57th Brigade	do	12.15.p.m. 11.30 a.m.

"Z" Battalion is the battalion on the right.

A Coy march out 8.0 am
B — 8.10
D — 8.18
C — 8.26
AB — 8.34 am

MA 3.

A   D
B   HQ   App XXXI b
C   R.M.

The Bn relieves 7th East Lancs in the trenches on 2nd Nov. Guides will be at R 32 b 7.9 where tramway cuts MOUQUET FM - THIEPVAL ROAD at 8.45 a.m.

A Coy. will march out from present camp 8.0 am. B 8.10 am D 8.18 am C 8.26, H.Q. 8.34 am. The L.G.O. will attach the two Bn. reserve guns to the front line Coys (A + B). Movements will be by platoons at 100 x distance.

Reports that relief in trenches is complete will be phoned "MA 3 complied with at ..." Dress will be as before. Packs must be clearly labelled.

Watts.

MA 4.

~~T~~

Transport Officer. & Q.M.S.

For the move into trenches on 2-11-16;—
in relief of 7th East Lancs.

① Blankets will be left in packs.
Packs will be stacked at Coy
H.Q. ready for collection by T.O.
They will then be taken to dump at
BOUZINCOURT.

② Mess Kits (as small as possible)
will be collected ~~at R~~
at Guard tent at 8.0 a.m.
onwards (One man in charge
each Coy). T.O. will provide
mules for conveyance to
Reserve Coy dump.

E Lord
Q
G. Cheshire

2/11/16

To 58th Bde. App XXXIC

No. MA 9.   3-11-1916.

1. Major Puxton and the Adjutant attempted to get down to the front line by daylight between 11.0 and 1.0 pm this morning. But the conditions of the communication trenches rendered this impossible.

They went down over land about 6.0 p.m. and found the front line almost impossible, and indeed, quite so by daylight as the mud was thigh deep.

Clearing of the mud is very difficult and almost impossible, as no sooner is one space cleared than the mud flows in from either side, or it gets churned up with the head lare. In consequence of this all carrying has to be done by night and reliefs by day are out of the question. I consider it very important that we should get duck boards and trestles put in the front line as soon as possible, and that the half cut communication trench from BAINBRIDGE to the western end of STUFF TRENCH should be put through and at the same time boarded as O.G.1. is not only ~~trench~~ in a terrible condition but is under accurate artillery fire from the enemy.

Conditions for the men in the front line are bad, as owing to the shortage of dugouts and the depth of the mud, they are wet through and it is very hard to carry out preventative measures against trench feet.

2. I would beg to request that permission be granted to keep a jar of RUM in the Aid Post, for issue under supervision of the M.O. to the wounded who have lain all day in the misery and mud of the front line.

2.11.71.

L.V.A.
Comdg 9th E Leshire R.

To 58 Bde

Aph XXXII

N° MA 10.   3-11-16.

I sent out an officer's patrol of five men tonight to reconnoitre the the German trench between C.G.1 and LUCKY WAY. They took with them a Lewis Gun, with the intention of inflicting casualties on any working parties they might come across.

The officer returned about 9.40 pm and reported that he went down the western side of C.G.1 and found that the enemy was firing Very lights from a point about 80x from our lines. He then worked to the left, over the crest, when he observed a large enemy party digging on the trench to be reconnoitred. His

Previous to going out one of our listening posts had reported a Boche patrol working towards our lines; and it the officer's intention to try and cut this off. As they were not encountered, the Lewis Gun was got in position and a drum was emptied into the working party. It is thought that many casualties were inflicted.

Our patrol then returned to our own lines, as an enemy patrol of a dozen men was seen to work forward; and, the previously reported patrol, not having been located, it was considered advisable to withdraw.

The going in NO MAN'S LAND is very bad indeed, being very different to the going on top between our support and front lines.

3-11-16. Comdg 9th Cheshires

App XXXii

Relief Table

Date	Units	From	To	In relief of	Guides to be provided by	Time of relief to start	Time of relief to be completed
	9th R.B. Tan.	Trench R.22.a.8.10 R.21.6.2.5	DONNET'S POST	Y.L. Royal Sumt	Grenelle Pit R.23.c. central	4.15 pm	4.55 pm
	6th W. Yorks	R.21.6.2.5 m R.20.6.4.6	AYELUY	Y.H. Cent. Lanca	do	do	4.55 pm
	9 Cheshires	R.20.y.6.6 R.20.a.8.2	DONNET'S POST HQ AYELUY	Y.11 South Lanc	R.20.6.4.3 where branched rd. Thiepval-Aveluy FARM road	6-7 pm	7.15 pm
	9 Welch	R.20.a.8.2b R.20.a.12.1	WOODPOST(R.9) LEIPZIG Redoubt (1 Coy) Y.11 N. Lancs	do	7 pm	
	53rd R.E. Fd Coy 56th M. Coy						8.30 pm

Arrangements to be made by OC 6 Lancs

App XXXIIIa

88th Brigade Order No. 90

Ref. CHAULNES S.E.   App III
LE GARD and DERNANCOURT 1/10,000   Copy No 8

1. The 87th Bde will be relieved tomorrow by the 88th Bde.
2. The relief will be carried out in accordance with attached table.
3. Routes will be overland and will be marked out by O.C. Battalions.
4. Lewis Guns will be relieved with their companies.
5. Billeting parties will be sent on in the morning to take over billets. They will also arrange to meet their units and lead them into camp. Billeting parties of 56 M.G. Coy and 58 S.M.Battery will report at Brigade H.Q. at 9 A.M.
6. Reports on completion to be sent as expeditiously as possible, and where practicable by wire in code.
7. Brigade H.Q. will be at X.2.a.5.5. till completion of relief, after at AVELUY.

Acknowledge.

W.H.Pott Captain
Brigade Major 88th Inf Brigade

Issued at

Copy No 1 A/A   Copy No 12 58 M.G.Coy
        2)   13 58 T.M.Bty
        3) War Diary   14 Staff Captain
        4 O.C.   15 Transport Offr
        5 Essex   16 Q.M. Coy R.E.
        6 5R Bde   17 S.S.O. "
        7 87 Bde   18 A.D.M.S.
        8 4 Cheshire   19 Bde Bombing Officer
        9 1/1 R.M.Fus
       10 1 Welsh
       11 R Wiltshire

Administrative Arrangements
for move

Trench Stores

Petrol tins in the line will be handed over to relieving units. Those at the transport lines will be handed over to the Transport Officers of the relieving units. Other trench stores will be handed over as usual. Receipts will be forwarded to this office early on the day after the relief. The 9th Bn. R.W. Fusiliers will bring out the tools and grenades which they carried in with them.

Gum Boots

Gum boots not in wear will be handed over to relieving units. Those at present in wear will be brought out and taken to the Drying Rooms at CRUCIFIX CORNER early on the morning of the 6th instant. Receipts will be taken.

SR 54
4/11/16

Staff Captain 58th Inf Brigade

Captain

App XXXIII a.

MA 13.   SECRET   Apx XXXIII 6.

1. The Bn. will be relieved on 15th inst by 7th S. hours; and on relief will move into camp at DONNETS POST. Bn H.Q. will be in AVELUY.

2. Guides for front Coys are being provided by Support and Reserve Coys. Billeting parties & guides have been arranged.

3. Mess Kits etc will be sent down by the front line coys as soon as possible after dusk to the Reserve Coy. Mule transport will be provided.

4. All empty water cans must be sent to Reserve Coy.
   Lists of Trench Stores will be prepared. These will be receipted and sent in to Orderly Room immediately on arrival in new camp.

5. Reports that relief is complete in trenches will be wired to H.Q. immediately on completion, in the form "THIRTEEN at ——————".

6. Reports of ARRIVAL in camp to be sent to H.Q. without delay. May be expected about 8.15 — 8.30 p.m.

6. Reports that Relief in Trenches is completed will be phoned to H.Q. in form "FOURTEEN done at _ _ _ _ _".

Reports of Arrival in Camp to be sent without delay.

4-11-16.

LaWatts Lt.
9th Cheshire R.

Note. All guides will report-

① O.C. C at 5.0 p.m.
O.C. C will detail an officer to be i/c guides & to meet the incoming Bn.

② All Gum boots in wear will be deposited at C Coy HQ.
They will then be transported by mule to drying rooms at transfer corner.

Watts

A 14.
1. The Bn. will be relieved in trenches by 7th S. Lancs on 5th. and will move into billets at DONNETS POST. Bn HQ. will be in AVELUY.
2. Guides will be provided :
   i   for RIGHT FIRE COY and RESERVE Coy (4 each) by C Coy.
   ii for LEFT COY and SUPPORT Coy (4 each) by D Coy.
   iii for H.Q. (3) by H.Q. Coy.
   Guides for SUPPORT, RESERVE and H.Q. will rendezvous at 5.0 p.m.
   Guides for Fire Coys will rendezvous at 7.0 p.m.
   Place of rendezvous is R32678 (where TRAMWAY meets THIEPVAL — MOUQUET FM road).
3. Kits will be sent to Reserve Coy as soon as possible after dusk. Mule transport will be provided.
4. Billeting parties are arranged.
5. Lists of Trench Stores will be receipted and sent to Orderly Room, immediately on arrival in new camp.

MA 15.

Transport Officer
9th Cheshire R.

1. BN. is relieved on 5th by 7th S. LANCS & moves into camp at DONNETS POST. BN. HQ will be in AVELUY.

2. Relief will be at night. First Coys will arrive in camp about 8.0 p.m.

3. Mules will be required for kits ; [and an extra mule for Gum Boots]. Mules should be at Reserve Coy about 5.30 pm (HQ & C) and 8.0 pm for A & B.

4. All water cans at the Depot must be handed over to 7th S. LANCS. Receipts will be obtained & forwarded to Orderly Room.

5. Billeting. You will take a party of one C.Q.M.S. [and 2 men per Coy to act as guides] in the morning and take over camp. Copy of receipts to be forwarded.
Inform RSM & QMS.

E. Watts.
4-11-16.

$\overline{XXXIII}$ б.

"A" Form.
MESSAGES AND SIGNALS.

Army Form C.2121 (in pads of 100).

This message is on a/c of:
.... Service.
App XXXIII C
(Signature of "Franking Officer.")

TO { T.R.

Sender's Number: AC 410
Day of Month: 5
AAA

T.R.O.O.90 complied with at 11.30 p.m.

From
Place: T.R.
Time:

XXXIII

"A" Form.
MESSAGES AND SIGNALS.

Army Form C.2121 (in pads of 100).

TO 58 Bde.

Sender's Number: ACU11
Day of Month: 6
AAA

The Bn. has arrived in camp at DONNET'S POST. Bn. HQ is in AVELUY. aaa. Relief was delayed owing to two platoons going astray. Time of arrival last platoons in camp 2.30 a.m.

From: 9th Cheshire
Time: 2.45 am

XXXIII d.

MESSAGES AND SIGNALS.

Army Form C.2121 (in pads of 100).

This message is on a/c of: **A**ᵖʰ Service. XXXIV

TO { All Coys. Transport Officer
R.S.M.

Sender's Number.	Day of Month.	In reply to Number.	
AC 414	8-11-1916.		A A A

The Battalion will move from the present camp area & move into the NISSEN HUTS at ~~[crossed out]~~ W12 c 5·4 tomorrow 9th inst. aaa The Nissen huts will be clear of the troops at present occupying by 12 noon aaa One N.C.O. per Coy will report to an officer to be detailed by O.C. "A" Coy at 10·0 a.m. for billeting aaa. This officer will take over huts and report as soon as possible aaa. ~~[crossed out]~~ The move will be made independently by Coys and should be completed by 1·0 p.m. Report of completion as soon as possible aaa One N.C.O. & 1 man per Coy to be left in old camp to clean & hand over aaa Time of C.O.'s Office Hours will be notified later aaa

From
Place
Time

Censor. Signature of Addressor or person authorised to telegraph in his name.

XXXIV

XXXIV

All Units.

The following copy of message from 19th Division is forwarded for your information.

Begins:-

"Following from Fifth Army begins aaa The Army Commander wishes to thank all ranks for their splendid efforts under most difficult circumstances aaa The great victory which they have won today will have very far reaching effects aaa To this success all the troops have contributed to the utmost of their power aaa Some have been more fortunate than others but this is always the case in war and is to be expected aaa Great results have been achieved and the Army Commanders confidence in the leaders and troops under his command has been more than justified aaa Ends.

Captain
Brigade Major 58th Infantry Brigade

Brigade H.Q.
14th Novr 1916.

SECRET   58th Brigade Order No 94.

Copy No 10

13.11.1916.

1. The 9th Cheshire and 9th Welch Regiments will relieve the 9th R.W.Fusiliers and 6th Wiltshire respectively in the Line tonight.

2. On relief the 9th R.W.Fusiliers will take over the NISSEN Huts from 9th Cheshire at X.12.C.5.4. and 6th Wiltshire will move to the dug-outs in X.2.a. and c now occupied by the 9th Welch Regiment.

3. Guides, 1 Officer, 1 per Battalion H.Q. and 1 per platoon will be at

	At	For
GRAVEL PIT	4.45.p.m.	9th Cheshire
R.27.C.central		
do	6.15.p.m.	9th Welch

4. 9th Cheshire and 9th Welch will take the following into the Line :-

   Tools
   Bombs (4 per man)   *everything*
   Smoke candles
   Flares.

5. Reports to Brigade H.Q. on completion by the word "STONE".

ACKNOWLEDGE.

Captain
Brigade Major 58th Infantry Brigade

Copy No 1 File   Copy No 13 58.M.G.Company
      2)   14 58.T.M.Battery
      3) War Diary   15 Staff Captain
      4 A.C.C.   16 Transport Officer
      5 19th Division   17 Signal Section
      6 56th Brigade   18 94th Coy R.E.
      7 57th Brigade   19 5.S.W.Borderers
      8 53rd Brigade   20 Bde Bombing Officer
      9 9.Welch   21 A.D.M.S.
     10 9.Cheshire
     11 9.R.W.Fus
     12 6.Wiltshire

Quartermasters have been informed.

First Coy will move 2.45 fm.
loans greatcoats who wore
packed blankets bdo. dumps

A   Ath fl
@   stole
B   Rot.
D   Urns
HQ. TH

"A" Form. Army Form C. 2121.
MESSAGES AND SIGNALS.

Priority

This message is on a/c of: ~~XXXVI~~ Service.

TO: O.C. 9th Cheshire
~~9th Welch Regt~~

Sender's Number: B.M. 172
Day of Month: 16 Nov.
AAA

You must prepared to be relieved tonight by a Batt<u>n</u> of the 18<u>th</u> Division. You will therefore collect guides 1 officer 17 O.R. and despatch them to the GRAVEL Pit on receipt of this. Their arrival at the GRAVEL Pit will be notified to Bde H.Q under arrangements already made by the Bde. Adds 9<u>th</u> Cheshire + 9<u>th</u> Welch

From Place: 58<u>th</u> Bde
Time: 2.30 p.m.

W Pott Capt

"A" Form.
MESSAGES AND SIGNALS.

Army Form C. 2121.

disposed.
1 Coy each in front line.
dividing line app. R 21 b 2.4.
1 Coy each in HESSIAN Trench.
dividing line app R 21 d 5.8.
4. Guides aheads arranged.
5. Relieved portion of 9th Welch
to dug outs X 2 a. & c.
9th Cheshire to NISSEN huts in
Marlborough Lines W 12 c.
6. Bde H.Q remains at X 2 b 0.4

Elliott Capt
58th Bde

"A" Form. Army Form C. 2121.

MESSAGES AND SIGNALS.

TO: O.C. 9th Cheshire.
9th Welch.

Sender's Number: B.M.103
Day of Month: 16 NOV.
AAA

The whole of 9th Cheshire Regt and that portion of 9th Welch Regt East of STUMP Road (incl to 9th Welch) will be relieved tonight as follows.

2. 9th Cheshire by 2 Corps 7th BUFFS
9th Welch by 2 Corps. 7th R. West Surrey.

3. Relieving Regts will be

SECRET.   Copy No 9

58th Brigade Order No 98.

                                                  17th Novr 1916.

1. The 58th Brigade will be relieved tonight from STUMP ROAD
   to BATTERY VALLEY R.14.C.9.0. by the 57th Brigade.
   STUMP ROAD will be inclusive to the 18th Division.

2. The 9th Welch Regiment will be relieved in the subsector
   STUMP ROAD - O.G.1. by 8th North Staffords.
   The 6th Wiltshire and 9th R.W.Fus O.G.1 - R.14.C.9.0. by
   the 10th R.Warwicks.

3. The relief will be carried out in accordance with attached
   Table.

4. 58th M.G.Company will rwmain in dugouts X.2.a.& c less four
   guns to proceed to the GRAVEL PIT as already ordered.

5. 58th T.M.Battery, less 2 guns and personnel attached to the
   57th Brigade, will move to billets which will be arranged
   by the Staff Captain

6. Brigade H.Q. will remain at X.2.b.0.4. tillcompletion of
   relief when it will move to AVELUY.

7. Completion of the relief by the word "NISSEN".

                                                  Captain

Issued at   Brigade Major 58th Infantry Brigade

Copy No 1 File   Copy No 13 58 M.G.Company
       2)   14   58.T.M.Battery
       3) War Diary   15   Staff Captain
       4. G.O.C.   16   Transport Officer
       5   19th Division   17   Signal Section
       6   56th Brigade   18   94th Coy R.E.
       7   57th Brigade   19   5.S.W.Borderers
       8   55th Brigade   20   Bde Bombing Officer
       9   9.Cheshire   21   A.D.M.S.
      10   9.R.W.Fus
      11   9.Welch
      12   6.Wiltshire

RELIEF TABLE.

Date	Unit	From	To	On relief by	Guides to be at Meeting place	Time	Remarks.
17th Nov	9.Welch (Part of)	Trenches STUMP ROAD - O.G.1.	Dugouts X 2 a & c	8th N.Staffords	GRAVEL PIT	5.p.m.	
do	6.Wilts	Trenches O.G.1 - R.20. b.3.8.	CROMWELL HUTS W.18.a.	10th R.Warwicks (part of)	do	6.30.p.m.	1 officer, 1 guide Battn H.Q., 8 guides from Front Line.
do	9th R.W.F.	Trenches R.20.b.3.8. - R.14.c.9.0.	AVELUY	10th R.Warwicks (part of)	do	6.30.p.m.	1 officer, 1 guide Battn H.Q., 8 guides from Front Line.
do	9th Cheshire	MARLBOROUGH HUTS W.12.C.	WELLINGTON HUTS W.12.d.	on vacation by Unit occupying WELLINGTON HUTS			
18Novr	9th Cheshire	Divisional Reserve	DUGOUTS X.2.a & c				
18.Novr	9th Welch	Dug-outs X.2.a.& C	WELLINGTON HUTS				Tomove at 9.a.m.

War Diary

"A" Form. Army Form C. 2121.
MESSAGES AND SIGNALS.

| Prefix | Code | m. | Words | Charge | This message is on a/c of: | Recd. at | m. |
| Office of Origin and Service Instructions. | | | Sent At m. To By | | XXXVIII ~~Service.~~ (Signature of "Franking Officer.") | Date From By | |

TO O.C. 9th Cheshire Regt ✓
    ~~58th~~

*	Sender's Number.	Day of Month	In reply to Number	AAA
	R M 22	17 Nov.		

R.t. O.O. 99. Zero hour is 6.10 a.m. ~~on~~ tomorrow 18th inst.

From
Place   58th Bde
Time

The above may be forwarded as now corrected. (Z)

Censor. Signature of Addressee or person authorised to telegraph in his name.

SECRET.   Copy No. 9

                    58th Brigade Order No 96.
                                                                     15.11.1916.
Ref:-   K.11. - M.23. 1/20,000
        1/10,000 Operation Map of 31.10.16.

1.   Operation Orders No's 87, 91 and 93 are cancelled.

2.   The 19th Division will attack GRANDCOURT TRENCH and GRANDCOURT
     in conjunction with an attack by the 18th Division (on our right)
     on GRANDCOURT TRENCH and by the V Corps on the PUISIEUX TRENCH
     and BAILLESCOURT FARM.

3.   The objective of the 19th Division will be from SIXTEEN ROAD
     at R.16.a.8.8. to the eastern end of GRANDCOURT village at
     R.10.A.0.0. and R.9.b.6.3., thence to R.9.b.1.4. and along the
     railway to R.8.d.4.8.

4.   The attack will be carried out by the 57th and 58th Brigades,
     the former being on the right, whilst the 56th Brigade will assist
     by attacking the enemy trenches in R.14.C. 9th Cheshire and 9th
     Welch Regiment will be in Divisional Reserve in the neighbourhood
     of the GRAVEL PIT R.27.C.central.

5.   The boundaries of the attacks will be as follows:-
     Right Boundary, 57th Brigade - The SIXTEEN ROAD (shown as such on
        1/5,000 only. From R.22.A.4.8. to R.16.a.8.8. all exclusive.
     Boundary between 57th and 58th Brigades - R.20.b.8.5. (inclusive to
        58th Brigade) - R.15.C.8.95 making the whole of O.G.1
        inclusive to 58th Brigade) - cross roads R.9.C.2.3. - road
        junction at R.9.C.1.8. - railway at R.9.A.2.1. where the river
        joins the railway before running parallel to it.
     Left Boundary, 58th Brigade - R.20.A.6.5. - railway at R.8.d.4.8.

     Dividing Line between Battalions - R.20.b.2½.6½. - junction of
     LUCKY WAY and bank at R.20.b.3½.9. thence along bank (inclusive to
     Left subsector) - R.14.b.6.7½. - S.E. corner of enclosure at
     R.8.d.8.2. - bridge at R.8.d.7.9.

6.   Preliminary Positions.
        The 6th Wilts will be on the right, the 9th R.W.Fusiliers on
     the left. The leading two waves will be in the trench newly dug
     by 56th Brigade, the two rear waves will be in artillery formation
     just behind the trench.
        These two rear waves may also be in the trench if there is
     room.
        58th M.G.Company - in STUFF Trench R.20.b.3.3.
        58th T.M.Battery - in STUFF Trench R.20.b.5.4.
        94th Field Coy R.E. in MINERIDGE Trench at its junction with
           BULGAR Trench at R.20.C.8.2.

7.   Objectives - of the 19th Division.
        1st Objective. - GRANDCOURT TRENCH R.16.A.8.8. - R.15.B.70.95
     - R.15.A.8.1. thence to R.15.C.0.5. 95. - R.14.D.90.15. - R.14.D.
     20.05 and thence a line running approximately R.14.B.3.3. -
     R.14.A.2.5.
        2nd Objective. - The SIXTEEN ROAD at R.16.A.8.8. to the
     eastern end of GRANDCOURT village at R.10.A.0.0. and R.9.B.6.3.,
     thence to R.9.b.1.4. and along the railway to R.8.d.4.8.

8.   ORDERS to Troops.
     (a) Infantry.   At ZERO the two leading waves at 25 yards distance
        will advance and capture the first objective, the two rear
        waves in artillery formation will follow at 25 yards distance.
        Special cleaning up parties will be told off to follow the
        assaulting troops, these must be given definite points or
        zones to clean up.   When their task is finished they will
        follow on and rejoin their units.

SECRET.   Copy No. 9

(2).

After the capture of the first objective, the leading wave will go right through to the second, being reinforced as required by the succeeding wave or waves.

(b) Machine Guns. As soon as the 1st objective is gained 8 guns of the 58th M.G.Company will move forward to the approximate line of the 150 contour hence they will:-
    (a) bring fire to bear on any likely machine gun positions on the slopes North of the river ANCRE.
    (b) bring fire to bear on PUISILUX Trench and its support line to assist the V Corps attack, if not already captured by V Corps.
    (c) take advantage of any target which presents itself on the opposite slopes.
    (d) keep the line BAILLESCOURT FARM - Quarry R.3.b.9.4. Quarry R.3.A.2.0.
    (e) engage any counter attack which may develop.
The O.C., 58th M.G.Company will move forward any of the remaining 8 guns at his discretion.

(c) Trench Mortars. O.C., 56th Trench Mortar Battery will send two mortars to follow closely each of the two Battalions, and to support them as required.

(d) 94th Field Company R.E. The O.C. 94th Field Coy R.E. will prepare routes for the pack transport of the Brigade.

9. Artillery Barrage.
The Artillery Barrage will be on the same lines as indicated in the original scheme, except that the halt on the 1st Objective will be for half an hour only.

10. The Objective from R.15.A.8.8. to the railway embankment about R.9.b.1.4. will be consolidated.
How much of the railway embankment is to be consolidated depends on the situation on our left.

11. After reaching the second objective i.e. the railway embankment both battalions will at once push out patrols to get touch with the V Corps.

12 FLARES. Flares will be lighted on reaching the GRANDCOURT TRENCH i.e. during the half hour's pause in the barrage, and on reaching the final objective. Also at any other times on demand by the aeroplane.

13 Routes for TANKS.
All ranks must be warned that on no account are they to wait for the Tanks to come up.
No 1 Tank from R.21.a.4.7. along the east side of STUMP ROAD to cross roads R.9.B.1.1½.
   2 " from R.21.A.4.7. to cross roads R.9.A.7.0.
   3 " from R.21.A.4.7. to cross roads R.9.C.0½.6.
   4 " from R.21.A.4.7. to the east end of GRANDCOURT.

14 DUMPS.
Dumps have been formed at following points:-
   (a) R.E.Stores - Grenades - Water   R.20.D.7.1.
   (b) R.E.Dump only   R.20.D.2.5.
   (c) T.M.Dumps   R.20.B.9.0. - R.26.B.0.2. R.19.D.8.4.

15 Carrying Parties.
Carrying parties of 50 men under an officer from 6th Wilts. and 9th R.W.Fus will assemble at Bde H.Q. R. 26.D.3.3. at 5.p.m. on evening prior to Zero. They will report there to Captain WILLIAMS, 9th R.W.Fusiliers.

(3).

16. Transport.

All Pack Transport animals with feeds, less sufficient to bring up Rations on the evening of Zero day, will assemble under the orders of the Brigade Transport Officer at the Tank R.26.b.5.1.

17. Medical arrangements.

 Regimental Aid Posts ......   R.25.A.6.8.
                  R.26.B.4.4.
         THIEPVAL R.25B.7.C.
                   R.25.D.6.8.

 Field Ambulance, Collecting Posts -- DONNETS POST
    Tram Terminus   X.7.A.0.2.

18. Signalling.

A Station will be established in STUFF Trench at R.26.B.3.3. and visual messages from the front will be received.

19. 56th Brigade Battle H.Q. will be at R.26.B.3.3.

 ACKNOWLEDGE

                        Captain

Issued at 7.30 a.m.

            Brigade Major 56th Infantry Brigade

Copy No 1 File
   2
   3 War Diary
   4 G.O.C.
   5 19th Division
   6 56th Bde
   7 57th Bde
   8 58th Bde
   9 8.Cheshire
  10 9.R. Fus
  11 9.Welch
  12 6.Wiltshire

Copy No 13 58.M.G.Company
  14 58.T.M.Battery
  15 Staff Captain
  16 Transport Officer
  17 Signal Section
  18 94th Coy R.E.
  19 5.S.W.Borderers
  20 Bde Bombing Officer
  21 A.D.M.S.

"A" Form.
MESSAGES AND SIGNALS.

XXXIX

Army Form C.2121 (in pads of 100).

Prefix .... Code .... m. Office of Origin and Service Instructions.	Words	Charge	This message is on a/c of: .... Service. (Signature of "Franking Officer.")	Recd. at.:........m. Date............. From............ By............
	Sent At.......m. To........ By........			

TO { FR.

Sender's Number.	Day of Month.	In reply to Number.	
* Blu 7 30	18½		AAA

Your message received. Please try to see OC OS (Lt Col Heath) and arrange with him as to the holding of the front line. If you are both satisfied that our original front line is held in sufficient strength you may withdraw your Battalion to STUFF & BAINBRIDGE Trenches for the night. In any case reorganise the battalion & report your action & disposition.

Col. Heath is at junction of LUCKY WAY & old front line. Your carrying party is being sent up with the bearer.

Your rations will be sent to Div HQ & will be forwarded to you.

From	TS		
Place			
Time	9.45 p		

The above may be forwarded as now corrected. (Z)

Censor.   M T Bulloch Major

Signature of Addressor or person authorised to telegraph in his name.

* This line should be erased if not required.

750,000. W 2186—M509. H. W. & V., Ld. 6/16.

HQ
O.C. 9/Cheshire Regt

Your HQ 3 of 18th received.
I have had one previous report, which I
acknowledged by the runner who brought it, &
sent at the same time orders to concert
with O.C. 10. R. War. R. as to holding the
line. His H.Q. at present are R 20 b 38 on
LUCKY WAY.
Two half Companies of yours, having lost their
way, are in STUFF & BAINBRIDGE trenches.
Take such measures as you think necessary for
holding our front line of yesterday morning.
There are only a few scattered detachments & some
M.G's & Lewis guns in it besides your batn.
Please try to keep me informed as to your position
& circumstances.

G.D. Jeffreys B.Genl
Comdg 57th Inf Bde

5.45 a.m.
19.10.16.

To Lt Col Worgan
                Comm'd 9th Cheshire

Sir
            Replying to your note I have
been along to the left & found a
large number of our fellows all
mixed up with other units & R.E. etc
   I did not stop to count them
exactly; but Mr Gadson
estimates the lot to be between
100 & 150.
      The officers here are: -

Mr Gadson — Beyer — Morrison
     Quale — Day — Gallie &
     Horsley.

   Mr Barnes came here last
night with twelve but went
straight on to the ard post.

8.20 am   J Higginbottom 2 Lt
19/11/16   L.Q.C.

"A" Form.
Army Form C. 2121.
MESSAGES AND SIGNALS.

TO: O.C. 9th Cheshire

Sender's Number: B.M. 223
Day of Month: 19 Nov.
AAA

Your Batt. is to occupy the dug outs in X2 a and c. Your transport officer has been informed.

From: 58th Bde

"A" Form.
MESSAGES AND SIGNALS.

Army Form C.2121 (in pads of 100).

Prefix ...... Code ...... m. Office of Origin and Service Instructions.	Words / Charge / Sent At .... m. To .... By	This message is on a/c of: ....Service. (Signature of "Franking Officer.")	Recd. at .... m. Date .... From .... By ....

TO — F R.

Sender's Number.	Day of Month.	In reply to Number.	
RM 735	19	F R. 4 + 2	A A A

Original of FR 2 was never received. The runner who brought your report on the attack was sent with a runner from your carrying party to pick them up and take them on to you. Apparently they and another lot of runners all lost their way.

There are two half companies of yours & three officers near the Hq of 1st L in BULGAR trench.

It is hoped that the Bde. will be relieved tonight.

From: TS
Place:
Time: 9.30 a.m.

SECRET.   Copy No

58th Brigade Order No 100.

Ref:- OPERATION MAP 1.5000   21st Novr 1916.
       57½D.N.E. 1/20,000

1. The 58th Brigade will be relieved on night of 22nd/23rd by the 13th Northumberland Fusiliers of the 34th Brigade.

2. The relief will be carried out in accordance with the attached table.

3. O.C., 13th N.F. will visit H.Q. tomorrow as follows:-
    9th R.W.Fusiliers .... 10.30.a.m.
    6th Wiltshire .... 11.a.m.
    O.C., 9th Welch Regiment will attend also at this hour.
    O.C. 34th Machine Gun Company will visit Brigade H.Q. at 10.a.m. to meet O.C., 58th Machine Gun Company.
    Separate instructions will be issued as regards the relief of the 58th Trench Mortar Battery.

4. Guides will meet the 13th N.F. on the NAB Road just below Brigade H.Q. at X.2.A.5.5. at 3.30.p.m. as follows:-
    <u>9th Welch Regt.</u>   1 Officer
                             4 guides from each of Front Line Coys
                             4 " from Support Coy in O.G.1.

    <u>6th Wiltshire Regt</u>   1 Officer
                             4 Guides from Company in Front Line from R.20.b.8.6. - LUCKY WAY
                             4 Guides from Support Coy in STUFF Trench

    <u>9th R.W.Fusiliers.</u>   1 Officer
                             4 Guides from the Company holding the New Trench from LUCKY WAY to R.14.d. 0.6½.

5. All aeroplane photos, and maps 1/5000, 1/10,000, and 1/20,000 not handed over to the incoming unit will be returned to Brigade H.Q. by 9.a.m. on 23rd inst.

6. Companies occupying ZOLLERN, FERGUSON, BAINBRIDGE and BULGAR trenches may withdraw after the incoming unit has passed through to the front line. Coy's occupying the trenches which are not being taken over will withdraw at the discretion of O's C Battalions.

7. Brigade H.Q. will move to AVELUY on completion of relief.

8. Reports by the word "LIMBER".

                                                                          Captain

Issued at   Brigade Major 58th Infantry Brigade

Copy No 1 File   Copy No 12 6.Wiltshire
        2)   13 58.M.G.Company
        3) War Diary   14 58.T.M.Battery
        4   G.O.C.   15 Staff Captain
        5   19th Division   16 Transport Officer
        6   56th Brigade   17 Signal Officer
        7   55th Brigade   18 94th Coy R.E.
        8   34th Brigade   19 S.W.Borderers
        9   9.Cheshire   20 Bde Bombing Officer
       10   9.R.W.Fusiliers   21 A.D.M.S.
       11   9.Welch

RELIEF TABLE.

Date	Unit	From	To	On relief by	Remarks.
22.Novr	9th Welch	Trenches STUMP ROAD (excl) to O.G.1 (excl) at R.20.b.8.5.	WELLINGTON HUTS.	2 Companies 13th Northumberland Fus	DISPOSITIONS of 13th N.F. 1 Coy in Front Line from STUMP ROAD to O.G.1. 1 Coy in O.G.1 from STUFF REDOUBT - STUFF TRENCH.
"	6th Wilts	From O.G.1 to LUCKY WAY (incl) at R.20. b.3.8. (approx)	CROMWELL HUTS (3 Huts to be kept vacant for T.M.Battery)	2 Companies 13th N.Fusiliers	1 Coy in Front Line from O.G.1 to R.14.d.O.6½ at R.14.d.O.6½
"	9th R.W.F.	LUCKY WAY (excl) to R.14.d.O.6½	AVELUY		1 Coy in STUFF TRENCH
"	9th Cheshire	Dugouts at X 2 a & c	MARLBOROUGH HUTS 5 Huts to be kept vacant for 58.M.G.Coy		To move at 10.a.m.
"	58.M.G.Coy) 58.T.M.) Battery)	Trenches	Huts as above		Reliefs to be arranged by OC's C concerned.

SECRET.   Copy No 7

58th Brigade Order No 101.

                                      22nd Novr 1916.

1. The Brigade will march to WARLOY on 23rd inst and will continue the march on the next day.

2. The Starting Point is Western exit of AVELUY W.16.b.8.3. and Units will pass it as below:-

	Time.	Route.
9th R.W.Fusiliers	11.15.a.m.	BOUZINCOURT → SENLIS
9th Cheshires	11.26.a.m.	do
6th Wiltshire	11.37.a.m.	do
9th Welch	11.48.a.m.	do
58th M.G.Company) 58th T.M.Battery) In order	11.59.a.m.	do

No 4 Coy A.S.C. will march in rear of the Column.

3. Movement will be by half Battalions, distances of 200 yards to be maintained between Half Battalions, 500 yards between Battalions.

4. Cookers, Water Carts and Mess Carts will accompany Units, the remainder of the transport will be Brigaded and will march under the orders of the Brigade Transport Officer.

5. Instructions re billeting will be issued by the Staff Captain.

6. The usual halts will be observed.

7. Brigade H.Q. will close at AVELUY at 11.a.m. and open at WARLOY at the same time.

Acknowledge.

                                                   Captain
Issued at. 11-30 AM   Brigade Major 58th Infantry Brigade.

Copy No 1 File   Copy No 11 58.M.G.Company
       2)   12 58.T.M.Battery
       3) War Diary   13 Staff Captain
       4   G.O.C.   14 Transport Officer
       5   19th Divn "G"   15 Signal Officer
       6   19th Divn "Q"   16 94th Coy R.E.
       7   9.Cheshire   17 5.S.W.Borderers
       8   9.R.W.Fusiliers   18 Bde Bombing Officer
       9   9.Welch   19 No 4 Coy A.S.C.
      10   6.Wiltshire   20 A.D.M.S.

MARCH TABLE.

Date	Unit	From	To	Route	Remarks.
24th Nov	Brigade H.Q.	WARLOY	AUTHIEULE	VARENNES-LEALVILLERS-ARQUEVES-MARIEUX - SARTON	
do	9.Cheshire	do	do	do	
do	6th Wiltshire) 9th Welch) 9th R.W.Fus)	do	DOULLENS	do	
do	58.M.G Company) 58.T.M.Battery)	do	FRESCHVILLERS	do	
do	59th F.Ambulance) No 4 Coy A.S.C.)	do	BRETEL	do	

XLIV

MARCH TABLE.

Date	Unit	From	To	Route	Remarks.
Nov 25th	Brigade H.Q.	AUTHIEULE	AUTHEUX	HEM - HARDINVAL	To move at 10.a.m.
	9th Cheshire	do	do	do	To move at 10.5.a.m.
	6th Wiltshire	DOULLENS	BOIS BERQUES	HEM - OUTRE BOIS	do 10.a.m.
	9th Welch	do	HEUZECOURT and GRIMONT	do	do 9.a.m.
	9th R.W.Fus	do	LE MEILLARD	do	do 9.30.a.m.
	58th M.G.Company	FRESCHEVILLERS	GRIMONT	do	do 10.20.a.m.) In order to
	58th T.M.Battery	do	LE QUESNEL F'ME	do	) follow 9 Cheshire
	59th F.Amb	BREUIL	LE MEILLARD	do	do 11.45.a.m.
	No 4 Coy A.S.C.	do	OUTRE BOIS (south of River)	do	do 12 noon

Units to move independently as above.

"A" Form.
MESSAGES AND SIGNALS.
Army Form C. 2121.

This message is on a/c of:
XLIVa Service.

TO | All Units
Bde Transport Officer

Sender's Number: MG921/A
Day of Month: 22.
AAA

Lorries will be at Church AVELUY at 8 a.m. guides from each unit should meet them there (1 per lorry) and guide them to Battalion H.Q. aaa 6 lorries will be available for 9th Cheshire 4 for 9 RWF 4 for 9th Welch and 5 for 6 Wilts. Busses will be at Church AVELUY at 8.30 a.m. 168 men of 9th R.W. Fus 168 of 9 Welch and 144 of 6 Wilts will parade there at that hour. Busses will do a double journey an officer of each of these 3 Battalions should accompany busses on return journey from WARLOY a similar number of men from each of these 3 Battalions will parade at Church AVELUY at 12 noon for the 2nd journey of busses to WARLOY

H Raymond Capt

(5396) Wt.W 2186/509 7/16 100,000 Pads. D.D.& L. E 111.

"B" Form.

Army Form C 2122.
(In pads of 150).

MESSAGES AND SIGNALS.

No. of Message..........

Prefix....... Code.............m.	Received	Sent	Office Stamp.
Office of Origin and Service Instructions. Words.	At................m.	At................m.	XLIV b
	From	To	
	By	By	

TO: All Units

Sender's Number	Day of Month	In reply to Number	AAA
SC442	24		

It has been arranged that 2 trains will convey men unable to march to DOULLENS today 1st train leaves ACHEUX at 1 PM 2nd train leaves ACHEUX at 5 PM for BEAUVAL + GEZAINCOURT 1st train holds 350 men 2nd train holds 550 men. 5 lorries have been obtained to convey men to trains and each unit will detail a guide to be at TOWN MAJORS office WARLOY at 7 AM to meet lorries + guide onto unit Units may send following numbers

From		
Place		
Time		

* This line should be erased if not required

"B" Form.
MESSAGES AND SIGNALS.

Army Form C 2122.

for conveyance by train
9 bhls — 250 men
9 RWF — 250 "
9 Welch — 150 "
6 Wilts — 150 "
58 MG Coy — 60 men
58 TMB — 30 "

Lorries will ply backwards and forwards between Warloy and Acheux. First journey to commence as soon as lorries are loaded up.

From: 58 Bde

Army Form C. 2118

WAR DIARY
9th Bn or Welsh Fusiliers 58/19
INTELLIGENCE SUMMARY

Volume 18
Page 1.

Vol 18

(Erase heading not required.)

Instructions regarding War Diaries and Intelligence Summaries are contained in F. S. Regs., Part II. and the Staff Manual respectively. Title Pages will be prepared in manuscript.

Place	Date	Hour	Summary of Events and Information	Remarks and references to Appendices
December	1st		In billets at LE MEILLARD	
	2nd			
	3rd			
	4th		Lt-Col. L.J. Sweatman M.C. arrived on this day and assumed command of the Battalion.	
	5th		In billets at LE MEILLARD	
			Major Lord Howard de Walden arrived on this day and assumed 2nd in Command of the Battalion.	
	6th		In billets at LE MEILLARD	
	7th		Received draft of 8 Other Ranks this day.	
	8th		In billets at LE MEILLARD	
	9th			
	10th			
	11th			
	12th			

Army Form C. 2118

WAR DIARY
of Major Welsh Fusiliers
INTELLIGENCE SUMMARY

Volume 16
Page 2

(Erase heading not required.)

Instructions regarding War Diaries and Intelligence Summaries are contained in F.S. Regs., Part II. and the Staff Manual respectively. Title Pages will be prepared in manuscript.

Place	Date	Hour	Summary of Events and Information	Remarks and references to Appendices
December	13		In billets at LE MEILLARD. The Battalion was inspected by the Corps Commander this day. Received draft of 8 other ranks from Base.	
	14		In billets at LE MEILLARD.	
	15		" " " "	
	16		" " " "	
	17		" " " "	
	18		" " " "	
	19		Received draft of 10 Other ranks this day from Base. In billets at LE MEILLARD.	
	20		" " " "	
	21st		" " " "	
	22nd		2/Lt. V. Eaglewood reported for duty. In billets at LE MEILLARD. 2/Lt. A. McD. Forbes reported for duty.	
	23rd		In billets at LE MEILLARD.	

WAR DIARY
9th Bat/alor Welch Fusiliers
INTELLIGENCE SUMMARY

Army Form C. 2118
Volume 18
Page 3

Place	Date	Hour	Summary of Events and Information	Remarks and references to Appendices
December	23rd		2/Lieuts. D.I. Thomas and I. Davies reported for duty with the Battalion.	
	24th		In billets at LE MEILLARD.	
	25th		" — Received draft of 22 other ranks from Base.	
	26th		" " " " "	
	27th		" " " " "	
	28th		" " " " "	
	29th		Received draft of 7 other ranks from Base.	
	30th		In billets at LE MEILLARD.	
	31st		" " " "	

Mr A Murchison
Lt. Col.
Commanding 9th R.W. Fus.

WAR DIARY
3rd Bn Welch Fusiliers
INTELLIGENCE SUMMARY

Vol 19

Place	Date	Hour	Summary of Events and Information	Remarks and references to Appendices
January	1		In billets at LE MEILLARD	
	2		2/Lt L.W. Jones reported for duty with the Battalion this day	
	3rd		In billets at LE MEILLARD	
	4			
	5		Capt C.P.B. Ruck joined the Battalion	
	6		In billets at LE MEILLARD	
	7			
	8			
	9		The Battalion marched to BEAUVAL arriving there about 12-0 noon. 2/Lt J.B Tibbitt joined this day. In billets at BEAUVAL.	
	10			
	11		The Battalion leaves BEAUVAL at 8.0 am in Motor Lorries en route for SULLY au BOIS arriving there at 11-0 am and relieved the 1/2 Batt. York & Lancaster Regt in billets at SULLY au BOIS, less 2 Coys. Wiltshire Regt who go into trenches with 6 Battalion Wiltshire Regt in 1 Sector.	
	12		2. Subsector.	

1875 Wt. W593/826 1,000,000 4/15 J.B.C. & A. A.D.S.S./Forms/C. 2118./

Army Form C. 2118

WAR DIARY
~~Naval or~~ Welch Fusiliers
INTELLIGENCE SUMMARY
(Erase heading not required.)

Vol 19
Page 2

Place	Date	Hour	Summary of Events and Information	Remarks and references to Appendices
January	12th 1917		In billets at SAILLY-au-BOIS, less 2 Companies who go into trenches with 6'Bn Wiltshire Regt in L Sector.	
			L.2 Subsector.	
	13"		Same as above.	
	14"		Same as above.	
	15"		The Battalion relieves the 6° Battalion Wiltshire Regt in L Sector. L.2 Subsector, relief being completed at 8.0 p.m.	
	16"		In trenches as above.	
	17"		ditto	
	18"		ditto	
	19"		The Battalion is relieved by the 9°Batt Welch Regt, the relief being completed at 7.30 p.m. Marched back to billets at POSSIGNOL FARM, less 2 Companies, who went to billets at SAILLY-au-BOIS	
	20"		In billets as above	

Army Form C. 2118

WAR DIARY
9th R.W.F. or Royal Welsh Fusiliers
INTELLIGENCE SUMMARY

(Erase heading not required.)

Volume 19
Page 3

Place	Date	Hour	Summary of Events and Information	Remarks and references to Appendices
January	23rd 1917		In the trenches at L Sector, L.I. Subsector.	
	24th			
	25th			
	26th		The Battalion was relieved by the 9th Batt. Cheshire Regt, relief being completed at 7.0pm, and marched to billets at COURCELLES.	
	27th		In billets at COURCELLES — 2/L A.J. Davies joined the Battalion. Received draft of 101 Other ranks from Base.	
	28th		In billets at COURCELLES.	
	29th			
	30th		The Battalion relieved the 9th Batt. Cheshire Regt in the trenches, the relief being completed at 7.30pm at L Sector, L.I. Subsector.	
	31st		In trenches at L Sector, L.I. Subsector.	

Arundel Walden Major
Comdg 9th Royal Welsh Fusiliers

WAR DIARY or INTELLIGENCE SUMMARY

9(S) Batt. Royal Welsh Fusiliers

Army Form C. 2118

Vol 20 Page 1.

Vol 20

Place	Date	Hour	Summary of Events and Information	Remarks and references to Appendices
Lebucquiere	1st		In trenches at L Sector. (Robecterne)	
	2nd		" " "	
	3rd		The Battalion was relieved in the trenches by the 10" Bn Royal Warwickshire Regt and marched to billets at COURCELLES. Relief was completed at 7.45pm.	
	4th		In billets at COURCELLES.	
	5th		do do do	
	6th		do do do	
	7th		do do do	
	8th		do do do	
	9th		do do do	
	10th		do do do	
	11th		do do do	
	12th		do do do	
	13th		do do do	

Army Form C. 2118

9' (C) B" WAR DIARY 9th Royal Welch Fusiliers
INTELLIGENCE SUMMARY
(Erase heading not required.)

Vol 20
Page 2

Instructions regarding War Diaries and Intelligence Summaries are contained in F. S. Regs., Part II. and the Staff Manual respectively. Title Pages will be prepared in manuscript.

Place	Date	Hour	Summary of Events and Information	Remarks and references to Appendices
Feb 14				
	15th		The Battalion relieved the 9' B" Cheshire Regiment in L Sector, D 2 Subsector trenches, the relief being completed at 7-0 p.m.	
	16th		In trenches as above.	
	17th		do do do	
	18th		do do do	
	19th		do do do	
	20		do do do.	
	21st		The Battalion is relieved by the 11th Bn East Yorks Regt. (31st Divisn), the relief being completed at 7.15 p.m., and marches to billets at LOUVENCOURT.	
	22nd		In billets at LOUVENCOURT.	
	23		do do do	
	24		do do do.	

Army Form C. 2118

Vol 20
Page 3

9'(S) Batt. Royal Welch Fusiliers.
WAR DIARY
INTELLIGENCE SUMMARY

(Erase heading not required.)

Instructions regarding War Diaries and Intelligence Summaries are contained in F. S. Regs., Part II. and the Staff Manual respectively. Title Pages will be prepared in manuscript.

Place	Date	Hour	Summary of Events and Information	Remarks and references to Appendices
Feb	25"		In billets at LOUVENCOURT.	
	26"		do do	
	27"		do do	
	28"		do do	

M.S. Muir Turner
Lieut-Colonel.
Comdg 9'(S) Bn Royal Welch Fus.

Army Form C. 2118

WAR DIARY or INTELLIGENCE SUMMARY

9 (S) Batt Royal Welch Fusiliers Volume 21 Page 1

Instructions regarding War Diaries and Intelligence Summaries are contained in F. S. Regs., Part II. and the Staff Manual respectively. Title Pages will be prepared in manuscript.

(Erase heading not required.)

Vol. 21

Place	Date	Hour	Summary of Events and Information	Remarks and references to Appendices
	March 2nd		Moved from LOUVENCOURT to COURCELLES. 3 new officers joined at COURCELLES 2/Lieut W. P. THOMAS 2/Lieut S. G. DAVIES 2/Lieut V. H. EVANS	
	3rd		Moved from COURCELLES to BUS-LES-ARTOIS	
	4th		In billets at BUS-LES-ARTOIS	
	5th		— do —	
	6th		Moved to fresh billets at JUNIPER CAMP just outside BUS-LES-ARTOIS	
	7th		In billets at JUNIPER CAMP	
	8th		do	
	9th		do	
	10th		do	
	10th		Moved to BEAUVAL via BUS-LES-ARTOIS, LOUVENCOURT, MARIEUX and BEAUQUESNE	
	11th		Moved to BARLY via DOULLENS and OCCOCHES	
	12th		In billets at BARLY	
	13th		Moved to BLANGERVAL and BLANGERMONT via BONNIÈRES, FREVENT NUNCQ, HAUTE-COTE and FLERS	
	14th		Moved to CONTEVILLE, via WINZEUX, OEUF, BEAUVOIS, PIERREMONT and WAVRANS	
	15th		In billets at CONTEVILLE	

WAR DIARY or INTELLIGENCE SUMMARY

Army Form C. 2118

GHQ (S) Battalion of the Buffs
Volume 21
Page 2

Place	Date	Hour	Summary of Events and Information	Remarks and references to Appendices
	Mar 16th		Moved to WESTREHEM via HESTRUS, TANGRY and FIEFS.	
	17th		In billets at WESTREHEM	
	18th		Moved to LES CISEAUX near LIGNY-LES-AIRE, RELY, LINGHEM, LAMBRES, AIRE and WIDDEBROUCK	
	19th		Moved to STRAZEELE via HAZEBROUCK and BORRÉ.	
	20th		Moved to CAESTRE via PRADELLES	
	21st		In billets at CAESTRE Training	
	22nd		do	
	23rd		do	
	24th		do	
	25th		do	
	26th		do	
	27th		Inspected by the 2nd Army Commander, General Sir Herbert C. O. Plumer GCMG, KCB, ADC.	
	28th		In billets at CAESTRE	
			do	
			3 Officers joined CAPT T. A. BAXTER from Hospital	
			2/Lieut C. D. JONES " "	
			Lieut D. G. ISAACS from 3rd Bat RW Fus	
	29th		In billets at CAESTRE	

WAR DIARY

9th (S) Batt Royal Welch Fusiliers

INTELLIGENCE SUMMARY

Volume 2, Page 3

(Erase heading not required.)

Place	Date	Hour	Summary of Events and Information	Remarks and references to Appendices
	Mar 30th		Moved to RIDGE WOOD (Ref Sheet 28 S.W. N.5.a) and relieved 2 Companies of the 8th Gloucester Regiment and 2 Companies of the 9th North Stafford Regt.	
	31st		Relieved the 10th Royal Warwickshire Regt in the line (1st Battalion) Relief complete by 11.45 am	

M J Meacham
Lieut Colonel
Commanding 9th Royal Welch Fusiliers

Army Form C. 2118

WAR DIARY
or
INTELLIGENCE SUMMARY

9th R.W. Fus.

Volume 22
Page 1

Place	Date	Hour	Summary of Events and Information	Remarks and references to Appendices
	April 3rd		In trenches Left Subsector (Sheet 28 N 7 b, a and c.)	
	4th		Relieved by 6th Wiltshire Regt and proceeded to RIDGE WOOD.	
	5th, 6th		In dugouts in RIDGE WOOD. 7 men wounded on working party.	
	7th		2 men wounded in wood.	
	8th		In dugouts in RIDGE WOOD. 1 man killed and 6 wounded in wood	
	9th to 11th		Relieved 9th Welsh Regt in Right Subsector	
			In trenches Right Subsector (VIERSTRAAT)	
	12th		Relieved by 9th Welsh Regt and proceeded to MURRAMBIDGE CAMP	
			LA CLYTTE (Brigade Reserve)	
	13th to 17th		MURRAMBIDGE CAMP (Brigade Reserve) 1 Officer 2/Lt- G F LEWIS joined from 3rd Batt R.W.F. on 17th.	
	18th		Relieved by 7th S Lancs and marched to WESTON CAMP near LOCRE	
	19th		Marched to SCHAEXKEN via MONT ROUGE, MONT NOIR and LE MONCHE.	
	20th to 28th		In billets at SCHAEXKEN, Brigade and Battalion Training	

WAR DIARY or INTELLIGENCE SUMMARY

Army Form C. 2118

Volume 22 Page 2

Place	Date	Hour	Summary of Events and Information	Remarks and references to Appendices
	Apr 29th		Marched to LINDE HOEK CAMP (Sheet 28. G.17.c) in relief of 6th Brigade.	
	30th		Relieved the 11th Northumberland Fusiliers in the HOOGE Sector.	
			Battalion Strength: 39 Officers, 721 Other Ranks.	

W. A. Muckleine
Lieut Colonel
Commanding 9 Royal Welch Fus.

9 R W F
Volume 23
Page 1

WAR DIARY
or
INTELLIGENCE SUMMARY
(Erase heading not required.)

9th R W F.

Army Form C. 2118

Place	Date	Hour	Summary of Events and Information	Remarks and references to Appendices
May	1st		In trenches in HOOGE trench.	
	2nd		do. 1 man wounded.	
	3rd		do. 1 man wounded.	
	4th		Relieved by 9th Welsh Regt and became Support Battalion	
	5th to 8th		1 Coy in YPRES, 1 Coy MAPLE STREET and 1 in RITZ STREET. Battalion H.Q in TULLERIES	
	9th		Moved Battalion H.Q to deep dugout near HALFWAY HOUSE In Support.	
	10th		do.	
	11th		do. Draft of 9 casuals rejoined.	
	12th		Relieved by 11th Sherwood Foresters and moved to HALIFAX CAMP near OUDERDOM. (4 killed and 5 wounded in YPRES.	
	13th		Marched to SCHAEXKEN near BERTHEN. In trenches at SCHAEXKEN. Draft of 55 joined.	
	14th			
	15th		Marched to EBBLINGHEM via HAZEBROUCK.	
	16th		Marched to ST MARTIN au LAERT via ARQUES.	
	17th		Marched to ZOUAFQUES near AUDRUICQ.	

Army Form C. 2118

WAR DIARY
or
INTELLIGENCE SUMMARY

(Erase heading not required.)

Instructions regarding War Diaries and Intelligence Summaries are contained in F. S. Regs., Part II. and the Staff Manual respectively. Title Pages will be prepared in manuscript.

9th R.W. Fus.

Volume 23.
Page 2.

Place	Date	Hour	Summary of Events and Information	Remarks and references to Appendices
May 19-	19th		Commenced training.	
	to 24th		Training at ZOUAFQUES (Drafts totalling 1142 arrived)	
	25th		Marched to WATTEN and entrained for BAILLEUL, afterwards marching to DE ZON CAMP near LA CLYTTE. (Draft of 14)	
	26th		Inspected by G.O.C., 19th Division. (Draft of 148) In tickets at DE ZON CAMP	
	27th		Company Platoon training. In tickets at DE ZON CAMP.	
	28th		do.	
	29th		Relieved 9th Cheshires in DIEPENDAAL Sector (Right Sub-sector)	
	30th		2 O.R. wounded, 1 of whom died in F.A.	
	31st		In trenches in Right Sub-sector.	
			do.	

Wm. Mackune
Lieut-Colonel
Commanding 9th Royal Welsh Fus.

S E C R E T.   PRELIMINARY INSTRUCTIONS FOR THE OFFENSIVE.

Reference WYTSCHAETE, Sheet 1/10,000.

1. GENERAL INTENTION.
   (1) The IXth. Corps will take part in an Offensive which has for its object, the capture of the MESSINES - WYTSCHAETE Ridge.
       The Attack will be preceded by a bombardment of unknown length.
   (2) ZERO day and hour will be notified later.
   (3) The 19th. Division will be the left of the 3 attacking Divisions of the 9th. Corps and will attack with 2 Brigades
       56th. Infantry Brigade on Left.
       58th. Infantry Brigade on Right.
       57th. Infantry Brigade (less 2 Battalions who are allotted to the assaulting Brigades for Mopping) in Divisional Reserve.
   (4) The 16th. Division will be on the Right of the 58th. Brigade. The 56th. Brigade on the Left.
   (5) The Battalion immediately on the left of the 9th. R.W.F. is the 7th. K.O. Royal Lancaster Regiment.

2. FRONTAGES AND BOUNDARIES.
   The Brigade will attack from the DIEPENDAAL Sector from the Sunken Road, N.18.a.7.8. to O.7.c.95.85., i.e. approximately the front at present held by the Right Battalion in the Line.
   The Left Boundary of the Brigade, which is the only one that concerns this Battalion and is the dividing line between this Battalion and the 56th. Brigade, is as follows :-
   Trench Junction O.7.c.6.4. - OBJECT ALLEY - Point where Trench Tramway cuts OBSERVATION SUPPORT, O.13.b.65.50. - ONRAET FARM - 2 kilometre stone on WYTSCHAETE - ST. ELOI Road - Trench Tramway to point where it cuts OOSTAVERNE Trench, O.14.d.35.63., all inclusive to this Battalion

   The Right Boundary of this Battalion (which is the dividing line between it and the Wiltshires on the Right) is as follows:-
   OBLIGE LANE - OBLIGE AVENUE (both inclusive to this Battalion) Point O.13.b.25.15. in OBSTRUCTION SUPPORT 50 yards S.W. of its junction with OBSTRUCTION DRIVE - Junction of OBVIOUS ALLEY and OBSTRUCTION DRIVE, O.14.c.3.3. - Trench Junction at O.14.c.78.28. to a point at O.13.a.65.60. where the latter trench leaves the edge of the GRAND BOIS and thence a straight line drawn along the edge of the GRAND BOIS to OBSTRUCTION TRENCH.

   The dividing line between Companies will be as follows :-
   Trench Junction N.12.d.8.7. - Junction of OBLIGE AVENUE and OBLIGE TRENCH (inclusive to Right Company) Track running from O.7.c.5.1. to O.13.a.9.7. (inclusive to Right Company).

3. GENERAL PLAN OF ATTACK.
   (1) The Attack will be carried out in 4 bounds of which only the 1st. and 2nd. concern this Battalion. The Objective to be gained by the 1st. bound is known as the 1st. objective and so on :-
       First Bound.............RED LINE.   1st. Objective.
       Second Bound...........BLUE LINE.   2nd. Objective.
       Third Bound............GREEN LINE. 3rd. Objective.
       Fourth Bound...........BLACK LINE. Final Objective.
   The 1st. Objective is taken by this Battalion and the Wilts. The 2nd & 3rd. by the Welch & Cheshires and the 4th. by the 57th. Brigade. (less 2 Battalions).

   RED LINE is a line drawn along OBSTRUCTION TRENCH from its junction with OBJECT ALLEY to its junction with OBSTRUCTION ALLEY and thence down OBSTRUCTION ALLEY to its junction with OBSTRUCTION LANE, thence along the S.E. Edge of GRAND BOIS to Northern Brickstack.

(Sheet II).

3. GENERAL PLAN OF ATTACK. (contd).

BLUE LINE is a line drawn along OBSTRUCTION SUPPORT from the R in RENTY FARM to its junction with OBVIOUS AVENUE.

GREEN LINE is generally the line of the YPRES - WYTSCHAETE Road, via ESTAMINET CORNER.

BLACK LINE is generally the line of OOSTAVERNE TRENCH to ESTAMINET CORNER and from there, in a S.W. direction, is the same as the GREEN LINE.

(2) (a) The RED LINE is to be reached at ZERO plus 35 minutes.
    (b) The advance from the RED LINE will take place at ZERO plus 65 minutes. There will therefore be a halt of 30 minutes on the RED LINE.
    (c) The BLUE LINE will be reached at ZERO plus 100 minutes. The advance from the BLUE LINE will take place at ZERO plus 3 hours 40 minutes. There will therefore be a halt of 2 hours on the BLUE LINE.
    (d) The GREEN LINE will be reached at ZERO plus 4 hours 10 mins:.
    (e) The advance from the GREEN LINE will take place at ZERO plus 4 hours 40 minutes.
    (f) The BLACK LINE will be reached at ZERO plus 5 hours.
    The RED, BLUE and BLACK LINES are to be consolidated for defence.

(3) (a) The Welch (on the Right) and the Cheshires (on the Left) will attack side by side, each Battalion taking half the BLUE LINE and subsequently half the GREEN LINE. Dividing lines will be the same as set out for Right Boundary of this Battalion.
    (b) These Battalions will advance from their Assembly trenches, (Support Line and in rear of it) so as to cross the British Front Line at ZERO plus 45 minutes.
    The leading Companies will advance so as to assault from the RED LINE, under the barrage, at ZERO plus 65 minutes.
    The two Battalions will advance from the BLUE LINE at ZERO plus 3 hours 40 minutes, to assault the GREEN LINE.
    (c) The formation for attack of these 2 Battalions will be the same as for the Wiltshires and R.W.Fus.
    (d) The Reserve Brigade will be brought up so as to cross the GREEN LINE at ZERO plus 4 hours 40 minutes and assault the BLACK LINE.

4. ASSEMBLY.

The Wiltshires (on the Right) and the R.W.Fus. (on the Left) will assemble as follows :-
(a) The 1st & 2nd. waves ("A" & "B" Coys:) in our Front Line.
(b) The 3rd & 4th. waves ("C" & "D" Coys: respectively) immediately behind our Front Line on a tape line to be marked out.
    Boards will be placed indicating each flank of each platoon.

5. DISTRIBUTION.

(a) Attack up to RED LINE.
"A" Coy. on Right and "B" Coy. (on Left) will form the 1st. & 2nd. waves. Each wave will consist of 1 line of men only. There will therefore be 4 Platoons (2 of "A" Coy. & 2 of "B") in one line forming the 1st. wave and 4 Platoons (2 of "A" Coy. and 2 of "B" Coy) forming the 2nd. wave. "D" Company will form the 3rd. wave, and "C" Company the 4th. wave.
    The 1st & 2nd. waves will proceed to, and take, the RED LINE. The 3rd. wave will stay in the General line of OBLIGE RESERVE. The 4th. wave will stay in the General line of the German Front Line.
    The 2nd. wave will, in all circumstances, stay in and consolidate the RED LINE until direct orders to the contrary are received from Battalion Headquarters.
    Outposts will be pushed forward from the RED LINE.

(Sheet 111).

5. DISTRIBUTION. (contd)
- (b) The Left Platoon of "D" Company will watch the flank of the attack and will be prepared to deal with any gap which may develop between the flank of the Brigade and the Brigade on our Left. Should the attack of the Brigade on our Left be held up, this platoon will be ready for form a defensive flank to enable our attack to proceed.
- (c) The Right Front Platoon of "A" Company will tell off a particular party to deal with OBLIGE AVENUE.
- (d) The Right Platoon of "D" Company will be ready in case of the Wiltshires being held up in the GRAND BOIS before reaching the RED LINE, to swing to their Right and attack from the GRAND BOIS from OBLIGE AVENUE to clear the front of the Wiltshires.
- (e) "C" and "D" Coys: will both be prepared to assist the attack on the RED LINE should this hang fire.
- (f) As soon as the 57th. Brigade has passed through the RED LINE, "C" Coy. will move forward through the GRAND BOIS to the BLUE LINE and will carry on the consolidation of the Line started by the 9th. Cheshires.

6. CONSOLIDATION.
- (1) The RED, BLUE and GREEN LINES will be strongly consolidated. The RED LINE and Strong Points in GREEN LINE are to be wired as soon as possible.

94th. Field Coy. R.E. (less 2 sections) and one half Coy, 5th. S.W.B. (Pioneers) are allotted to this Brigade to assist in this work. These troops will work under the orders of the O.C. 94th. Field Coy. R.E. and will be employed on :-
- (a) Construction of 2 Strong Points on RED LINE and 2 on GREEN LINE as mentioned below. These are to be commenced as soon as the respective objectives have been captured. The O.C., 94th. Field Coy. R.E. will arrange for the material for the work to be dumped in a position from which it can be carried forward without delay.

As soon as the construction of a strong point is complete, The R.E. Officer in charge will report the fact to O.C. Battalion in whose area the Strong Point is. The Post will then be occupied by a garrison of 1 platoon with its Lewis Gun. O's.C. "A" & "B" Coys: will each detail 1 Platoon to occupy these Strong Points when made.

1. RED LINE. The line to be consolidated will be at least 100 yards in advance of existing trench if ground suits. This can only be decided by Officers on the spot.
   (1) The O.C., 94th. Field Coy. R.E. will arrange to construct 2 Strong Points on the RED LINE. The actual points can only be decided on the ground after reconnaisance but they should be sited about the following localities :-
   O.13.a.55.25.,   O.13.b.2.3.
   The R.E. Parties (and Pioneers) detailed for the construction of these Strong Points will move forward at ZERO plus 3 hours 40 minutes to construct S.P's on GREEN LINE. O's.C. Wiltshires will be responsible for completing S.P. at O.13.a.55.25. and R.W.Fus: the one at O.13.b.2.3. Parties for this work to be told off beforehand. In addition to above S.P., O.C. Wilts: will arrange to construct one small S.P. about O.13.a.35.65.

2. BLUE LINE.
The consolidation of the BLUE LINE will be commenced by the Welch and Cheshire Regts. When these two Battalions move forward the work will be continued by one Company of each of Wilts: and R.W.Fus.
In consolidating on the BLUE LINE, a new trench should be dug 100 to 150 yards beyond the S.E. edge of GRAND BOIS.

(Sheet IV)

7. **MOPPING UP.**
   (a) "D" Company will be responsible for the Mopping of OBLIGE RESERVE and the trenches forward of this to the RED LINE.
   Special Parties will be detailed to deal with :-
   (1) OBJECT ALLEY.   (2) OBLIGE AVENUE.   (3) OBLIGE SWITCH.
   (b) "C" Company will be responsible for the Mopping up the German Front Line and the trenches forward of this to the Line of OBLIGE RESERVE.
   Special Parties will be detailed to deal with :-
   (1) CROONAERT CHAPEL.   (2) OBJECT ALLEY.
   (3) OBLIGE LANE.   (4) OBLIGE AVENUE.
   (5) OBLIGE SWITCH.

8. **CARRYING.**
   (1) A party of 5 men and 1 N.C.O. per Company will assemble under 2/Lieut. FORBES at Battalion H.Q. who will carry the following:-
      (a) Spare Lewis Gun Drums.
      (b) Bombs (10 boxes)
      (c) S.A.A. (5 boxes).
   This party will go forward in rear of the 4th wave and will carry all their material to the Advanced Battalion Dump at a point as near the junction of OBLIGE SWITCH and OBLIGE RESERVE as possible.

   The exact position will be chosen by 2/Lieut. FORBES, who will send a guide to the O's C. "A" & "B" Coys to bring back carrying parties for any material these Companies may require.
   O.C. "C" & "D" Companies will find the Battalion Dump for themselves.   2/Lieut. FORBES with his party of 24 will be responsible that the Battalion Dump is kept filled with:-
      (1) Bombs.   (2) S.A.A.   (3) Stakes.
      (4) Wire.   (5) Mallets.   (6) S.O.S. Rockets.
   He will supply the RED LINE Companies first and then "D" and "C" Companies.
   The position of the Advanced Brigade Stores from which Ammunition of all kinds and R.E. material may be drawn will be notified later.
   (2) 15 men and 1 N.C.O. from the Band, to be detailed by Major Lord Howard de Walden, will act as Brigade Carrying party.
   Details as to this party will be issued later.

9a. **AMMUNITION, BOMBS, ETC.**
   (1) A table showing the amounts to be held in various dumps will be issued shortly.
   (2) All S.A.A. and Bomb limbers (both Battalions and M.G.Coy.) will be ready loaded at ZERO hour and will not be unloaded without orders from Brigade.
      S.A.A. expended before Z day is to be replaced.
   (3) Position of dumps is as follows :-
      (a) Advanced Divisional Dump, House in N.5.b. (on telephone).
      (b) Main Brigade Dump, N.11.b.3.5. VIERSTRAAT SWITCH, just North of POPPY LANE.
      (c) Advanced Brigade Dumps, N.12.c.7.5., near junction of POPPY LANE and SUPPORT TRENCH.

                  N.12.b.8.7. in Front Line, about 100 yards South of junction of STUART TRENCH.
   (4) Dumps formed in German Lines are to be marked with a 12" square Board, painted white with a black D in the centre.
      These will be provided by Brigade.

9. **R.E. STORES.**
   The main Brigade R.E. Dump is near the rear end of POPPY LANE, N.11.b.1.4. Forward dumps will be made in the First Line trenches and their position notified later.

(Sheet V)

10. **MACHINE GUNS.**
   A. 2 sections (8 guns) of 58th. M.G. Coy: are allotted for covering fire. The arrangements for these guns will be co-ordinated by the Corps. They will:-
   (1) Establish a creeping barrage either direct, enfilade or oblique, 200 yards in front of the Artillery Barrage. After the capture of the RED and BLUE LINES, the barrage will halt 500 yards in front of each of these lines respectively until the advance re-commences.
   (2) Fire on selected targets such as Strong Points, Cuttings or Ravines.
   (3) Sweep all ground in front and rear of the enemy's main line of resistance from the commencement of the attack. Arrangements will also be made for special concentration on likely lines of enemy counter attacks, also to answer "S.O.S." Signals. Further details with regard to these guns are being issued to O.C., 58th. Machine Gun Coy.

   NOTE:- Lewis Guns are responsible for keeping open gaps cut in the enemy's front line wire.

   B. The remaining 2 sections will act as follows:-
   (a) One section will follow last wave of attack of Wiltshires. One section last wave of attack of R.W.F.
      The general role of these guns will be:-
   (1) To protect the assaulting Battalions against counter attack during the assault.
   (2) To cover any gap which may occur during the advance, either in our attack or between our attack and Brigades on our Right and Left.
   (3) After capture of Objectives to sweep the ground in front of that line till advance against the next Objective commences.
      To perform these duties, the best formation for the advance will be by sub-sections, sub-sections selecting a line of advance towards the flanks of the Battalions they are supporting.
   (b) When the advance from RED LINE takes place, the inner sub-sections of each section will advance immediately behind the attack of the Welch and Cheshires respectively and, on capture of the BLUE LINE, will occupy positions in or near that line from which they can sweep the ground between BLUE and GREEN LINES until advance from BLUE LINE commences.
      These two sub-sections will again advance in rear of the Welch and Cheshire Regts from the BLUE to GREEN LINE, following approximately the centre of the Battalions they are supporting. When the GREEN LINE is taken they will be disposed for its defence, the sub-section with Welch Regt. taking up a position about O.14.c.30.05., the sub-section with the Cheshire Regt taking up a position near the Northern end of the Cutting, about O.14.c.6.5.
   (c) The two sub-sections left behind in the RED LINE will move forward as soon as the GREEN LINE is captured.
   (d) The guns will be under their own section commanders and not under the direct orders of O's C. Battalions they are supporting. O's C. Sections will work in close co-operation with these Battalions and as far as possible keep Battalions concerned informed of their whereabouts.
   (e) Every opportunity is to be taken of engaging suitable targets as so to inflict as much loss as possible on the enemy. Especial care is to be taken to prevent the enemy gradually drifting forward in small parties and so collecting considerable forces, under cover, for counter attack.

(Sheet VI).

11. **STOKES MORTARS.**
    Stokes Mortars will be allotted as follows :-
    (1) For the Attack on the RED LINE, 2 mortars are allotted to each of Wiltshires and R.W.F. These mortars will be under the orders of the O.C. Battalion concerned. They will advance immediately in rear of the last wave of the attack and behind the centre of the Battalions to which they are attached.

    The two R.W.F. mortars will follow the dividing line between "A" & "B" Coys. up to the RED LINE. As soon as the RED LINE is taken, the mortars will move to positions near junction of OBSTRUCTION LANE and OBSTRUCTION ALLEY, and near junction of OBJECT ALLEY and OBSTRUCTION TRENCH.

    When the attack from RED to BLUE LINE takes place, the mortars will follow the last wave of this attack, the two left mortars moving approximately along the line of OBJECT ALLEY to a position near junction of OBJECT ALLEY and OBSTRUCTION SUPPORT. For the advance from RED LINE, the two right mortars will be attached to Welch, and the two left mortars to the Cheshire Regt. When the advance from BLUE LINE takes place, the mortars will follow the last wave of the attack, approximately along lines as under :-

    One Mortar............OBVIOUS AVENUE.
    One Mortar............OBSTRUCTION DRIVE.
    Two Mortars...........OBJECT ALLEY.

    When the GREEN LINE is captured, the mortars will be disposed for its defence under orders of O's.C. Battalions concerned.
    (2) The remaining 4 mortars will be in reserve. They will advance in rear of Welch and Cheshire Regts: to the RED LINE where they will remain in reserve, occupying positions; two mortars near junction od OBSTRUCTION LANE and OBSTRUCTION ALLEY; and two mortars near junction of OBJECT ALLEY and OBSTRUCTION TRENCH.
    (3) It is most important that all Officers and N.C.O's know where the mortars will be during the advance and after capture of objectives in order that they can get assistance from them quickly if required.

12. **POSITION OF HEADQUARTERS BEFORE ASSAULT AND ASSEMBLY AREAS.**

	Headquarters.	Position of Assembly.
(a) Brigade H.Q.	Dug-outs. N.10.b.3.9.	
(b) Wiltshires.	N.12.d.0.2.	Front Line & behind it.
(c) R.W.Fus.	N.12.c.9.6.	-do-
(d) Welch Regt.	New Reserve in vicinity of N.11.b.9.2.	In Support Line & ground between Support Line and WYTSCHAETEBEEK. (Exclusive of WYTSCHAETEBEEK)
(e) Cheshires.	-do-	-do-

13. **BOUNDARIES IN ASSEMBLY AREAS.**
    <u>In Front Line</u>.
    Right Brigade Boundary. - VIERSTRAAT - WYTSCHAETE Road.
    Left Brigade Boundary. - O.7.c.03.67.

    <u>In Support Line</u>.
    Right Brigade Boundary. - VIERSTRAAT - WYTSCHAETE Road.
    Left Brigade Boundary. - N.12.b.78.14.

    <u>Dividing Line between Battalions</u>.
    Front Line.   - N.12.d.48.46.
    Support Trench.   - N.12.d.08.80.

(Sheet VII).

14. ARTILLERY.
   (1) The Front of the Brigade during the attack will be covered by the Right Group, consisting of :-
       104 - 18 pdr. Guns.   18 - 4.5 Howitzers.
   (2) There will be a senior Artillery Liason Officer from the Group with Brigade Headquarters. A junior Artillery Liason Officer will be with each Battalion.
   (3) The creeping barrage on the Brigade Front will open on the German Front Line, OBLIGE TRENCH - OBJECT SUPPORT at ZERO hour and will lift from it at ZERO plus 4 minutes, except on the Right (NAGS NOSE) from which it will lift at ZERO plus two minutes, on to the line point where NAG's NOSE cuts the Road OBLIGE TRENCH). From this line it will lift at the rate of 100 yards in 2 minutes until it reaches the line of OBLIGE RESERVE where it will remain till ZERO plus 12 minutes. Thence it will lift uniformly throughout the advance at 100 yh yards every 4 minutes until it reaches each successive objective (RED, BLUE, GREEN, BLACK LINES). As it arrives on each objective it will pile up and remain until the hour fixed for it to lift off (viz: RED 0-35, BLUE 1-40, GREEN 4-10, BLACK 5-0) so as to let the Infantry enter into the objective (RED, BLUE, GREEN and BLACK) simultaneously along the whole Brigade Front.
   (4) After lifting off the Objectives RED, BLUE, GREEN & BLACK LINES, (on which halts are to be made) it will form a protective barrage as follows :-
       The first lift will be normal 100 yards, where it will remain for 4 minutes, after which a portion of the barrage will be placed on those points in the enemy trench system from which fire can be directed against troops halted on the Objectives. The remaining portion will lift another 50 yards and form a barrage 150 yards beyond the objective.
   (5) At the hour at which the Infantry are due to advance from each line (RED, BLUE and GREEN) the barrage will reform on the line of the protective barrage (150 yards in front of the RED, BLUE or GREEN LINES).
       After reforming, it will rest for the normal 4 minutes before lifting. During the first 2 minutes, the rate of fire will be moderate, for the last two minutes intense.
       The reforming of the creeping barrage at 150 yards ahead of the trench will be the signal to the Infantry to move out to the barrage and form for the next advance.
       e.g. Creeping barrage recalled from more distant targets reforms at 3-40 on the line of the protective barrage 150 yards beyond the BLUE LINE and fire is delivered at a moderate rate until 3-42. From 3-42 to 3-44 the fire is intense.
       At 3-44 the barrage lifts 100 yards and then lifts 100 yards every 4 minutes. The Infantry, on seeing the barrage reform at 3-40, will move close up to it so as to follow it forward when it lifts at 3-44.

15. REFERENCE TO TIMES.
    In making reference to times, before or after which operations will commence, the following nomenclature will be adopted in future :-
    (a) Referring to Days.
        "Z" is the day on which Operations take place.
        1 day before Z equals Y day.
        2 days   "   Z   "   X   "
        3 "   "   Z   "   W   "
        4 "   "   Z   "   V   "
        5 "   "   Z   "   U   "
        Days before U will be referred to as :-
            Z - 6, Z - 7, Z - 8, Z - 9, etc.
        One day after Z = A, 2 days after = B, 3 days after = C.
        Days after C will be referred to as Z plus 4, Z plus 5, Z plus 6, etc.

(Sheet VIII).

15. REFERENCE TO TIMES. (contd.)
    (b) Referring to hours on "Z" Day.
        ZERO is the exact time at which Operations will commence, and times will be designated in hours and minutes plus or minus from ZERO, even if they encroach on "Y" Day.

16. COMMUNICATIONS.
    (a) Before Battle.
        In order to prevent leakage of information and to ensure that other methods of communication are practised, all communications by telephone and messages sent on buzzer will cease in advance of present Battalion H.Q. until the hour of ZERO. The Telephones which may be used by Corps and Divisional Signal Coys: and Army Area Parties will be exempt.
        The following methods of communication will be permitted in front of Battalion Headquarters:-
            Pigeons, Visual, Runners, Fullerphone for "S.O.S." calls, Rockets for "S.O.S." calls
        N.B. All fullerphones in front of Battalion H.Q. will either be issued without hand sets or have the microphones removed from the speaking circuits.
        Existing "S.O.S." lines, Battery to Company with the excepting of buried lines will be removed, and the Batteries connected to Battalion H.Q. only. These lines must be recovered to save cable and lessen the probability of messages being carried forward by induction.
        No message is to be sent by pigeon which contains anything in the address "to" or "from" or body of message which would be of value if it fell into the hands of the enemy, until after ZERO hour.
    (b) During Attack.
        A Forward Command Post will be established under the command of Lieut. IRWIN. His duties will be to collect and transmit all information and to keep communication with Company and Battalion H.Q. He will also get in touch with the Brigade Forward Station. The personnel under his Command will be as follows:-
            6 Signallers, (including 1 N.C.O.), 4 Runners, 6 Scouts (including 1 N.C.O.), 1 Pigeoneer with two pigeons, 1 Rifleman per Company. The Command Post will follow the 4th wave and occupy a position near the junction of OBLIGE SWITCH and OBLIGE RESERVE. After the RED LINE has been captured, Battalion H.Q. will move to this point. The signalling equipment to be carried will be as laid down on page 17, of S.S. 148.

17. SUPPLIES.
    (a) Divisional Supply Railhead will be at WIPPENHOEK.
    (b) Refilling Point will be at R.5.c.8.8. (½ mile N.E. of BOESCHEPE)
    (c) The days supply usually held by the Supply Column will be held by the Divisional Train and turned over daily so that however late the Railway train may arrive, rations may be delivered early and regularly to the First Line Transport Lines of Units.
    (d) The normal system will be adhered to as long as possible.
        To provide for eventualities, 14,000 Iron Rations will be stored near the BRASSERIE under Lieut. ARCHER, A.S.C. If on any day after "U" Day, the supplies for any Unit fail to arrive, application will be made to the Brigade Commander who will telegraph authority to Lieut ARCHER to issue.
    (e) It is hoped to issue to the assaulting troops 2 day's Oxo Ration and a "Tommy's Cooker" per two men and to arrange for each man to go into action at ZERO hour with his current days ration and his Iron Rations.

(Sheet IX).

18. WATER.
(a) It is proposed to store water in tanks in the front line system. These tanks will be situated as follows:-
4 - 80 gallon tanks in Front Line.
4 - 80 gallon tanks in NEW RESERVE LINE, between POPPY and CARRE FARM.
If time and material allow, water will be piped to these tanks, otherwise they will be filled prior to the bombardment under Brigade arrangements.
During the bombardment they will not be used by troops holding the line, unless the ordinary water supply fails.
(b) It is hoped that all tanks (except those destroyed by hostile fire) will be full at the time when the assaulting troops take over the line, and there will thus be a reserve in the tanks available for the assaulting troops in the event of pipes being broken.
(c) 800 full tins of water will also be stored in the Front Line System. These will form a reserve of 1 day's supply for the Brigade in case it is not possible to carry up water into the captured positions from further back on Z and A night. These tins will be distributed in batches near the tanks, and kept under a guard. They will on no account be touched before "Z" day.
A further Brigade Reserve of 800 full tins will be kept in rear of the Front Line System.
(d) A reserve Dump of water tins will also be formed under Divisional Arrangements at a point to be notified later where empty tins can be exchanged for full ones.
(e) It is hoped to send up water on Z/A and subsequent nights on pack animals under Brigade arrangements and to provide for this every Battalion should be in possession of 200 water tins and crates for carrying 100 of them on pack saddles. Should these crates not be available, they should be constructed from ration boxes under Unit arrangements. Units will be informed should this be the case.

19. MEDICAL.
(a) Two Regimental Aid posts will be established at:-
N.18.b.2.5.   STUART Trench.
N.11.a.5.7.   POPPY.
An advanced Dressing Station will be situated at KLEINE VIERSTRAAT (N.10.a.0.9.) whence lying or sitting cases will be evacuated to the Main Dressing Station at WESTOUTRE.
A Walking Wounded Collecting Post will be established at N.3.d.5.8. and the Main Dressing Station for Walking Wounded will be at LACLYTTE.
(b) Wounded will be brought to the Regimental Aid Posts by Regimental Stretcher Bearers. The services of any German prisoners that may be captured should be used to assist.
(c) As soon as practicable after the attack, fresh Regimental Aid Posts, to be known as Battle Aid Posts will be improvised in or beyond the present Front Line. If Battn M.O's require extra assistance in carrying wounded to the Regimental Aid Posts they will apply to the O's C. Battns. in the RED LINE any time after the BLUE LINE has been taken.
(d) Carrying from the Battle Aid Posts to the old Aid Posts and thence to the Advanced Dressing Station will be done by the R.A.M.C. personnel. But if there is congestion at the Battle Aid Posts calls for help in clearing these will be sent to Brigade H.Q. who will obtain the necessary bearers from the O.C. Bearers (Lieut.-Col. J.POWELL, 57th Field Ambulance) at A.D.S. KLEINE VIERSTRAAT. The Officer making the request will invariably send a guide to conduct the party to where it is required.

(Sheet X).

19. **MEDICAL.** (contd.)
   (e) Each Battalion will detail 3 men to report to% the A.D.S. at KLEINE VIERSTRAAT at 9-0 a.m. on "Y" day, to assist in evacuating wounded on the Tramway system.
   (f) Two dumps of 12 reserve stretchers will be established in the Front Line near the heads of STUART and POPPY Communication Trenches.
   (g) For routes from the Front line to the Regimental Aid Posts, see para 27.
   (h) Instructions for Regimental Medical Officers and their Stretcher Bearers Appendix "A.1 has been issued to each Battalion Medical Officer by the A.D.M.S.

20. **PRISONERS OF WAR.**
   (a) A Brigade Prisoners Cage will be established at N.11.a.7.5.
   (b) It will be in charge of an Officer to be detailed by O.C., 9th. Cheshire Regt; and will be selected from a number of those to be left out of the line.
   His name will be submitted to this Officer by 1st. prox.
   (c) Each Battalion will detail 4 men as a guard for the cage.
   (d) Prisoners will be sent by Battalions capturing them to the Brigade cage by cross country tracks. Escorts should consist of slightly wounded men, if possible, and should not be stronger than 1 man to 10 prisoners.
   (e) After an escort has handed over its prisoners to the Officer 1/c Prisoners' cage, this Officer will send such of the escort as are fit back to their Units, ordering them to report on their way up POPPY LANE at the Main Brigade Bomb Store, N.11.b.3.4., where they will get their waterbottles refilled, their S.A.A. replenished and will be given bombs or other ammunition to carry forward to the line. Slightly wounded men will be sent to the Walking wounded Collecting Station at N.3.d.5.8.
   (f) The Officer 1/c Prisoners' Cage will send on prisoners, in batches, to the Divisional Collecting Station at N.3.b.3.3. and hand them over to the A.P.M. He will use men of his own guard as escort between the Brigade Cage and Divl: Station.
   (g) Officers and N.C.O. prisoners will be kept seperate from their men and not be allowed to converse with them.
   (h) Nothing will be taken from prisoners except arms and equipment. If, however, a prisoner is seen attempting to destroy papers, etc., that he may have, they may be taken from him by the escort who will hand them over to the Officer 1/c Prisoners' Cage or to the A.P.M.

21. **STRAGGLERS' POSTS.**
   Stragglers' Posts will be established at the BRASSERIE.
   N.3.a.1.2.   N.3.d.5.9.

22. **LIASON.**
   Major Lord Howard de Walden will be with H.Q., 58th. Brigade.
   2/Lieut. Turner will be with H.Q., 56th. Brigade.

23. **RESERVES.**
   The following Officers, N.C.O's and men will remain with Depot and Transport Lines :-
   Captain H.L. WILLIAMS, M.C.   The R.S.M.
   Captain I.A. BAXTER, M.C.   C.S.M. Burridge.
   Lieut. J.W. PHILLIPS.   C.S.M. Owens.
                                      Cpl. Davies. (Bomber)

   The Provo Sergeant.
   3 Signallers (1 N.C.O.) to be detailed by 2/Lt. FOX.
   2 Scouts. (1 N.C.O.) to be detailed by Lieut. IRWIN.
   2 Orderly Room Staff.

   <u>In each Company.</u>, to be detailed by O.C. Company,
       1 Sgt. 1 Lewis Gun Instructor. 1 Cpl. 2 L/Cpls.

   <u>In each Platoon.</u>   1 Rifle Grenadierx. 2 Lewis Gunners.

(Sheet XI)

23. RESERVES. CONTD.

Four Officers per Company will go in with "B" & "C" Coys and three with "A" & "D" Coys, including the O.C. Company.

Officers over and above this strength (to be detailed by O's C. Companies concerned) will remain with the Transport. Officers, N.C.O's and men left out (apart from usual Transport and Depot) will remain in Camp at M.4.c.5.0.

24. CLOTHING AND EQUIPMENT.
- (a) **Officers.** Same as for other ranks with revolver.
- (a) **Other ranks.**
  - (1) Clothing as issued.
  - (2) Arms as issued.
  - (3) Entrenching Tool as issued.
  - (4) Accoutrements as issued, with the exception of the Pack. The Haversack will be carried on the back in place of the Pack.
  - (5) Box Respirator and Tube Helmet.
  - (6) Articles carried in the Haversack.
    - (a) Towel and Soap.
    - (b) Spare Oil Tin.
    - (c) Holdall Complete.
    - (d) Iron Rations.
    - (e) Two day's OXO Rations.
    - (f) Every other man, 1 "Tommy's Cooker".
  - (7) The Mess Tin and Cover will be slung outside the Haversack. The Macintosh Sheet will be carried, rolled on the belt below the Haversack.
  - (8) Ammunition, 170 rounds, except for Bombers, 120 rounds., Signallers 50 rds., Scouts 50 rds., Runners 50 rds., Lewis Gunners 120 rds., Carrying Parties 50 rds.,
  - (9) Mills Grenades. Two carried, 1 in each top pocket of the jacket. These grenades are intended to be collected into a dump as soon as the Objective has been carried and are not to be used by the individual except in emergency.
  - (10) Aeroplane Flares. 50 per Company to be carried in the bottom pocket of the jacket.
  - (11) Sandbags. 4 per man, carried slung through the belt.
  - (12) Rations and Water. 1 Iron Ration in Haversack, the unexpended portion of current day's ration in Mess Tin. 1 Filled Waterbottle. Men must be warned to drink sparingly.
  - (13) Wirecutter & Breakers, in the percentage of 4 in each of the 1st and 2nd waves, to 1 in each of the 3rd and 4th waves.
  - (14) Picks and Shovels. in the proportion of 1 pick to 3 shovels for every man in the 2nd, 3rd, and 4th waves.
  - (15) Very Pistols and 1½" guns. Two pistols and 1 Gun with each Company H.Q. Two pistols and 1 gun with Battalion H.Q. Three green Very Lights per Cot. and 6 green gun lights per Coy. The same for Battn H.Q.

Bombers.
Men in Bombing sections will carry bombs as follows:-
5 per Bayonet Man, 10 per Thrower, 12 per Carrier, 10 per N.C.O.

Rifle Grenadiers.
12 Grenades and blank cartridges per man.

Parties told off for Mopping Up. will in addition carry:-
"P" Bombs, Smoke Bombs, M.S.K. Grenades.
These will be issued as follows:-

Coy	"P" Bombs	Smoke Bombs	M"S"K" Bombs
"A"	5	20	4
"B"	5	20	4
"C"	10	20	4
"D"	10	20	4

The greatest care will be taken that the M.S.K. Grenades are only carried by men who thoroughly understand their use.

(Sheet XII).

25. DISTINGUISHING MARKS.
    (a) Yellow tab to be sewn on back of each Haversack.
    (b) Scouts. Green band on Left forearm.
    (c) Runners. Red Band   -do-
    (d) Signallers. Blue Band on Shoulder Strap.
    (e) Carrying Parties. Yellow Band on Left forearm.
    (f) Mopping Up Parties. White Band   -do-
    (g) Men equipped with wirecutters or wirebreakers will wear a piece of white tape tied to the right shoulder strap.
    (h) The flags to be carried will be :-
        (a) Yellow and Black (diagonal flag 18" square carried by Platoon commander and Platoon Sgts: in order to assist the Infantry to locate their own Infantry.).
        (b) Yellow and Red (horizontal) flag 9" square carried by N.C.O. of Bombing Squad.
        (c) Strict orders will be issued that these flags are not to be stuck in the ground, in order to avoid mistakes which might be caused by flags being left behind when evacuating positions.

26. SURPLUS KIT.
    (a) At least 48 hours prior to the commencement of the bombardment all Government kit and Stores, surplus to what is authorised to be carried on existing transport, will be stored as laid down in "Scheme for the Collection of Stores in the event of an Advance", issued under S.C.2448, dated 21-5-17, of which the Quartermaster has a copy.
    (b) Private kit, beyond what is authorised to be carried, will be stored at the Divisional Stores, 192 Rue de la Gare, BAILLEUL.
    (c) Greatcoats and packs of men, together with authorised equipment, will be left in the Quartermaster's Stores so that, if they are required in the line, they can be got at at once.
    (d) It is improbable that any lorries will be available to assist the authorised transport when the Division is relieved and therefore it is necessary for these instructions to be followed in every detail.

27. DOCUMENTS and MAPS.
    All ranks, taking part in the assault, are forbidden to carry any letters, papers, orders or sketches which, in the event of their capture, would be likely to give any information to the enemy. Officers should only carry the trench map of the actual area and possibly the local 1/100,000 sheet.

28. BRIDGES.
    The Wilts: and R.W.Fus: will, in order to enable the troops in rear to cross the Front Line, place 18 bridges in position in each of their assembly trenches.
    "D" Company will be responsible for this.
    These bridges will be drawn from the 94th. Field Coy, R.E. and placed in trenches at points at which they will be required They will only be put into position after dark on Y/Z night.

29. THE "S.O.S" Signal will remain RED signal cartridges as at present. GREEN 1" and 1½" cartridges will be kept in reserve for use should it become necessary to make a change.

30. IN THE event of any Brigade being held up, the unit on the flanks will on no account check their advance but will form defensive flanks in that direction and press forward themselves so as to envelope the Strong Point or centre of resistance which is preventing the advance. With this object in view, reservesw will be pushed in behind those portions of the line that are successful rather than those which are held up.

(Sheet XIII).

31. All Commanders, down to the Platoon Commanders, will keep in touch throughout with the Commander of the similar formation on his flanks. They must know the disposition and action being taken by their neighbours and more particularly so when the units on the flanks belong to another Division.

32. Commanders are reminded of the necessity of impressing on all ranks under their Command that it is of the utmost importance to keep Dicisional Headquarters constantly informed of the state of affairs in order that higher authority may be informed and arrangements made in time to take advantage of success as well as to give efficient support.

33. The necessity of pushing forward to their objective regardless of the progress of units on either flank must be impressed on all ranks. It should also be made known to them that the care of the wounded is not in their province as special people are detailed for this purpose.

34. All men should be warned against the probable misuse of white flags and signs of surrender by the enemy. They have also been known to sham death and then to shoot into the back of our assault. The possibility of the enemy using ruses, such as giving the word "retire", must be impressed on all ranks.

35. POPPY LANE, BOIS CARRE trench and CHICORY LANE will be reserved as IN trenches.
STUART TRENCH, P & O trench will be reserved as OUT trenches. The 57th Brigade will provide the police posts necessary to control traffic throughout the whole length of these trenches from ZERO hour.
   After ZERO hour, no one except Officers of the Divisional or Brigad Staffs will be permitted to use these trenches in an opposite direction to the traffic.
   O.C. 94th Field Coy.R.E. will be responsible for the maintenance of POPPY LANE and STUART Trench East of the WYTSCHAETEBEEK to the Front Line.

36. ACCOMODATION OF SURPLUS PERSONNEL.
   (1) A Camp has been established at M.4.c.5.0. for the accomodation of surplus Officers and Other Ranks not going into action. Re-inforcements will also be sent there.
   (2) The Senior Field Officer will be Camp Commandant. His name will be notified to formations.
   (3) Any subsequent amendments of numbers already submitted as being sent to the Camp will be notified to this Office without delay.
   (4) The Camp will be an independent unit for administrative purposes, and will be rationed direct by the Divisional Train. It will have a Medical Officer detailed for duty by the A.D.M.S.
   (5) Personnel to be accomodated in the camp will report there by 6-0 p.m. on "W" Day, carrying rations for consumption on next day.

37. TRANSPORT.
   (1) The Brigade Transport Officer (Captain H.G.Percival, 9th Welsh Regt) will take charge of the Brigade Transport Lines and act as Brigade Staff Officer for Transport. The Duties of Transport Officer of his Battalion will be carried out by another Officer detailed by O.C., 9th Welsh Regt.
   (2) The Brigade Transport Officer will be connected by telephone with D.H.Q. who will keep him informed as far as possible of the position of units in the Brigade.

(Sheet XIV).

37. TRANSPORT. CONTD.

(3) No extra pack animals are being allotted to the Brigade, and in the event of all units in the Brigade being in advance of the present Front Line on Z/A night, every available animal in the Brigade including Officers' horses will have to be requisitioned for pack work, and a certain number will probably have to do a double trip forward carrying ammunition etc., to dumps behind the captured positions. The Brigade Transport Officer will be informed by the Brigade as early as possible how many animals are needed for carrying ammunition, and guides will be provided.

(4) It may be possible for the pack trains to go forward by day. In this case the Brigade Transport Officer will be notified by the Brigade and rations should be ready for loading by noon.

(5) Two guides will be sent back from each Battalion as soon as possible after reaching its objective. They will report to Brigade H.Q. and await the arrival of their Battalions' ration mules, then guide them to the point selected for off-loading. Each Transport Officer will therefore call at Brigade H.Q. on his way up to the line with rations and if no guide from his Battalion is awaiting him, it will be his duty to lead his animals to a point indicated by the Brigade, off-load the rations, leave a man in charge of them, send the animals back, and get in touch with his Battalion.

38. TRACKS.

Three mule tracks will be available from the VIERSTRAAT - KEMMEL Road to the present front line.

(a) A continuation of "Y" track, starting from N.11.c.5.4. and joining the VIERSTRAAT - WYTSCHAETE ROAD at N.11.d.50.45. This track is marked with "Y" boards and could be used by limbers up to the front line.

(b) Track "X.1" From VIERSTRAAT - KEMMEL Road at N.11.b.3.5. via N.11.b.75.40., - N.12.a.0.5., crossing the WYTSCHAETEBEEK at the tallest tree N.12.c.8.9., thence to the Front Line, running parrallel to POPPY LANE, The track is marked with white stakes.

(c) Track "X.2" from VIERSTRAAT - KEMMEL Road at N.11.b.4.5 via N.11.b.95.70, N.12.a.20.70., N.12.a.5.3., (just South of pond) thence to Front Line running parrallel to and 100 to 150 yards S.W. of STUART Trench. The track is marked with white inverted triangles on sticks.

These tracks should be reconnoitred forthwith by as many Officers as possible. They will be used for reaching position of assembly, as well as for pack transport. Stretcher cases could also be carried up "X.2" track from "NO MANS LAND" and along the rear of the New Reserve Trench to Regimental Aid Posts at N.12.b.2.5., or up "X.1" or "Y" Tracks to Regimental Aid Posts at N.11.a.5.7.

39. SALVAGE.

All parties and individuals returning from the front line must carry some salvaged article with them which may be dumped at the Salvage Dump at HALLEBAST CORNER or at CANADA CORNER.

The Salvage Officer will arrange for Notice Boards to be put up at these places. All carrying parties coming back to Brigade Dumps at Tramheads will bring salvage to these places, from where they will be returned by tram. Perishable things such as unboxed ammunition, grenades, food. etc; should be salvaged first.

40. SANITATION.

(1) All sources of water must be carefully conserved and Units will search for and label all sources of water supply in the captured trenches.

(2) Indiscriminate fouling of the ground by using shell holes as latrines should be prevented and latrines dug as early as possible.

(Sheet XV).

41. ORDNANCE.
   The Divisional Ordnance Store remains at WESTOUTRE.
   All captured war material will be sent back as early as possible. Attention is drawn to the instructions with regard to any captured war material which Units wish to claim.
   The purport of these instructions was that all articles must be clearly labelled and a claim submitted to this Office, stating the circumstances under which they were captured.
   If possible the official number and marks on the captured article should be stated in the claim,

42. R.E. STORES.
   The forward dump of R.E. material of all kinds is at the junction of POPPY LANE with the Front Line.

Lieut. & Adjt.,
9th. (Service) Battalion R.W. Fusiliers.

COPY No. 2
Issued at 9:30 a.m.

(Sheet XVI).

42. **PRELIMINARY INSTRUCTIONS FOR THE OFFENSIVE.** (contd)

43. **WATER SUPPLY FOR DRINKING.**
Para 16 is cancelled and the following substituted :-
(1) Water is stored in tanks or barrels at the following places :-
   (a) Front Line. N.12.d.8.7. Approximate amount 200 gallons.
   (b) Junction of POPPY and Support Line N.12.c.7.4. Approximate amount 250 gallons.
   (c) New Reserve N.12.a.1.2. Approximate amount 200 gallons.
   These are provided as a reserve supply and should not be drawn upon before Y/Z night unless all other sources of supply fail. O.C. Battalion in the Line is responsible for guarding these supplies.
(2) 1200 Petrol tins have been allotted to the Brigade. This number includes those already on charge of the Brigade or in possession of Battalions. The number of petrol tins at present held by Battalions will therefore be made up to 300 per Batth:. These are sufficient for a 3 days supply and will be distributed as follows :-
  (1) 100 will be dumped full by Units arrangements at some point to be selected by the Unit, in or near the assembly trenches which the Unit will occupy on Y/Z night. A point near one of the mule tracks should be selected in order to enable the Transport Officer of that Unit readily to collect the empties on the removing night.
  O's.C. Units will issue strict orders that no man is to drink out of his waterbottle before ZERO hour, and they will make arrangements for each man to be given a drink in the assembly trenches, using the water in the tanks and as many of the 100 water tins as are necessary for this purpose.
  (2) The remaining 200 will be kept at the Transport Lines, 100 to be taken up on Z/A night and 100 on A/B night.
  10 pairs of crates are being issued to each Battalion for carrying water tins on mules (8 tins per mule). Some sort of tin carriers will, therefore, have to be improvised by Units for at least 3 more mules.
  11 extra pack saddles and 12 saddle bags per Battalion are also being issued.
  (3) A reserve dump of water tins is being formed, under Divisional arrangements, at the BRASSERIE.
  Empty tins can be exchanged for full ones there.

With reference to the above the Battalion Dumps will be at the junction of STUART Trench and the Front Line.

44. **RATIONS.**
(1) Each man will be carrying at ZERO hour :-
   (a) Rations for consumption on ZERO day.
   (b) His Iron Ration.
   (c) One OXO Cube.
(2) A hot meal will be given to the men, under Unit arrangements, before leaving their camp on the evening of "Y" day. RUM will be issued, under Unit arrangements, in the assembly trenches half an hour before ZERO.

45. **MEDICAL.**
In continuation of para 19, sub para g.
(g) Walking wounded will go via "X.1" and "X" Tracks to the Aid Post in POPPY N.11.a.5.7.
  Stretcher cases will go to STUART Aid Post N.12.b.2.5., either up STUART Trench or up "X.2" Track as far as the WYTSCHAETEBEEK, thence due North to the Aid Post.
  Signboards will be placed along these routes under Brigade arrangements.

(Sheet XVII)

45. **MEDICAL.** (contd)
In continuation of para 26, sub-para 'h',
(h) "Instructions for Regimental Officers and their Stretcher Bearers Appendix "A" (1), has been issued to each Battalion M.O's by the A.D.M.S. 19th Division. Battalion M.O's will show these instructions to the O.s C. their Battalions, who will see there in detail the Medical Arrangements for the Offensive and the responsibilities of each Battalion with respect to these.

With reference to paras 1 and 7, of Appendix "A" (1), 1 and 2 M.O's of the 58th Brigade will be those of the 9th R.W.Fus. and 6th Wiltshires. 3 and 4 those of the 9th Cheshire and 9 Welsh.

Lieut. & Adjt.,
9th (S) Bn Royal Welch Fusiliers.

WAR DIARY of Gyaesch Bn
or
INTELLIGENCE SUMMARY.

Army Form C. 2118.
Volume 24
Page 1

Vol 24

Place	Date	Hour	Summary of Events and Information	Remarks and references to Appendices
June	10th to 5th		In billets at WESTON CAMP near LOCRE	
			C & D Companies relieved 2 Companies of the 9th Welsh Regt in the DIEPENDAAL Sector. Relief commenced at 9-0 a.m.	
			A raid was made by the whole of C Company under 2/Lieut E O ROBERTS and 2/Lieut D W THOMAS with the object of securing identifications. The raid was very successful.	
			Copies of the report on and of the orders for the raid are attached.	
	6th		A & B Companies in WESTON CAMP and C and D Coys in line	
			A & B Companies moved up to line at 8-30 p.m. to positions of assembly. Assembly was complete by 10-30 p.m.	
	7th		At 3-10 a.m. the attack on the WYTSCHAETE – MESSINES RIDGE was launched. A copy of the orders for the attack are attached.	
			Little resistance was encountered except in isolated cases, the Germans surrendering on the whole quickly. Eighty prisoners and four machine guns were captured	

WAR DIARY of RW Fusiliers
INTELLIGENCE SUMMARY.
(Erase heading not required.)

Army Form C. 2118.
Volume 24
Page 2.

Place	Date	Hour	Summary of Events and Information	Remarks and references to Appendices
June	7th	(cont)	by the time the 1st Objective had been taken. There was very little barrage fire from the Germans. The 1st Objective (the RED LINE) was captured according to time table and consolidated and a further line, 200 yards in rear of this was also consolidated. Our own barrage was excellent. ZERO hour at 3-10 am was too early, it being still quite dark.	
		3 pm	At 3.0 pm orders were received to move forward to the GREEN LINE. This line had been partly consolidated by the 9th Welsh Regt and consolidation was carried on was carried on by our own troops until 8.0 pm when further orders were received to move forward in relief of the 9th Welsh Regt to the BLACK LINE. This move was soon started with difficulty owing to heavy shelling from the enemy at this time the 9th Cheshire Regt was on the left of the Battalion and in touch and elements of the 16th Division on right with an entrainment	

Rml[?] Rushworth

WAR DIARY
INTELLIGENCE SUMMARY.
(Erase heading not required.)

Army Form C. 2118.

9th W Yorks
Volume 24
Page 3

Place	Date	Hour	Summary of Events and Information	Remarks and references to Appendices
June	7th (Contd)		of 300 yards between	
			Battalion HQ. was moved at 3-0 pm up to ONRAET FARM	
			where it remained until the 9th June 1917.	
	8th		Holding and consolidating the BLACK LINE	
			It was found that this line was too thickly held and in	
			consequence ½ of B Coy and ½ of D Company was moved to a	
			trench 200 yards East of the BLACK LINE. The enemy	
			shelled intermittently and at times heavily	
	9th		Consolidation on BLACK LINE continued. The Battalion was	
			relieved by the 10th Warwicks from the 57th Brigade, relieving	
			to the old British front trenches. Relief was completed by	
			9.0 pm. The total casualties to date were:—	
			2nd Lieut J B TIPPETTS Wounded 7th. Other Ranks KILLED 15	
			2nd Lieut V HAZLEWOOD Wounded 7th WOUNDED 99	
			2nd Lieut S G MANDERS Wounded 8th MISSING 3	
			2nd Lieut A G BROMMAGE Wounded 7th	

A M [signature]

WAR DIARY
or INTELLIGENCE SUMMARY.

Army Form C. 2118.

Volume 24
Page 4

Instructions regarding War Diaries and Intelligence Summaries are contained in F. S. Regs., Part II. and the Staff Manual respectively. Title pages will be prepared in manuscript.

(Erase heading not required.)

Place	Date	Hour	Summary of Events and Information	Remarks and references to Appendices
June	10th		The Battalion relieved the 3rd Rifle Brigade on the left of the previous position commencing at 9.0 pm. There was a very heavy hostile artillery bombardment while the relief was in progress considerable delay being caused. The relief was completed by 2-30 am on the 11th June. The Battalion then occupied by the Battalion areas - D Company in OBSTACLE SWITCH from its junction with the OOSTAVERNE - ST ELOI road to GOUDEZEUNE FARM. B Company in a new trench partially dug from this point to DENYS FARM on the South side of the road joining these two points and A and C Companies in OBSTACLE TRENCH. Battalion HQ being in a small copse 100 yards South of LESIGHE FARM.	
	11th		The Battalion was in support of the 9th Welsh Regt in the same trenches, much work being done in consolidating the	Col J M. Murchy [?]

Army Form C. 2118.

WAR DIARY
or
INTELLIGENCE SUMMARY.
(Erase heading not required.)

Army _____ Volume 2d
Page 5

Place	Date	Hour	Summary of Events and Information	Remarks and references to Appendices
June	11th (Contd)		Shelling was very heavy all day from guns of all calibres mostly from guns apparently placed North of the YPRES-ostend line was great trouble caused activity.	
	12th		On outskirts of the 9th Welsh Regt on the same trench shelling still continued. Anti[?] activity of the enemy increased much. Consolidation and wiring was done. Battalion had some heavy shells and was sent to DOMI HOUSE to the DAMSTRASSE. A communication trench was commenced from OBSTACLE TRENCH to OBSTACLE SWITCH to connect up A and D Companies.	
	13th		In support to the 9th Welsh Regt in the same trenches. Consolidation was continued.	
	14th		The Battalion relieved the 9th Welsh in the front line the relief commencing at 10.0 p.m and was completed by 12 mid night. The Battalion occupied a very long trench
A.M. McMurtrie[?] Lt	

A6945 Wt. W14422/M1160 330,000 12/16 D. D. & L. Forms/C./2118/14.

WAR DIARY
or
INTELLIGENCE SUMMARY.
(Erase heading not required.)

Army Form C. 2118.

[regiment] Welch Fus...
Volume 24
Page 6

Place	Date	Hour	Summary of Events and Information	Remarks and references to Appendices
June	14th (contd)		tactically dug pearced to ODYSSEY TRENCH and 100 yards to the East extending from North of ROSE WOOD to a point due East of the North end of BUG WOOD. This line was held by B and D Companies. A Company being in OBSTACLE SWITCH and C Company in OBSTACLE SUPPORT	
	15th		Battalion H.Q. close to the RAVINE near OBSTACLE SWITCH. Further digging of new front trench and communication trench. Intermittent shelling.	
	16th		Consolidation continued. Heavy damage by hostile artillery on our front and support lines. An officer's patrol was sent to the WESTERN edge of GREEN WOOD encountering no opposition.	
	17th		Early quiet except between 6.0 pm and 7.0 pm when a rather heavy barrage was put on the front and support lines. Another officer's patrol again proceeded towards Northern edge of GREEN WOOD encountering no opposition	

WAR DIARY
or INTELLIGENCE SUMMARY.

Army Form C. 2118.

Volume 2nd Page 7

Place	Date	Hour	Summary of Events and Information	Remarks and references to Appendices
	June 18th		The Battalion was relieved by the 8th Gloucester Regt (57th Brigade) commencing at 10 pm. Relief was complete by 11.30 pm. The Battalion proceeded to GARDEN FARM CAMP (N 13 a.8.7 Sheet 28 SW) The total casualties for the tour in the trenches were 11 Other Ranks KILLED 59 Other Ranks WOUNDED	
	19th		The Battalion marched to a camp in Corps Reserve near BAILLEUL (N 8 a & 3 Sheet 28 SW)	
	20th to 30th		The Battalion in camp. Close training	

A M MacClintock
Lieut Colonel
Commanding 9th Royal Welch Fus

SECRET.

9th. (S) Bn. ROYAL WELCH FUSILIERS.
INSTRUCTIONS FOR THE OFFENSIVE.

1. All orders and instructions for the Offensive issued previous to the Actual Operation Orders will be sent out in the form of instructions in accordance with S.S.135 "Instructions for the Training of Divisions for Offensive Action", sect 1, paras 3 & 4.

2. All recipients of these instructions are responsible for the custody of the dicuments and maps and that only such portions of these contents are issued to subordinates as the situation demands.

3. Copies issued to :-

   Copy No. 1. File.
   2.¹2a War Diary.
   3. O.C. "A" Coy.
   4. "   "B" "
   5. "   "C" "
   6. "   "D" "
   7. Scout Officer.
   8. Signalling Officer.
   9. Bombing Officer.
   10. Transport Officer.
   11. Medical Officer
   12. Quartermaster.
   13. Commanding Officer.
   14. Second-in-command.
   15. 58th. Infantry Brigade.
   16. 58th. Trench Mortar Battery.

Headquarters.,
4ᵗʰ June 1917.

SECRET.	OPERATION ORDERS
by
Lieut.-Colonel L.F. Smeathman, M.C.
Commanding 9th (S) Bn. Royal Welch Fusiliers.	4/6/17.

1. INFORMATION.
"C" Company 9th. R.W.F. will carry out a raid on the enemy lines on the 5th. inst. Two Companies of the 56th. Brigade will, at the same time, raid on the immediate left of "C" Company. Touch will be maintained with these Companies throughout the operation.
There will be no raiding party on the right of "C" Company.

2. OBJECTIVE.
OBLIGE SWITCH from O.13.a.50.82 to O.7.c.65.30.

3. INTENTION.
To capture (not to kill) Germans.

4. FORMATION.
"C" Coy: will attack with 3 platoons in one wave (1 line of men only) and 1 platoon in the second wave. The second wave will be on the right rear of the 1st. wave.

5. BARRAGE.
The barrage will open on the enemy front line at ZERO, will lift 100 yards at ZERO plus 04, remain there for 2 minutes (to ZERO plus 06) lift 100 yards and remain there till ZERO plus 0.10, lift 100 yards and remain there until ZERO plus 0.25.
The Objective will probably not be able to be assaulted until ZERO plus 0.10, but if the barrage allows, men will get into the Objective before this lift takes place.

6. ZERO.
ZERO hour will be notified later but the Company will be in position by 2-30 p.m.

7. TIME IN OBJECTIVE.
The Objective will be reached at ZERO plus 0.11 and will be cleared at ZERO plus 16. This will give 9 minutes for the Company to withdraw to our own lines.

8. SIGNALS.
Two Very Lights will be fired in quick succession from our own Front line by 2/Lieut. S.G. MANDERS at ZERO plus 16 as a signal for withdrawal. At the same time a Bugle will be blown, under the orders of 2/Lieut. MANDERS in our own front line, and two Very pistol lights will be sent up by 2/Lieut. E.O. ROBERTS in the enemy lines.

9. DRESS.
Coats will not be worn, otherwise Drill Order.

10 Equipment.
One bomb per man will be carried in the trousers pocket but the greatest care will be taken that these are only used as a means of defence and that they will not be thrown except in exceptional circumstances. No identifications will be carried on the man and men must be cautioned that, in the unlikely event of their being captured, they must on no account give any information beyond their names. Bombers, in bombing sections, will carry 5 bombs each in the haversack, rifle grenadiers will not carry Rifle grenades.
Lewis Gunners will carry gun and 8 magazines only. Smoke bombs (1 per Section) will be carried. These will be used a make a smoke barrage when withdrawing from the enemy trench.

11 OFFICERS.
2/Lieut. E.O. ROBERTS and 2/Lieut. D.W. THOMAS.

12. WITHDRAWAL.
Upon withdrawal from the enemy line, the 1st. wave will withdraw through the 2nd wave to our own lines and men will return down POPPY LANE and assemble in the NEW RESERVE LINE independently.

(Sheet 2).

13. **SECOND WAVE.**

    The 2nd. wave will occupy a position in the German front line at approximate junction of OBLIGE LANE and OBLIGE TRENCH and WX will be responsible for the right flank. They will carry 4 smoke candles to create a flank smoke screen if weather conditions permit.

    This wave will withdraw at ZERO plus 0.20. or as soon as the first wave has passed through them.

14. **RIGHT FLANK.**

    (1) A Lewis Gun section from the first wave will be told off to reach the junction of OBLIGE LANE and OBLIGE AVENUE, to guard the right flank.

    (2) O.C. "D" Company will be responsible for mounting two Lewis Guns in our own line to sweep the right flank and neutralise any possible fire from the NAG's NOSE.

15. **PRISONERS.**

    Any prisoners captured will be immediately brought back to Battalion Headquarters.

16. **SYNCHRONISATION OF WATCHES.**

    This will be arranged by 2/Lieut. S.G. MANDERS, at 2-30 p.m.

17. **MEDICAL.**

    Wounded will be brought back to our own Front Line. No one must, on any account, be left behind.

                                                 (sd) G.L. KIRBY., Lieut & Adjt.,

                              9th. (Service) Bn. Royal Welch Fusiliers.

REPORT ON RAID.

1. The raid on the whole was a great success.
2. A Copy of Battalion Orders for the raid is attached.
3. The objective was easily reached.
4. 37 prisoners passed by Battalion Headquarters but it is known that a considerable number of the prisoners captured by this Battalion were cleared down CHICORY TRENCH and thus went through the 56th Brigade.
5. It is impossible to say at present really how many casualties have occurred. The following are known :-
    - 1 Officer seriously wounded. (2/Lt. D.W. THOMAS.)
    - 2 Men Killed. One of these was brought in.
    - 9 Men Wounded.
    - 1 Man Missing., but a party of 1 N.C.O. and 2 men have, it is thought, found him in "NO MANS LAND" and are waiting to bring him in to-night.
6. No gap occurred between the Battalion on the Left and this Battalion, but a gap occurred between the two platoons of this Battalion.
7. The gap was caused by a 4.5 in. Howitzer Battery shooting short.
8. The Barrage was not so good as that put up three days ago.
9. No difficulty was experienced in following the barrage, the alignment of which was good but pauses (not gaps) occurred in it.
10. The Front Line German Trench is almost demolished. Three dug-outs were found in it, two of which were concrete and contained Germans. The OBLIGE SWITCH LINE contained dug-outs and was in fairly good condition.
11. The Wire was no obstacle anywhere.
12. One German Machine Gun fired from the NAGS NOSE; position not identified but thought to be on the edge of the GRAND BOIS.
    One German Machine Gun was destroyed in a dug-out in the NAGS NOSE by two Sergeants of this Battalion.
13. Germans only put up a fight in two places.
14. No Germans were found on watch; they were all in dug-outs or close against the walls.
15. The enemy shelled his own Front Line on the Right and Very Lights (RED) were fired by him in a Northerly direction from the NAGS NOSE.
16. 15 Germans are known to have been killed with the bayonet.

(Sgd) L.F. SMEATHMAN, Lieut.-Colonel,

5/6/17.   Commanding 9th (S) Bn. Royal Welch Fusiliers.

O.C. 9th R.W.Fusiliers.

   Major General SHUTE wishes to convey his congratulations and thanks to the Battalion for the part they took in the Raid to-day. The result was splendid.

O.C. 9th R.W.Fusiliers.

   Convey to "C" Company, 9th R.W.Fus, Brigadiers Hearty Congratulations on excellent work this afternoon.

AWARDS GRANTED FOR THE RAID ON 5TH JUNE 1917.

2/Lieut. Douglas Walter Thomas. awarded Military Cross for the
following act :-
"During a raid on the enemy lines in the WYTSCHAETE Area
"on the 5th June 1917, set a magnificent example to all
"N.C.O's and men.
"   It is known that he shot two Germans and stunned
"another with the butt of his revolver.
"He was seriously wounded. This Officer has on numerous
"previous occasions done most excellent patrol work in the
"enemy line."

16880 Sergt. C. Bannister. awarded Distinguished Conduct Medal, for
the following act :-
"During a raid on the enemy lines in the WYTSCHAETE Sector
"on the 5th June 1917, this Sergt. was in command of a
"platoon, the duty of which was to guard the right flank
"of the Battalion.
"   Owing to his able-leadership, this platoon thoroughly
"performed its allotted task.
"   This Sergt., with Sergt. Evans then, with a complete
"disregard of hos own safety, attacked and destroyed a
"German Machine Gun in a concrete emplacement, which was
"firing on the flank of the raiding party.
"   His plucky action undoubtedly saved many lives.

9366 Sergt. XXXXXXXX Evans. T. awarded Military Medal for the
following act :-
"During a raid on the enemy trenches in the WYTSCHAETE
"Sector on the 5th June 1917, he, in company with Sergt.
"Bannister, and with a complete disregard of his personal
"safety, attacked and destroyed a German Machine Gun
"which was causing much trouble to the Right flank of the
"raiding party."

33463 Cpl. Bonsall. H. awarded Military Medal for the following act:-
"This N.C.O., during a raid on the German Lines in the XX
"WYTSCHAETE Sector on the 5th June 1917, displayed the
"greatest ability in leading his section. It is established
"beyond doubt that he killed two Germans with the bayonet
"and captured 5 more personally."

16652 Pte. Siviter. E. awarded the Military Medal for the
following act :-
"During a raid on the enemy trenches in the WYTSCHAETE
"Sector on the 5th June 1917, he performed numerous acts
"of great gallantry.
"   He continuously left our own line to help and dress
"wounded in spite of heavy Machine Gun fire from the enemy.
"   He ultimately crawled out in full daylight up to the
"enemy front line to a Lance Corporal who was wounded and
"gave him water.
"   He has previously been recommended 4 times, but so
"far, has not had any recognition of his most valuable
"services."

13803 Pte. Weeks. F., awarded the Military Medal for the following
act :-
"During a raid on the enemy trenches in the WYTSCHAETE
"Area on the 5th June 1917, this man was the last to leave
"the enemy lines. He found a wounded Lance Corporal who he
"could not carry, came in and reported and returned to the
"Lance Corporal, across NO MAN's LAND in broad daylight
"and in spite of heavy enemy Machine Gun fire.
"   He also assisted in the saving of a badly wounded
"Officer on the same occasion."

14367 Pte. Jones. T. awarded xxxx a Bar to his Military Medal for
for the following act :-
"When 2/Lieut. D.W. Thomas was badly wounded during a
"raid on the enemy lines in the WYTSCHAETE Sector on the
"5th June 1917, this man, in spite of heavy enemy
"xxxxxxxxxx fire from Machine Guns, and with complete
"disregard of his own personal safety dashed out from
"our own lines and brought 2/Lieut. THOMAS in.
"On four other occasions during the same raid he brought
"in wounded men at great personal risk.
    He had already been awarded a Military Medal.

O.C. 9th R.W. Fusiliers.

Following copy of message received from 19th Division is forwarded for your information.

Begins :-

"Military Cross awarded to T/2/Lieut. D.W. THOMAS, 9th R.W.F. Convey Army Corps and Divisional Commanders' congratulations to recipient. The Brigadier adds his hearty congratulations.

AWARDS GRANTED FOR RAID, 5th JUNE 1917.

2/Lieut. D.W. THOMAS,	Military Cross.
16680 Sgt. BANNISTER, C.	Distinguished Conduct Medal.
9366 Sgt. EVANS. T.	Military Medal.
33463 Cpl. BONSALL, H.	Military Medal.
16652 Pte. SIVITER. E.	Military Medal.
13503 Pte. WEEKS. F.	Military Medal.
13367 Pte. JONES. T.	Bar to Military Medal.

To all Units.

The following letter which has been received by the Divisional Commander from the Corps Commander is passed for the information of all :-

IX Corps H.Q. 6th June 1917.

"My dear Shute,
   Just a line to wish you all the best of luck. This is no time for words, but I should be glad if you would, on my behalf, wish every Officer, non-commissioned officer and man of the 19th Division all the good fortune he deserves as a reward for his long patience and hard work".
                                 v. sincerely yours
6/6/17.   (sd) A.H. GORDON.

SPECIAL ORDER OF THE DAY.
by
Major General C.D. SHUTE, C.B., C.M.G.
Commanding 19th Division.   10/6/17.

The G.O.C. 19th Division has pleasure in publishing the following telegram from H.M. The King received by the G.O.C. Second Army (through the Field Marshal, Commanding-in-Chief):-

"I rejoice that thanks to thorough preparation and splendid co-operation of all arms, the important MESSINES RIDGE which has been the scene od so many memorable struggles is again in our hands. Tell General Plumer and the Second Army how proud we are of the achievements by which in a few hours the enemy was driven out of strongly entrenched positions held by him for two and a half years."

All Units.

Following Message received from Division. Following message from Corps Commander. Well done 19th Division. Heartiest congratulations on capture of BLACK LINE. I fully realise what a magnificent effort by each individual this has been.

All Units.

The following copy of message received from General BRIDGES is forwarded for your information.

"Please tender heartiest congratulations in my name to all ranks for magnificent success in recent operations.

WAR DIARY
6/Royal Welsh Fusiliers
INTELLIGENCE SUMMARY.

Volume 25
Page 1

No 25

Place	Date	Hour	Summary of Events and Information	Remarks and references to Appendices
	1917 July 1st		In billets camp near BAILLEUL S.E. a 8.3 (Sheet 28 SW)	
	2nd		moved to camp at N.17.a.2.6. H.Q at PARRET FARM	
	3rd		Moved to camp at N.10.d.2½.1½.	
	4th 6.10th		In camp at N.10.d.2½.1½.	
	11th		moved to trenches in support of 6th Wiltshire Regt. Disposition as follows. "A" Coy. 2 platoons in OBLONG RESERVE 0.10.a.5.2 to 0.10.a.9.5. 1 platoon in OBSCURE TRENCH 0.9.d.7.8 to 0.9.d.10.10 and 1 platoon in OBSCURE SUPPORT 0.9.d.6.5 to 0.9.d.10.7. A Coys Headquarters at DELBSKI FARM 0.10. to 1.2.	
			"B" Coy in BLUE LINE 0.10.a.6½.5 to 0.9.b.9.3½.	
			"C" Coy in trench 0.15.b.0.5 to 0.15.b.5.0. Company Headquarters at GOUDEZEUNE FARM 0.15.6.1.4	
			"D" Coy in BLUE LINE 0.9.c.9.9 to 0.10.a.1.6 along the edge of PHEASANT WOOD	
			Battalion Headquarters in DENYS WOOD 0.9.d.6½.4½	
	12th		In support to 6th Wiltshire Regt. Major D.J. PEREGRINE-JONES arrived	

Rn? A. Awadger

Army Form C. 2118.

WAR DIARY
INTELLIGENCE SUMMARY.
9th (S) Bn Royal Welch Fusiliers
Volume 2.5
Page 2

(Erase heading not required.)

Place	Date	Hour	Summary of Events and Information	Remarks and references to Appendices
	July 13th/14th		In support to 6th Wiltshire Regiment.	
	15th		Relieved 6th Wiltshire Regt in front line trenches. 2/Lieut	
			T. HOWELL arrived. Dispositions of Companies as follows	
			'A' Coy Right Front Coy. 2 platoons in front line from O.17.a.25.0	
			— O.17.a.30.55 — O.17.a.35.70, 2 platoons in support O.16.b.80.10	
			to O.16.b.80.40 Coy H.Q. at O.16.b.80.25. The following points	
			were also held, O.17.a.5.5, O.17.a.7.4½, O.17.a.8.5, O.17.a.6.7	
			(by day only) and O.17.a.7.7½ (by night only)	
			'B' Coy Centre Front Coy. 3 platoons in front line from O.17.a.35.70	
			to O.11.C.35.40, 1 platoon in Support from O.10.d.45.45 to	
			O.10.d.40.70. A Lewis Gun post was held by night at O.11.c.6.2.	
			Company Headquarters at O.10.d.1.6. (with 'C' Coy).	
			'C' Coy Left Front Coy. 3 platoons in front line from O.11.C.3.5	
			to O.11.a.30.05, 1 platoon in support from O.10.d.6.5 to O.10.d.60.10	
			1 Lewis Gun post at O.11.C.6½.4½. Company Headquarters O.10.d.1.6.	
			D Coy. Support Coy. 1 platoon South of ROOZEBEEK and 3	

[signature]

WAR DIARY
INTELLIGENCE SUMMARY.

9th (S) Bn Royal Welch Fusiliers Volume 25 Page 3

Army Form C. 2118.

Place	Date	Hour	Summary of Events and Information	Remarks and references to Appendices
	July 15th	(Contd)	"D" Coy Contd Platoons North of ROOSEBEEK from 0.16.a.92.20 to 0.16.a.9.9 Company Headquarters at 0.16.a.8.7 Battalion Headquarters in DENYS WOOD at 0.9.a.5.5.	
	16th		In Front Line	
	17th		In Front Line. A Party of 27 o/Ranks under Lieut. T.W. PHILLIPS attempted a raid on an enemy post at 0.11.c.9½.2½ at 11-30 p.m. The post was found to be unoccupied but a enemy outside KROLLEBEKE about 100yds EAST of FORRET FARM which was strongly manned. The party was fired on and had to return. 3 men were wounded.	
built held up in a trench				
	18th		In Front Line.	

	19th		Relieved in trenches by 56th Brigade. 'A' + 'D' Coys were relieved by 7th East Lancashire Regt. and 'B' + 'C' Coys by 9th L. North. Lanc. Regt.
			The Battalion on relief proceeded to BUTTERFLY CAMP near LOCRE.
			Total casualties for 8 days tour in trenches were
			    1 Other Rank Killed
			    25 Other Ranks Wounded	

AW Mackinnon
Lt Col

Army Form C. 2118.

WAR DIARY
9th (S) Bn Royal Welsh Fusiliers Volume 25
INTELLIGENCE SUMMARY.
(Erase heading not required.)

Page 4.

Place	Date	Hour	Summary of Events and Information	Remarks and references to Appendices
	July 20th & 21st		In tents and huts at BUTTERFLY CAMP	
	" 22nd		Moved to S.P.12, O.17.c.7.0. for working parties in line	
	23rd		Working parties over 400 men nightly. (The Bath had 2 nights stop in the attached.)	
	25th		Relieved by 9th Cheshire Regt.; proceeded to KENNEL SHELTERS	
	26th to 28th		KENNEL SHELTERS Training.	
	29th		Moved to IRISH HOUSE O.23.c.8½.7½.	
	30th		The Battalion moved to its assembly position in reserve to 56th Brigade. Copy of Battalion Orders for Assembly attached. Assembly was complete by 12.10 am on 31st	
	31st		The 56 Brigade attacked a line known as the blue line together with attached orders. The objective was easily reached with few casualties but a wound within from potters. Men the objective. Enemy entered this evening heavy casualties occurred in consolidation. During the morning one other was received (appendix) at 9 am stating that our Company of the 7th Kings were being	

Army Form C. 2118.

WAR DIARY or INTELLIGENCE SUMMARY.

Royal Ulster Division
Volume ?
Page 5

(Erase heading not required.)

Place	Date	Hour	Summary of Events and Information	Remarks and references to Appendices
	July 31st (Contd)		surrounded and cut off. 2/Lt. D. Phillips was sent up to reconnoitre the position and orders were issued to B Coy (Captain N. C. IRWIN) to do the same and support by counter attack if necessary.	
			The bombardment appeared to be out our Company on the right of the 36th Brigade (on the left Company of the 63rd Bgde) who contre attacked and fallen back to the line they had started from. No movement had been observed on the right flank of the 74th Bgde and no company line right and appears to have been late entirely at this time. The enemy seemed to push on in small parties up hedges and ditches and was beaded with by machine gun fire along the second "BLUE LINE" with no movement. After reconnoitering the position Captain IRWIN decided to counterattack which he did at once driving the enemy back and ultimately digging in along the line	

A5915 Wt. W1422/M1160 350,000 12/16 D. D. & I. Forms/C./2118/14.

WAR DIARY or INTELLIGENCE SUMMARY

Army Form C. 2118.

1st Battalion A.B.[?] Volume 15

Page 6

(Erase heading not required)

Place	Date	Hour	Summary of Events and Information	Remarks and references to Appendices
	July 31st (contd.)		of a ridge from O.17.d.3.h. to O.17.a.0.3. thus forming a defensive flank. Meanwhile unsuccessful efforts to connect with the Company on the right at O.17.d.4.5 being wounded and cut off were all probably prevented the whole line from being pushed out. Lieut. Atkinson D. Company was placed at the disposal of the 7th Kings Scots and were known as the gap between the right of C. Company and the left of the Remnants of two companies of the Kings Scots who were holding to original British trench from a point at JACK FARM inclusive. This movement took place at about dark (9.45 p.m.) B. Company were at the time in the VAN HOVE FARM line (old British 2nd line) and A. Coy. at ODONTO LINE.	
	Aug 1st		The Battalion was relieved by the 9th Welsh Regt. Casualties Killed 2/Lt H. KILVERT, 2/Lieut. A.G. DAVIES, 2/Lieut S.G. DAVIES and 24 Other Ranks. Wounded 2/Lt N.A. BUCK and 32 Other Ranks. 1 Other Rank missing.	

OPERATION ORDERS
by
Lieut.-Colonel L.F. Smeathman, M.C.
Commanding 9th (S) Bn. Royal Welch Fusiliers.   29/7/17.

1. MOVE.
    The 9th R.W.F. will move today to IRISH HOUSE, N.23.c.8.8.

2. ROUTE.
    Main LOCRE - KEMMEL Road to KEMMEL, thence by the KEMMEL - VIERSTRAAT Road and the Road running along the Southern edge of ROSSIGNOL WOOD.

3. DRESS. Fighting Order.

4. FORMATION.
    Companies will move off in the following order, "A", "B", "C", "D", "H.Q", by platoons at 100 paces interval.

5. TIME.
    Leading platoon of "A" Company will leave camp at 5-15 p.m.

6. PACKS.   packed
    Will be ~~loaded~~ and carried to FERMOY FARM under ~~Company arrangements~~ arrangements to be made by Q.M. All packs to be ~~carried by 4-0 p.m.~~ ready for loading at Coy H.Q. by 2.0 pm

7. VALISES.
    Will be packed ready for loading at Company and Battalion H.Q. by 4-0 p.m. They will be brought to the new camp.

8. LEWIS GUNS AND MESS KIT.
    One limber per Company and one for Battalion H.Q. will be in camp by 4-0 p.m. ready for loading. These limbers will follow Companies.

9. COOKERS. Will follow Companies.

10. BILLETING PARTY.
    Under 2/Lieut. D.W. TURNER has already proceded and will meet incoming Companies at ROSSIGNOL WOOD.

11. TRANSPORT.
    Will move, under orders to be issued by Brigade Transport Officer, to SEIGE FARM.

12. SURPLUS PERSONNEL.
    Will report to FERMOY FARM today and will not accompany the Battalion to the new camp.

13. BOMBS" PICKS" ETC.
    Taken over from the 8th Glosters at SEIGE FARM will be brought to the new camp under arrangements to be made by Captain D.C.W.J. BROOKS by 10-0 a.m. tomorrow.

14. TENTS AND HUTS.
    All tents and huts will be left scrupulously clean.

G.L.Kirby.
Lieut. & Adjt.,
9th (S) Bn. Royal Welch Fusiliers.

S E C R E T.   Reference 1/10,000, WYTSCHAETE,
OPERATION ORDERS   28. S.W.2.
by
Lieut.-Colonel L.F. Smeathman, M.C.
Commanding 9th (S) Bn. Royal Welch Fusiliers.   29/7/17.

1. **ASSEMBLY.**
    The 9th R.W.Fus. will assemble on a night to be notified later in the positions set out in "Instructions for the Offensive"

2. **ROUTE.**
    IRISH HOUSE - Road junction N.23.a.5.5. - Junction of Road and Track N.17.c.1.1. - Road Junction N.12.c.1.2. - Main VIERSTRAAT WYTSCHAETE Road to HOSPICE - New Wooden Road from this point to ESTAMINET CORNER - IN DE STERKTE CAB and thence by the nearest route to their assembly trenches.

3. **ORDER AND TIME OF MARCH.**
    "C" Company - 9-20 p.m.   "D" Company - 9-30 p.m.
    "A" Company - 9-40 p.m.   "B" Company - 9-50 p.m.
    Headquarters Company - 10-0 p.m.

4. **MOVEMENT.**
    Movement will be by platoons at 100 paces interval.

5. **TRANSPORT.**
    (a) One limber for "C" & "D" Companies' Lewis Guns and Mess Kit will accompany the leading platoon of "C" Company and will be unloaded at IN DE STERKTE CAB.
    (b) Ditto for "A" & "B" Coys, to follow leading platoon of "A" Coy.
    (c) One Pack Mule for "H.Q" will accompany "H.Q" Company.
    All the above will report at IRISH HOUSE at 8-0 p.m.
    (d) Two limbers loaded with full water cans will report at IRISH HOUSE at 10-0 p.m. These will accompany "H.Q" Coy to the Battalion Headquarters where they will be unloaded under the supervision of 2/Lieut. D.W. TURNER.
    (e) Valise wagon will report at IRISH HOUSE at 8-0 p.m. and valises will be packed ready for loading at IRISH HOUSE at 7-30 p.m.
    (f) One limber will report at IRISH HOUSE at 8-30 p.m. to take down surplus kit and Orderly Room Kit.
    (g) Cooker Horses will report at IRISH HOUSE at 8-0 p.m.

6. **REPORTS.**
    Companies will report by runner to Battalion Headquarters when assembly is complete.

7. **SYNCHRONISATION OF WATCHES.**
    Watches will be synchronised with 2/Lieut. A.J.C. FOX (who will synchronise beforehand with Brigade) as Companies pass IRISH HOUSE.

8. **TRENCH MORTAR BATTERY.**
    The affiliated section of the 58th T.M.Battery will be in position by 12-0 midnight and will report arrival to Battalion H.Q. by runner, at which time watches will be synchronised.

9. **CASUALTIES.**
    Any casualties during assembly will be reported when assembly complete is reported.

10. **SMOKING, ETC.**
    There will be no smoking and the assembly will take place in strict silence.

Copies to all recipients of "Instructions for the Offensive".

                                 G.L.Kirby.
                                         Lieut. & Adjt.,
                    9th (S) Bn. Royal Welch Fusiliers.

Issued at 10-0 p.m.

Date... 29.7.17.

WAR DIARY
INTELLIGENCE SUMMARY

9th Royal Welsh Fus. Volume 26 Page 1

Vol 26

Place	Date	Hour	Summary of Events and Information	Remarks and references to Appendices
	1917 Aug 1st		Relieved in trenches by 9th Welch Regt and proceeded to Brigade Reserve, C & D Coys to IRISH HOUSE and A & B Coys H.Qrs to ESTAMINET CORNER	
	2nd		A & B Coys H.Q. moved to IRISH HOUSE	
	3rd		Relieved 9th Welch Regt in trenches	
	4th 5th		In front line trenches	
	5th		Relieved by 9th Welch Regt and proceeded to Bde Reserve A & B Coys at ESTAMINET CORNER and C & D Coys H.Q. to OOSTAVERNE WOOD	
	6 & 7		In Brigade Reserve	
	7		Relieved by Battalion of 37th Division and proceeded to ROSSIGNOL WOOD	
	8th		Proceeded to camp at S.8.a.5.3 (Sheet 27) near BAILLEUL	
	9th		In camp Draft of 9 other ranks joined	
	10th		Entrained at BAILLEUL and detrained at WIZERNES, afterwards marching to AFFRINGUES	
	11th 27th		Training with the following exception	

Army Form C. 2118.

WAR DIARY
9 Royal Welch Fusiliers Volume 26
INTELLIGENCE SUMMARY.
Page 1

(Erase heading not required.)

Instructions regarding War Diaries and Intelligence Summaries are contained in F. S. Regs., Part II. and the Staff Manual respectively. Title pages will be prepared in manuscript.

Place	Date	Hour	Summary of Events and Information	Remarks and references to Appendices
	Aug 13th		Inspected by G.O.C. Second Army.	
	15th		Presentation of medal Ribbons by G.O.C. 19th Division	
	28th		Entrained at WIZERNES. On arrival at BAILLEUL marched	
			to STAFFORD CAMP. R at a.o.s. (Sheet 27) Draft of 17 O.R. arrived	
	29th-31st		Training. Draft of 106 O.Ranks arrived on 31st	
	25th		Inspected by Commander in Chief.	

AMMcMeachnie
Lieut Colonel
Commanding 9 Royal Welch Fus

9th (S) Bn. ROYAL WELCH FUSILIERS.

INSTRUCTIONS FOR THE OFFENSIVE.

Copy No. 2.

Copy Nos.	1.	File.
	2.)	War Diary.
	3.)	
	4.	O.C. "A" Company.
	5.	" "B" "
	6.	" "C" "
	7.	" "D" "
	8.	Scout Officer.
	9.	Bombing Officer.
	10.	Transport Officer.
	11.	Medical Officer.
	12.	Quartermaster.
	13.	Commanding Officer.
	14.	2nd-in-Command.
	15.	58th Infantry Brigade.
	16.	56th Infantry Brigade.
	17.	58th Trench Mortar Battery.
	18.	
	19.	
	20.	

Lieut.-Colonel,
Commanding 9th (S) Bn. Royal Welch Fusiliers.

Issued on ....

(Sheet I.)   S E C R E T.

INSTRUCTIONS FOR THE OFFENSIVE.

Reference 1/10,000 Map,
   Sheet 28 S.W.2. (attached "A")

1. GENERAL PLAN.
   The IX Corps, in conjunction with the Corps on right and left, is to undertake offensive operations on Zero day, the date of which will be notified later.
   It is the intention that these operations, which will be preceded by several days' bombardment, should create the impression of a serious attempt to capture the WARNETON - ZANDVOORDE Line.

2. PLAN OF ATTACK BY IX CORPS.
   The immediate objective of the IX Corps is the capture and consolidation of the line known as the BLUE LINE running as follows from North to South. - Bend in Road O.11.b.6.9. - O.11.d.4.8. - O.11.d.5.2. - O.11.d.4.0. - O.17.b.4.5. - O.17.b.5.0. - O.17.d.4.8. - O.17.d.4.9. - O.23.b.4.6. - O.23.b.3.4. (Fork Roads)
   The immediate objective of the X Corps is a line joining this line on the North. This Line runs East of HOLLEBEKE and crosses the canal at O.6.c.8.2.
   The attack against the BLUE LINE on the IX Corps front will be delivered in two phases :-

   1st Phase.
   Attack against that portion of the BLUE LINE from HOUSE at O.23.d.05.65. to road at O.11.b.55.00., will be delivered at ZERO hour by 19th Division and by two Battalions of 37th Division, which will be under the orders of 19th Division.
   The attack by 41st Division (X Corps) on the left of the 19th Division, will be made simultaneously with this attack.

   2nd Phase.
   Attack against the BLUE LINE South of the HOUSE at O.23.d.05.65 will be delivered against by 37th Division at a later hour.

3. PLAN OF ATTACK BY 19TH DIVISION.
   (a) The infantry advance will be made under artillery barrage from the line O.23.c.20.35. to O.11.a.5.X.
   (b) The attack will be made by two battalions 63rd Infantry Bde (37th Division) on Right, and by 56th Brigade (19th Division) on left.
       As the advance is made, the 63rd Brigade will form a Defensive Flank on the line O.23.c.20.35. to HOUSE at O.23.d.05.65.
       The Dividing line between Brigades during the advance will be the road O.23.a.3.3. to O.23.b.8.4 (inclusive to 63rd Bde
   (c) 63rd Brigade will attack with one Battalion in Front Line and one Battalion in Support 56th Brigade will attack with 3 Battalions in Front Line and one in Support
   (d) Troops will assemble for attack on the night Y/Z in existing trenches on the line O.23.c.40.35. to O.11.a.5.1
       Dividing Line between Brigades in assembly area will be the line O.23.a.50.40. - V.HOVE F.R. - POLK E.T I.ST - Bend in Road O.21.central. (all inclusive to 56th Bde)

(Sheet II.)

3. PLAN OF ATTACK (Cont'd)

(e) <u>Movement of reserve battalion of 58th Brigade</u>

The Battalion in Reserve of 58th Brigade which is assembled in the old British Front Line, namely, ROSE WOOD – V . HOVE ? will move forward at ZERO Hour to the present front line from which the attack by the remainder of the Brigade is launched. This Battalion will be replaced in the old British front line by 9th Royal Welch Fusiliers who will be placed at the disposal of G.O.C. 56th Brigade at ZERO Hour

(f) (1) The 58th Infantry Brigade will be assembled by ZERO hour as under :– Head uarters – The WARREN, ONE ET WOOD

9th R.W. Fus. and 2 Sections of 58th T...B. will assemble as follows, times to be notified later, :–

Battalion H.Q – Dug-outs at 0.15.c.59
"A" Coy: in the trench running through 0.15.b and d with their left on GOUDBERG F.R. – H. ? at or near this Farm,
"B" Company – OIL TRENCH
"C" Company – ODONTO TRENCH with their Right on PRESTON ROAD. (0.22.a.3.7.)
"D" Company – ODONTO TRENCH with their Left on PRESTON Road. (0.22.a.3.7.)

At ZERO Hour "C" & "D" Companies will move forward and occupy the old British Front Line – "C" Coy: with its Right on PRESTON ROAD at 0.22.b.1.8. and "D" Coy: with its Left on this point,
"A" Coy: will occupy the trench vacated by "C" Company,
"B" Coy: will occupy the trench vacated by "D" Company,

Movement will be overland by half platoons and will be completed as soon as possible.
Routes will be carefully reconnoitred beforehand by all platoon commanders.

<u>TRENCH MORTAR BATTERY.</u>

Two sections of the 58th. T.M. Battery will assemble and remain at the junction of ODONTO TRENCH and PRESTON ROAD. (0.22.a.3.7.)

The remaining units of the Brigade – RIDGE DEFENCES.
Details for the move will be issued later.
The 9th. R.W. Fus: will not be employed without reference to Divisional Headquarters.

(ii) On the morning of ZERO day the 57th Brigade will move forward to the Support Brigade Area, Headquarters S.P. 12.

(iii) 2 Sections of the 246th M.G. Company will occupy positions detailed by the D.M.G.O. vacated by sections of the 57th and 58th M.G. Companies which move forward to positions to form the barrage to cover the infantry attack.

The remainder of the 246th M.G. Company will assemble West of the RIDGE Defences at a position to be selected by the D.M.G.O.

4. CONSOLIDATION OF BLUE LINE

(a) The best position in the vicinity of the BLUE LINE will be consolidated. The point of junction with the 37th Division on the right will be at the road junction at 0.23.b.2.4.
The point of junction with the 41st Division on the left will be at 0.11.b.85.00.

(b) That portion of 63rd Brigade placed under orders of 19th Division for the advance will come again under orders of 37th Division at ZERO plus   hours, and the consolidation of the BLUE LINE by 63 rd Brigade will therefore be carried out under the orders of the 37th Division.

Sheet 3.)

5. ARTILLERY INSTRUCTIONS.

The preliminary bombardment commenced 16th. July under orders of the G.O.C., R.A., IXth. Corps.

Two practice barrages will be carried out between 16th. July and Z day in co-operation with the Corps on each flank, under arrangements which will be made by the G.O.C., R.A., IXth. Corps.

6. MACHINE GUNS.

(a) 56th. M.G.Coy: will remain at the disposal of G.O.C., 56th. Infantry Brigade.
(b) 57th. and 58th. M.G.Coys: will provide covering fire during the Infantry advance, and a protective barrage during consolidation under instructions which will be issued later.
   Instructions as to the positions to be prepared will be issued to Machine Gun Companies by the D.M.G.O.
(c) Harassing fire prior to ZERO day will be carried out by 57th. and 58th. M.G. Coys: under instructions issued by D.M.G.O.
(d) 8 Guns of 19th. Motor M.G. Battery will be attached to the Division to deal especially with the slope running from BEE FARM - RIFLE FARM towards PILL FARM.
   Positions for these Guns will be selected about the cutting East of VIERSTRAAT FARM. Their task will be to open at ZERO, fire on a line from RIFLE FARM - WASP FARM to Road 100 yards North of latter and creep forward to a line running through PILL FARM.
(e) The 37th. Division will, from a position South of ANZAC FARM, employ 4 guns to put down at ZERO an oblique creeping barrage 300 yards in depth, the centre line of which will run through Rifle Farm to the North West corner of LAKE FARM.
   Both groups will maintain fire on the LAKE FARM and PILL FARM salients for one hour after the BLUE LINE is reached, and will then gradually cease.

7. BURIED CABLE SYSTEM.

The buried cable system is given on a map which has been handed to the Signalling Officer. The cable head is situated in a dug-out at O.15.D.8.7. Twenty-one pairs of lines are available on all routes for the Division. Units requiring lines should apply to the Division by wire, to 19th. Division Signals.
Linesmen will be stationed at the following dug-outs :-
   WH, OW, DA, GZ, (Map B).

8. FORWARD STATIONS.

The 55th. Brigade are establishing a Forward Station at GOUDEZEUNE FARM and will be responsible for the communications up to Battalion Headquarters. 55th. Brigade are also establishing a Signal Station near the TOWER about O.16.d.8.2. This station will be provided with a Power Buzzer and Amplifier by the Division and will also be a Visual Station. The centre and Right Battalion will each send one Orderly to this station three hours before ZERO so that in the event of their lines being cut, messages may be received via this Station. The Station call will be SE.

9. DIVISIONAL O.P.

The Divisional O.P. will be situated at about O.10.d.4.8. It will be connected to the Division by telephone and will also be a Power Buzzer and Visual Station. The Divisional Signal Company will be responsible for this Station.

(Sheet IV)

10. **BATTALION FORWARD COMMUNICATIONS** (This applies only to 56th Bde)
Each Battalion will lay and maintain not more than two forward trunks from its Headquarters to a point in rear of its final objective. In the event of Battalion communications failing, messages may be sent either to the Signal Station at the TOWER, O.16.d.8.2. or to the Divisional O.P. at about O.10.d.4.6.

11. **VISUAL SCHEME.**

NO.	POSITION OF STATION.	Unit i/c STATION.	INSTRUMENTS.	STATION CALL.
1.	KEMMEL.	DIVISION.	1 Helio 2 Lucas Lamps.	K N
2.	GOUDEZEUNE FM.	56th Bde.	Helio 2 Lucas Lamps.	G Z
3.	TOWER at O.16.d.8.2.	56th Bde.	Lucas Lamp.	T R
4.	O.P. in OLIVE Trench.	Division.	Shutter Lucas Lamp.	O L

In order to help units to pick up the KEMMEL Station, at night, a Green light will be shown every half hour.
Units working to KEMMEL by night will use a Red glass.

12. **POWER BUZZERS AND AMPLIFIERS.**
Four amplifiers and six power buzzers are available. These will be distributed as shown in the following table :-

POSITION.	INSTRUMENT.	PERSONNEL SUPPLIED BY
GOUDEZEUNE FM.	Amplifier and Power Buzzer.	Division.
TOWER at O.16.d.8.2.	Amplifier and Power Buzzer.	Division.
OLIVE TRENCH.	Amplifier and Buzzer.	Division.
Advancing Infantry.	2 Power Buzzers.	Battalions.

One Amplifier and Power Buzzer will be held in reserve at Brigade Headquarters.

13. **PIGEONS.**
44 pigeons will be delivered at 56th Infantry Bde. H.Q. at 4-0 p.m. on "Y" Day. This will give an allotment of 8 per Battalion for 56th Brigade and 12 in reserve to be used by the 57th Brigade if they require them.

14. **SIGNAL STORES.**
A dump of cable and signal stores will be formed at the CABLE HEAD at O.15.b.2.7. This will be under the charge of the 56th Bde. Signal Officer, who will issue as required.

15. **CODE CALLS.**
Units which do not move their Headquarters will use their position calls. Units which move will use their IX Corps Code Calls after moving.
Power Buzzers will use the Station Calls given in para 11.

(Sheet F.)

15. **FORWARD STATIONS.**
Three Brigade Forward Stations will be established with any of which it is optional for Units to communicate. Messages sent to these Stations by runner will be forwarded under Brigade arrangements. There is a buried cable head at GOUDAZEUNE FARM. These Stations will not move forward.

(a) Central Station (Code call G.Z.) - Dug-outs near GOUDAZEUNE FARM. (O.15.b.0.4.).
From this Station the following methods will be available forward :-
  Telephone to all Battalions.
  Visual On an arc of 82° - 150° (T.B.) The Southern limit of visibility being formed by the crest of the Ridge from O.15.d.9.0. - O.17.c.2.2.
  Amplifier & Power Buzzer, to two Stations (b) & (c) below.
  Runners.
(b) Right Station. (Code call T.R.) - O.16.d.90.25.
(c) Left Station. (Code call O.L.) - O.10.d.2.6.)
  Both Stations (b) & (c) are fitted with Visual and Amplifier and Power Buzzer.
  The above three stations will open at 9-0 p.m. "Y" day.

16. **ARTILLERY ALLOTMENT.**
1. The attack of 19th. Division is to be covered by the 19th. Divisional Artillery which will be divided into two groups.
Right Group. commanded by Lieut-Colonel W.J. KENT, R.F.A.
  Headquarters N.17.d.3.4.
Left Group. commanded by Lieut-Colonel G.S. TOVEY, D.S.O.,
  R.F.A. Headquarters O.13.b.0.9.

17. **LIAISON.**
(a) A senior Liaison Officer will be with H.Q. of the Infantry Brigade carrying out the Attack.
(b) A Junior Liaison Officer and a Forward Liaison Officer will be with each assaulting Battalion.
(c) There will be a Forward Intelligence Officer with each Artillery group.

18. **BARRAGES.**
The Attack will be carried out under a Creeping Barrage opening at ZERO on the Line O.23.c.85.60. - O.23.b.62.45. - O.17.c.50.90, - O.17.d.00.85. - O.17.b.00.90. - O.11.c.80.30. - O.11.a.87.15.
The Barrage will advance with lifts of 100 yards generally at the rate of 100 yards in 4 minutes.
It will halt on the Objective from ZERO plus 18 to ZERO plus 40 when it will again advance to the protective barrage line which it will reach at ZERO plus 55.

19. **S.O.S. Lines.**
After the Operations the S.O.S. Lines will be on a line from O.14.a.88.12. - O.15.c.76.88.

19a. **PRISONERS OF WAR.**
1. A Divisional Prisoners Cage will be established at N.18.b.2.4.
2. Prisoners (with the exception of those enumerated in para 3) will be marched to this Cage from the 58th. Inf. Bde: Collecting Station (O.15.a.85.15.) under an escort not exceeding 10% (these should if possible consist of slightly wounded men).

(Sheet VI.)

19a. PRISONERS OF WAR. (contd)
(3) Officers, N.C.O's and such privates as are considered intelligent who are captured, will be detached from the main party of prisoners at the 56th. Inf: Bde: Collecting Station; these will be marched without delay under an escort of similar strength to 56th. Inf: Bde: H.Q. where they will be examined by the Divisional Intelligence Officer. This Officer will keep in close touch with G.O.C., 56th. Inf: Bde: so that he may receive all information obtained from prisoners first hand.

After examination by the Div: Intelligence Officer, prisoners will be marched to the cage at N.18.b.2.4. under an escort to be found by 56th. Inf: Bde:

(4) A receipt will be obtained from the A.P.M. for his representive by the N.C.O. i/c escort, for all prisoners handed over at the Divisional Cage.

(5) With the exception of those enumerated in para 3, prisoners will not be searched before arrival at the Cage. Should a prisoner endeavour to destroy any document he will be searched by the N.C.O. i/c Escort who will hand over the documents to the A.P.M. or his representive at the Cage. He will obtain a receipt for these.

(6) Weapons and ammunition will be taken from prisoners on surrendering.

(7) Officers and N.C.O's will be kept seperate from Private soldiers as far as possible and will be placed in seperate pens in the cage.

20. MAPS.
In addition to those Maps already held by Brigades the following Maps will be issued :-
   A. 1/10,000 Special Map giving British Front Line and Bounderies - enemy front line, strong points, dug-outs, and the objective line.
   B. 1/10,000 Special Situation Map giving enemy front line, strong points and dug-outs. These are intended to mark the situation and facilitate forwarding reports.
   C. Wax Scribbling Maps.

DISTRIBUTION.	A.	B.	C.
Each Battalion.	10	25	20

21. ASSEMBLY OF 56th. INFANTRY BRIGADE.
(a) The boundaries between Battalions in the assembly area position will be :-
   7th. R.Lanc.R. Right on Brigade Right Boundary, viz :- O.23.a.5.4. - VAN HOVE FARM - POLKA ESTAMINET - Bend in Road O.21.central. (inclusive to 7th. R.Lanc.R.)
   7th. E.Lanc.R. Right at S.E. of small wood at O.17.c.33.68. thence due Westward.
   7th. N.Lanc.R. Right at junction of present front line and ROOZEBEEK, thence due Westward.
   Left on O.11.a.5.1. and thence Westwards along the line of the Divisional Northern Boundary.
   The above three Battalions will assemble in the present front line and the line of supporting points in rear.
(b) The Brigade will be holding the line on the night Y/Z on a three Battalion frontage.

(Sheet VII)

22. PLAN OF ATTACK OF 55th. INFANTRY BRIGADE.
    (a) At a ZERO hour to be notified later the three leading battalions of the Brigade will advance under an Artillery barrage which is to move forward in accordance with details referred to in para 18 and will capture the objective in accordance with para ....
    (b) The boundaries between Battalions on the Objective will be:-
        7th. E.Lanc.R. and 7th. E.Lanc.R. - Point in the BLUE LINE due West of House at O.17.d.80.75.
        7th. E.Lanc.R. and 7th. N.Lanc.R. - Road Junction at O.17.b.5.8.
        (inclusive to 7th. E.Lanc.Regt.).
    (c) 7th. N.Lanc.R. and 7th. E.Lanc.R. and 7th. E.Lanc.R. will each have 4 Companies in the line - each Company being on a frontage of two half platoons. The first line will move in extended order - the second line will move in sections in file. These two lines comprise the first waves which will assault the objective.
        The third line will also go in file and will be detailed for mopping up. The remaining platoon of each Company will be detailed for carrying but will not automatically advance at ZERO Hour.
    (d) 7th. S.Lanc.Regt. will assemble in the O.B.L. with four Coys: in the line. At ZERO hour these four Companies will advance in Artillery formation and occupy the front line system which will have been evacuated by the three assaulting Battalions.
        When distributed in this line at least three Companies will be South of the ROOZEBEEK.
    (e) Each Battalion will be responsible for mopping up the area over which it advances, with the exception that 7th. E.Lanc.Regt. will be responsible for dealing with the low lying ground lying between the left of their advance and the ROOZEBEEK, including GIM FARM and the adjoining dug-outs, O.17.b.80.95.
    (f) Each Battalion will consolidate the objective allotted to it - work being commenced as far as possible during daylight. The line consolidated will be approximately along the BLUE LINE - but the new trench will be dug at least 70 yards in front of, or behind, any conspicuous landmarks, e.g. houses or hedges.
        In order to assist them in finding the line of the Objective where there are no clear landmarks, Battalions will arrange to find their approximate places on the BLUE LINE by means of measured strings pulled out as they advance.
        Junction will be effected with 57th. Division at O.23.b.2.4. and with 4th. Division on Left at O.11.b.55.00.
        Consolidation will be carried out on the following lines :-
        (1) FRONT LINE. - Fire bays will be dug first each about 8 yards long with gaps 5 yards wide between each fire bay. These gaps will subsequently be made into traverses.
            This front line will be consolidated by the leading wave, who will also be responsible for finding covering party and patrols after the capture of the objective.
        (2) SUPPORT LINE. - will be dug at first as a series of small posts, which will not be connected until the digging and wiring of the new front line are well advanced.
            The digging of these posts will be begun by the mopping platoon from each Company who will be the first garrison of such posts.

23. **AFFILIATED TECHNICAL TROOPS.**

Two Field Coys: R.E. and two Coys: 5th. S.W.B. (Pioneers) will be affiliated to the 56th. Infantry Brigade to assist in consolidation.
(a) Field Coys: will be employed in the construction of strong points. There will be two of these strong points in rear of the front held by each of the three leading Battalions, which will be situated from 200 to 300 yards in rear of the new front line. The Map reference of approximate sites selected for these strong points will be notified later.
(b) Pioneers will be employed in the prolongation of the existing communication trenches to the new front line.

24. **HEADQUARTERS.**

19th. Divisional H.Q.	SCHERPENBERG.
56th. Brigade H.Q.	DAMMSTRAASE. O.9.c.3.8.
7th. R.Lanc.Regt.	POLKA ESTAMINET. O.22.a.3.2.
7th. E.Lanc. Regt.	Dug-outs at O.16.d.1.6.
7th. N.Lanc.Regt.	Dug-outs in the RAVINE O.10.d.15.55.
7th. S.Lanc.Regt.	O.18.a.8.6.

25. **WATER AND RATIONS.**

The ordinary method of supply of water and rations will be continued. A Battalion dump of petrol tins will be formed at Battalion H.Q. under 2/Lieut. D.W. TURNER, as soon as possible after ZERO HOUR. Companies will send to this point when they require water. Great care will however be taken that men start the day with full waterbottles. A small Divisional reserve of 500 tins will be formed at the head of the pipe line at O.14.c.7.7. this will be in charge of the Divisional Train and empty tins can there be exchanged for full ones.
One days rations will be carried on the man.

26. **STRAGGLER'S POSTS.**

Straggler's Posts will be established at :-
O.20.a.3.8.
O.15.a.35.15.
O.8.d.9.9.
OOSTAVERNE, O.21.b.6.7.

27. **BOMB STORES.**

The position of Bomb Stores will be as follows :-
Divisional Bomb Store.	YORK HOUSE. N.16.c.9.2.
Advanced Divl: Bomb Store	BOIS QUARANTE, O.7.c.5.9.
Brigade Bomb Stores.	O.22.a.5.9. & O.16.a.40.95.
Store on Right Flank.	PICK HOUSE, N.26.a.45.50,. (37th. Division),
Store on Left Flank,.	O.4.a.4.7. (41st. Division.).

After ZERO HOUR the Divisional Bombing Officer will be responsible for delivering bombs to tramhead at IN de STERKTE Cross Roads.

28. **SURPLUS PERSONNEL.**

Officers and men not accompanying the Units into action will be accomodated at First Line Transport Lines. Orders will be issued if, and when, this personnel is to be sent to the Transport Lines.
Units will inform Brigade H.Q. as early as possible whether any extra tents will be required.

(Sheet IX.)

29. R.E. DUMPS.
The main dump will remain at N.18.a.9.7. with advanced dumps at O.16.a.4.9. and O.22.a.20.95.

30. PACK TRAINS.
12 Pack Saddles will be drawn at once by Battalions from Brigade H.Q. and retained for use of Pack Trains. Battalions and M.G.Coys: will each be prepared to provide at short notice 6 animals complete with Pack saddles to form a Brigade Pack Train for work with the Brigade carrying party. The N.C.O. i/c and half the drivers (3 per Battalion and M.G.Coy) will be provided from transport personnel of Units and half from the Brigade carrying party. All Pack trains will be under the orders of the Brigade Transport Officer, Captain H.G. PERCIVAL., 9th. Bn. Welch Regt.

Details as to method of work will be issued if necessary but, in order to save carrying, pack transport will be used in preference to wheeled, whenever it is possible to push it forward further than wheeled transport could go.

31. MEDICAL.
The Regimental Medical Officer will be at Battalion Headquarters. Advanced Dressing Stations will be at DAMMSTRAASE, O.9.a.3.o, and ONRAET FARM, O.14.a.25.05.

Main Dressing Station will be in KEMMEL VILLAGE.

Walking Wounded Collecting Posts :- NORTH HOUSE, O.19.b.9.9. Routes from Regimental Aid Posts to Advanced Dressing Stations and Collecting Post will be labelled under arrangements to be made by the A.D.M.S.

Sites for Regimental Aid Posts have been selected by 56th. Infantry Brigade at :-
Right Battalion.   O.22.a.1.2.   ) Clear to A.D.S.
Centre Battalion. O.16.c.4.8.   )   ONRAET WOOD,
Left Battalion.   O.10.d.1½.6,   Clear to A.D.S., DAMMSTRAASE.

32. SALVAGE.
Salvage will be collected by Battalions. Material likely to be immediately required will be salved forward to where it can be made use of. All other material will be collected to the place where First Line Transport brings rations and evacuated by the returning Transport.

It is to be impressed on all troops that the question of salvage is daily becoming more important owing to the increased difficulties of production and oversea transport.

33. BATTALION CARRYING PARTY.
A party of four men per Company with four Regimental Police will report to 2/Lieut. TURNER on Y night. They will be accomodated with Battalion Headquarters. One Bombing N.C.O., to be detailed by 2/Lieut. TURNER, will be with this party.

34. LIAISON.
Captain A.F. CROSS will be with H.Q., 56th. Brigade. He will report there on the evening of Y day and will remain there until the Battalion leave the 56th. Brigade, when he will report to Headquarters, 58th. Infantry Brigade.

(Sheet X0.

35. RESERVES.
The following Officers, and N.C.O's will remain at the Transport Lines, (in the numbers will be included all N.C.O's and men on Courses and Leave).

Captain Brookes, M.O. who will act as Transport Officer.
2nd Lieut A.M.Forbes.
Regtl Sergt-Major,
C.S.M. Hoare,
C.S.M. Doyle.
One Bombing Instructor to be detailed by 2nd Lieut D.W. Turner
Provost Sergeant.
6 Signallers (1 N.C.O) to be detailed by 2nd Lieut Fox.
2 Scouts to be detailed by Lieut Phillips.
2 Orderly Room Staff.
Sergt Hewitt,

IN EACH COMPANY To be detailed by O.C. Company.
1 Sergeant, 1 Lewis Gun Instructor, 1 Corporal, 1 Lcpl,
In each platoon. Two Lewis Gunners.

Three Officers per Company will go in with each Company.

36. BRIGADE CARRYING PARTY.
Fifteen men of the Band to be detailed by the Adjutant will act as Brigade carrying party and will report to the Brigade Bombing Officer Captain May at N.23.b.6.6. at 2.30 p.m. on Y day bringing with them rations for Z Day - From A day inclusive they will be rationed by Brigade H.Q., They will wear yellow arm bands.
This party will probably not be used unless the Brigade is called upon to take part in active operations and will remain near S.P.12 until required.

37. CLOTHING AND EQUIPMENT.
(a) Officers. Same as for other ranks with revolver.
(b) Other Ranks
  (1) Clothing as issued.
  (2) Arms as issued.
  (3) Entrenching Tool as issued.
  (4) Accoutrements as issued, with the exception of the Pack. The Haversack will be carried on the back in place of the Pack.
  (5) Box Respirator and Tube Helmet.
  (6) Articles carried in the Haversack.
    (a) Towel and Soap,.
    (b) Spare Oil tin.
    (c) Holdall complete.
    (d) Iron rations.
    (e) Two day's OXO rations.
    (f) Every other man, 1 "Tommy" cooker.
  (7) The Mess tin and cover will be slung outside the haversack. The waterproof sheet will be carried, rolled on the belt, below the haversack.
  (8) Ammunition, 170 rounds, except for bombers 120 rounds. Signallers, Scouts and Runners. 50 rounds each. Lewis Gunners 120 rounds, Carrying party 50 rounds.
  (9) MILLS Grenades. 2 carried, 1 in each top pocket of the Jacket. These grenades are intended to be collected into a dump as soon as the Objective has been carried and are not to be used by the individual except in emergency.
  (10) Sandbags. 4 per man carried slung through the belt.
  (11) Rations & Water 1 Iron ration in haversack, the unexpended portion of the current day's ration in Mess tin. Filled Waterbottle. Men must be warned to drink sparingly.

(Sheet XI.)

37. CLOTHING & EQUIPMENT. (contd).
  12. Wirecutters and Breakers.
  13. Picks and shovels in the proportion of 1 pick to 3 shovels for every man.
  14. Very Pistols & 1½" Guns. Two pistols and one gun with each Company H.Q. Two pistols and one gun for Battalion H.Q. 6 S.O.S. lights per Company, the same for Battalion H.Q.

  Bombers.
       Men in bombing sections will carry 6 bombs per man.
  Rifle Grenadiers - 6 grenades and blank cartridges per man.

38. DISTINGUISHING MARKS.
  (a) Scouts - Green band on left forearm.
  (b) Runners - Red band -do-
  (c) Signallers. Blue band on shoulder strap.
  (d) Carrying parties. - Yellow band on left forearm.
  (e) Men equipped with wire cutters or wire breakers will wear a piece of white tape tied to their right shoulder straps.
  (f) The flags to be carried will be :-
      (a) Yellow and Black (Diagonal flag 18" square carried by platoon commander and platoon Sgts: in order to assist the Infantry to locate their own Infantry).
      (b) Yellow and Red (horizontal) flag 9" square carried by N.C.O. of bombing squad.
      (c) Strict orders will be issued that these flags are not to be stuck in the ground in order to avoid mistakes which might be caused by flags being left behind in evacuating positions.

39. FORWARD DUMPS OF WIRE.
  The 57th. Infantry Brigade have arranged to form dumps of wire and pickets at the following places :-
       Right Battalion at TOOL FARM, O.17.c.3.3½.
       Centre Battalion in the Cutting at O.17.a.M.2.
       Left Battalion at HOPE FARM, O.11.c.3.3½.

40. TRANSPORT LINES.
  On the 29th. inst: the 58th. Infantry Brigade will take over the Transport Lines of the 57th. Infantry Brigade at SEIGE FARM. Units will take over Transport Lines, Quartermaster's Stores and tents as follows :-

       9th. Cheshire Regt from 10th. R.War.Regt.
       9th. BN. R.W.Fus: from 8th. Glos: Regt.
       9th. Welch Regt. from 10th. Worc: Regt.
       6th. Wilts: Regt. from 9th. N.Staffs.

41. STORES TO BE CARRIED ON THE MAN.
  The Battalion will take over the following stores at SIEGE FARM :-

No. 5 MILLS boxes.	115.
Hales No. 24 " X	9
Mills No 23 " X	46
X. Cartridges and rods issued with these.	
S.A.A. Boxes.	25
Sandbags.	1,850
Hedging Gloves.	30
Long handled wire cutters.	35
Mark V wire cutters.	10
S.A. -do-	40
Tommy Cookers.	225
Revolver Amm: Rounds.	492

(Sheet XII).

1. **STORES TO BE CARRIED ON THE MAN.** (contd).

    In addition to the above 500 sandbags, 100 picks and 300 shovels are being added to each Battalion Store tomorrow morning.

    As no further issue of "Tommy" cookers is to be expected, the 225 taken over by each Battalion will be held in reserve until the Brigade is sent into the line.

    2/Lieut. D.W. TURNER will be responsible for the equal division of these stores between Companies.

2. **COLLECTION AND BURIAL OF DEAD.**

    Two Cemeteries will be established in the forward area at about O.16.c.5.1. and O.16.a.5.9.

    One Chaplain and 10 O.R. have been detailed by G.H.Q. to assist in the burial of the dead in the forward area. All ranks will be informed that the Green Identity Disc is in no circumstances to be removed from bodies. If for any reason a body has been stripped of personal belongings, a note to that effect will be left with the body stating the Rank and Unit of the person who has removed the effects.

    OPERATION ORDERS ADDENDUM.

    Operation Order No. 3 (f) will be ammendedcas follows :-

    "C" Company will occupy ODONTO TRENCH with their Left and H.Q. at a dug-out at approximately O.16.c.5.6.

    "D" Company will occupy ODONTO TRENCH with one platoon South of PRESTON ROAD and the remaining three platoons North of this point. Headquarters at the junction of ODONTO and PRESTON ROAD.

    At ZERO hour "C" & "D" Companies will move forward and occupy the old British Front line, "C" Company with its right on the Road at O.16.d.3.4. and "D" Company with its Left at this point.

    Two Battalion runners will be with "A" Coy: H.Q. and two with "B" Coy: H.Q. Messages will be sent to "A" & "B" Coy: H.Q. by telephone and sent on from there by runner.

    Kirby. Lieut & Adjt,
    9th. (S) Bn. Royal Welch Fusiliers.

WAR DIARY
INTELLIGENCE SUMMARY.
(Erase heading not required.)

Army Form C. 2118.

9th (S) Batt. [Loyal] North Lancs Fusiliers Volume 27 Page 1

Vol 27

Place	Date	Hour	Summary of Events and Information	Remarks and references to Appendices
	September 10th & 10th		In tents at STAFFORD CAMP, R.24.a.0.5 (Ref Sheet 27) near BERTHEN. 2/Lieut T.E. JONES arrived.	
	11th		Moved to CORUNNA CAMP, M.15.c.5.2 (Ref Sheet 28) near WESTOUTRE.	
	12th		In camp at CORUNNA CAMP.	
	13th		Moved to camp at N.16.c.2.3 (Ref Sheet 26) near KEMMEL.	
	14th		In tents at N.16.c.2.3.	
	15th		Moved to camp at N.20.a.3.3. Battalion in bivouacs.	
	16th		"A" company moved to IRISH HOUSE and were attached to 9th Bn Cheshire Regiment for operations. Rest of Battalion in camp at N.20.a.3.3.	
	"17/18th"		In camp as on 16th. The 58th Brigade was inspected at training by Sir Douglas Haig, G.O.C.-in-Chief, on the 18th.	
	19th		The Battalion moved to Assembly Position in preparation for Offensive. (Details attached)	
	20th		Assembly was complete at 1-15 am on 20th. Zero hour was at 5-40 am The Battalion was in Brigade	

WAR DIARY
INTELLIGENCE SUMMARY.

Army Form C. 2118.

9th (S) Batt Royal Welch Fusiliers Volume 27 Page 2

Place	Date	Hour	Summary of Events and Information	Remarks and references to Appendices
	Sept 20th (Contd)		Reserve. At 12.30 p.m. "B" Company reinforced front Line at HESSIAN WOOD, P.I.c.2.8 (Ref Sheet 28)	
		2.30 p.m	"D" Company reinforced front line on right of "B" Company Battalion Headquarters was established in IMPERFECT COPSE, I.36.d.4.3 with "C" Company in reserve. These positions were held during the night The Battalion remained in same position till night when the Front Line was re-adjusted and then handed over to the 56th Infantry Brigade. The total casualties for the 20th and 21st were:- Officers: Wounded. 2/Lieut. H.R. DAVIES, 2/Lieut. N.A. BUCK and Lieut. J.W. PHILLIPS. Other Ranks. Killed 21 (including 7 Died of Wounds) Wounded 73 Missing 12	
	21st			

Army Form C. 2118.

WAR DIARY

9th(S)Bn Royal Welch Fusiliers Volume 27

INTELLIGENCE SUMMARY.

Page 3

(Erase heading not required.)

Instructions regarding War Diaries and Intelligence Summaries are contained in F. S. Regs., Part II. and the Staff Manual respectively. Title pages will be prepared in manuscript.

Place	Date	Hour	Summary of Events and Information	Remarks and references to Appendices
	Sept 22nd		The Battalion in Support to 58th Brigade, in dugouts between THE BLUFF, I.34.c.5.5 and NORFOLK BRIDGE. I.33.d.5.5	
	23rd		Battalion moved to dugouts between NORFOLK BRIDGE I.33.d.5.5 and SPOIL BANK. I.33.a.3.0.	
	24th		The Battalion was relieved and proceeded to camp at N.16.a.2.3.	
	25th & 27th		In camp at N.16.c.2.3.	
	28th		Moved to SPOIL BANK. 'A' and 'B' Coys in SPOIL BANK and 'C' and 'D' Companies in BUFFS BANK and GASPERS CLIFF. 2/LIEUTS. D.R.JONES, L.JONES and W.T.ELLIS joined	
	29th		In support to 58th Brigade	
	30th		2/LIEUTS. F.J.WHITEMAN, W.E.BEDDOW, D.J.JONES, R.W.G.JONES and R.A.C. BAKER joined Battalion. In support	

Howard de Walden Major
Commanding 9th Royal Welch Fus

                                    Date of award.
D.S.O.   Capt. N.L.C. IRWIN.   15-9-17.   (Hospital.)

D.C.M.   16455 Sgt. Corcoran. H.   15-9-17.   (Wd. to England)
            54871 L/C. Barnett. H.   "   (On Leave.)
            13484 Pte. Davies. D.   "
            54304 "   Fisher. G.H.   "
            15888 Sgt. Morgan. J.   19-10-17.
            16680 "   Bannister. C. 14-6-17.

M.M.   7784 Pte. Yendall. G.E. 4-9-17.
            12941 Sgt. Brotherstone. D. "   (Sick to Eng.)
             4353 L/C. Lewis. W.H.   "   (Hospital)
            54182 Sgt. Davies. F.   "   (Second Army School
            13432 "   Phillips. S.   "   (Instructor.)
            13129 Cpl. Treharne. G.   "
            56348 Pte. Clarke. C.   "
            54235 "   Maher. J.   14-10-17.
            23338 Cpl. Hill. J.   "   (Att: T.M.B.)
            17719 Sgt. Miles. C.   "
           235118 L/C. Davies. E.   "
            13822 "   Briers. J.   "   (58th. Bde. H.Q)
            39232 Pte. Hughes. T.   "
            54195 "   Beddoe. D.T.   "
            38094 Cpl. Anthony. J.   "
            24463 L/C. Budd. J.T.   "
            37658 Pte. Williams. R.O.   "
            33331 "   Williams. B.   "
            14194 "   Pierce. J.   "
            39381 "   Evison. J.R.   "   (On Leave.)
            54345 "   Thompson. J.H. 14-8-17.   (Wounded.)
            33463 Cpl. Bonsall. H.   14-7-17.
            15703 Pte. Weeks. F.   "

SECRET   Copy No. 3

9th (S) Bn. Royal Welch Fusiliers
INSTRUCTIONS FOR THE OFFENSIVE.

The recipients of the above instructions is responsible for the custody of the documents and maps and that only such portions of their contents as may be necessary are communicated from time to time to their subordinates as the situation demands.

These instructions will be issued in two sections, Part I, Operations; Part II, Administrative.

Particular attention will be paid to maintaining strict secrecy with regard to impending operations.

Copies issued to :-

    Copy No. 1. File.
              2)
              3) War Diary.
              4. O.C. "A" Company.
              5.   " "B"   "
              6.   " "C"   "
              7.   " "D"   "
              8. Scout Officer.
              9. Signalling Officer.
             10. Bombing Officer.
             11. Transport Officer.
             12. Medical Officer.
             13. Quartermaster.
             14. Commanding Officer.
             15. Second-in-Command.
             16. 50th Infantry Brigade.

                          Howard Walder   Major,
                     Commanding 9th (S) Bn. Royal Welch Fusiliers.

APPENDIX I.   CONTACT PATROLS.

1. Aeroplanes for Contacts Patrols will be R.E.8 type and will be specially marked by a black flap attached to the rear of each Lower Plane. Photographs of aeroplanes are being issued. The contact patrol will fly over the line and call for flares at the following hours and any hours subsequent to them at which special aeroplanes may be ordered by the Corps. Troops will also be prepared to put out flares at any other time if the aeroplane calls for them.
    Zero plus 45 minutes.
    Zero plus 115 minutes.

3. Aeroplanes will call for flares and watson fans by sounding a Klaxon horn and firing a Very Light or by giving either of those two signals.

4. Red flares will be used. They should be lit in bunches of 3 each at about 50 yards apart. Watson fans will be used in conjunction with flares. The fans should be turned over every two seconds and not quicker, that is, the white side will be exposed to the aeroplane for two seconds and the dark side for two seconds and so on. This signal will be made for periods of not less than two minutes at a time as the observer is sometimes in a position from which he cannot see the fans.

5. The Corps Dropping Ground will be in the Field S.E. of the LA CLYTTE - LOCRE Road in N.17.b. and d, just west of the S in SCHERPENBURG, and will be in charge of Lieut. Henry, 9th Corps Cyclists.
    Camp Commandant will detail 6 runners to report at 9-0 a.m. on the day before Attack Day at Divisional H.Q.

6. A Schedule of Code calls for aeroplanes to be used is shown below.

7. Xth Corps Contact Aeroplanes will be distinguished by three broad white bands on the fuselage and also by a black board on the lower left plane.
    VIII Corps Contact Aeroplane will be distinguished by two black streamers on the lower right hand plane.

CODE LETTERS FOR LIAISON BETWEEN INFANTRY AND AIRCRAFT.

    58th Brigade............ L I V
    9th Cheshire Regt....... L I W
    9th R.W.Fusiliers....... L I X
    9th Welsh Regt.......... L I Y
    6th Wilts............... L I Z

S E C R E T.   9th Royal Welch Fusiliers.

INSTRUCTIONS FOR THE OFFENSIVE – PART I.

Reference Map HOLLEBEKE 1/10,000.

1. The IXth Corps is to take part in the Second Army Offensive.
   The main object of the attack of the IXth Corps is to secure the right flank of the Xth Corps.
   The attack from the IXth Corps front of attack (viz., YPRES – COMINES CANAL – J.31.a.75.75. is to be carried out by the 19th Division. The 30th Division is to hold the defensive portion of the IXth Corps front from the line of the YPRES-COMINES CANAL to the BLAUWEPOORTBEEK.
   (a) The 19th Division will attack on a two Brigade front :-
       56th Brigade on the Right.
       57th Brigade on the Left.
       58th Brigade will be in Divisional Reserve.
   (b) The 58th Brigade will attack on a three-Battalion front with one Battalion in reserve:-
       6th Wiltshire Regt on the Right.
       9th Welch Regiment on the Centre.
       9th Cheshire Regt. on the Left.
       9th Royal Welch Fusiliers will be in reserve.
   (c) The Southern Boundary of the 19th Division from the present front line back to YORK ROAD will be, O.6.c.80.70. – Along canal to O.4.b.30.50. – O.4.c.40.40. – DOLE HOUSE – CATTEAU FARM – O.7.d.35.10. – O.13.a.45.80. – N.18.a.30.80. – Along road to N.33.b.40.78. – Along road to N.33.a.00.10.
       The boundary between the 57th and 58th Brigades will be a line from P.1.b.35.55. to J.31.c.0.5, thence due West.
       The boundary between the centre and left Battalions of the 58th Brigade will be the line P.1.a.6.0. to N I.36.d.4.0.
       The boundary between the Right and Centre Battalions will be the line O.6.d.8.7. – O.6.d.65.95. – O.6.a.95.35.
       58th Brigade H.Q. will be at Dug-outs in Railway Cutting at about D.35.b.0.5.
       One M.G. Company each of the 30th and 37th Divisions and the IX Corps Motor M.G. Battery are placed at the disposal of the 19th Division for the attack.
       Headquarters are as follows :-
           6th Wilts. Regt.   Present double Company H.Q. at O.6.a.4.7.
           9th Welsh Regt.   3 dugouts at I.36.d.35.20. and I.36.d.39.10.
           9th Cheshire Regt. Dugout I.36.d.40.40.
           9th R.W.Fusiliers. Battalion H.Q. I.36.c.3.0.

2. DATES AND TIMES.
   The day on which operations will be carried out will be designated the "Attack Day" and the date will be indicated by a Code Letter. This letter code of dates will be communicated only to those Officers whose duties require them to be in possession of this information.
   "Zero" is the exact time on "Attack Day" at which the Artillery Barrage commences and the Infantry advance to the attack. Other references to times will be given in hours and minutes A.M. or P.M.

3. METHOD OF ATTACK.
   (a) The Artillery Creeping Barrage will open at ZERO from 150 yds in front of the line of assembly and will move by lifts of 100 yards. Subject to final adjustment, the first lift will be made at ZERO plus 4 minutes, second lift at ZERO plus 6, the third and all subsequent lifts will be made every 6 minutes.

(Sheet II.)

3. METHOD OF ATTACK. (Continued).
   (b) A pause of 30 minutes will be made by the creeping barrage on a line drawn roughly through POTSDAM FARM and the western edge of BELGIAN WOOD. This will enable the two right Battalions to go through to their objectives. The left Battalion will have a 30 minutes pause in which to re-organise for the attack on POTSDAM FARM.
   (c) The Creeping Barrage, after reaching the final objective, will rest for one hour as a close protective barrage, under cover of which, the defence of the position can be organised and consolidation commensed... During this period, guns will search and sweep.
   (d) After this pause of one hour, the artillery will lift on to the line
   to enable battle patrols to clear the immediate foreground and blow up dug-outs.
   The Artillery programme will be arranged so that one hour is available for this mopping up of the ground in front of the objective. At the end of this hour, the protective barrage will be put down again in front of the final objective.
   (e) During the operations, any point of resistance which holds up a frontal assault should be surrounded and must not delay the general advance.
   (f) In all stages of the advance, it is most important that all commanders (down to platoon and section commanders) should keep their men in hand, re-organising whenever possible.

4. OCCUPATION OF POSITION AFTER CAPTURE.
   The area allotted to each Brigade will, after capture, be held in depth. Two lines of resistance will be formed.
   (a) Line OPAQUE WOOD - Dug-outs about O.6.b.70.15. - East of Cross Roads at J.31.d.3.9. - GROENBURG FARM.
   (b) Line THE CEMETERY - HESSIAN WOOD - POTSDAM FARM - WOOD FARM - TOP HOUSE.

   Each of these lines should consist of a series of posts arranged in depth. On the right, posts will be established south of the Cemetery and touch established with troops of the 30th Division holding the line on the west of the CANAL.

5. COUNTER ATTACK AND USE OF RESERVES.
   It must be remembered that counter-attack is almost inevitable and reserves should therefore be close up and ready to act. The fire power of units must be fully developed. A situation must not be allowed to remain obscure. Positions taken must be held at all costs. It is the duty of commanders in rear, should they see men coming back, to push forward at once without waiting for orders.

6. MACHINE GUNS.
   Two sections and one subsection will be employed as follows :-
   (a) One subsection will be attached to each of the three attacking Battalions and will come under the direct command of Officers Commanding Battalions.
   (b) One subsection will move up in rear of the last wave of the left attacking Battalion. It will look out for any gaps that may occur between the 57th and 58th Brigades. In the event of the 57th Brigade being held up, it will give every assistance possible with flanking fire and will cover the exposed flank of our Left Battalion until a proper defensive flank is formed.
   This subsection will eventually be established in the intermediate line (See para 4 (a))about P.1.a.6.7.

(Sheet III.)

6. **MACHINE GUNS. (Continued).**
   (c) One subsection will move forward at ZERO in rear of the last wave of the Centre attacking battalion and will establish themselves on the spur about the intermediate line near the junction of the Centre and Left Battalions.
   (d) One section and one subsection of the 56th Machine Gun Coy will be at the disposal of the D.M.G.O. for barrage work during the initial advance. When no longer required, one section will move forward to the original front line and one subsection to the intermediate line to reinforce the guns which will already be there. These guns will take up a position about the junction of the Centre and Right Battalions

7. **TRENCH MORTARS.**
   Two mortars will be attached to each of the three attacking Battns. The remaining two mortars will be held in reserve in their present positions at O.6.a.4.5.
   On the final objective being gained, the mortars attached to Battalions will take up a defensive position in the intermediate line.

8. **ARTILLERY LIASON.**
   Each attacking Battalion will be accompanied by a Junior Liason Officer and a Forward Liason Officer. The Junior Liason Officer will remain at Battalion H.Q. until relieved and on relief of the Battalion, will transfer his liason to the relieving Battalion.
   The Forward Liason Officer will co-operate with the Junior Liason Officer in collecting information by going forward to positions from which he can watch the situation and so keep the Junior Liason Officer informed of the position of the Infantry and progress of the fight.

9. **COMMUNICATIONS.**
   In order to prevent leakage of information, all communication by telephone and messages sent by buzzer will cease in advance of the line HILL 60 - O.4.central - O.15.central - O.27.central, till the hour of Zero. The following methods of communication may be practiced in front of Brigade H.Q.
   Pigeons, Visual, Runners, Fullerphones for "S.O.S" calls, Rockets for "S.O.S" calls, Power Buzzers for "S.O.S" calls and urgent tactical messages.
   All Fullerphones in front of Brigade H.Q. will either be issued without handsets or have the microphones removed from the speaking circuits.
   No message will be sent by pigeon which contains anything in the address "To" or "From" or body of message which would be of value if it fell into the hands of the enemy until after Zero hour.

10. In the event of hostile aeroplanes flying low over our lines to ascertain whether our trenches are more strongly manned than usual, all ranks will remain still and will not look up.

11. **TANKS.** Tanks will not be employed in the attack on the 19th Division front.

                                                  Captain & Adjt.,
                                                  9th (S) Bn. Royal Welch Fusiliers.

9th (S) Bn. Royal Welch Fusiliers.

INSTRUCTIONS FOR THE OFFENSIVE - PART I, OPERATIONS.

12. **FORWARD COMMAND POSTS.**
 Forward Command Posts will be formed in the vicinity of :-
 (a) 6th Bn. Wilts. Regt.   S.E. side of OPAQUE WOOD or in Railway Embankment.
 (b) 9th Bn. Welsh Regt.   O.6.b.85.60.
 (c) 9th Cheshire Regt.   PIONEER HOUSE.

 O.C. 9th Welsh Regt., will move up after the attack to his Forward Command Post whence he will control the fight and report frequently to Brigade H.Q. Commanding Officers may, of course, move if temporarily necessary, he may call on the Brigade Reserve. In this latter case, he will immediately inform Brigade H.Q.
 A detachment of Brigade Forward Station will accompany 9th Bn. Welsh Regt to the Forward Command Post.

13. **COMMUNICATIONS.**
 (a) **Cable Supply.** Each Battalion will be issued with 2 miles D.8. on small drums which will be issued to Battalions before going into the line. 5 miles of cable will be at Brigade Forward Station for the use of the Brigade Forward party and a reserve of 5 miles will be kept at CABLE HEAD. No cable from the reserves will be issued to Battalions without a note from either the Officer i/c Brigade Forward Party or Brigade Signal Officer.
 (b) **Telephone System.** Cable Head will be at I.36.c.3.0. From the cable-head Brigade Signal Section will lay by 10 p.m. 18th inst. one metallic circuit to each of the Battalion Battle H.Q. Brigade Forward Station will be established at minus 3 hours in the dugout at I.36.d.40.25. On the Headquarters of the 9th Welsh Regt moving forward, a detachment of 1 N.C.O. and 5 men from the Brigade Forward Station will lay two metallic circuits one Infantry and one Artillery, to the selected command post. Brigade Signal Section will work and maintain these lines. Runners at the Command Post will be found by the 9th Welsh Regt.
 (c) **Station Calls.** Before Zero position calls will be used. After Zero, code calls called down in my B.M.3171 of 16/9/17. Existing position calls will be allotte to the Battalion Battle H.Q. Owing to the danger of giving away the assembly the telephone lines from Battalion Battle H.Q. will on no account be used except for "S.O.S" All testing of lines will be done from cable head.
 (d) **Visual Signal Scheme.** Brigade Signal Section will establish a Brigade Visual Station at O.5.b.5.5½. This Station will receive D.D.messages from Battalion H.Q., Brigade Forward Station, and Forward Command Post. When the situation permits, R.D. will be given to messages. Where no acknowledgement is possible, messages will be sent through 3 times. Messages received at Brigade Visual Station will be sent on by telephone or visual to Brigade Headquarters.

 (e) Runners will be distributed as follows :-
   Brigade H.Q. 8
   No. 3 Bde. Relay Post... 6   I.35.c.1.6.
   No. 1 "   "   "   " 6   I.36.c.9.4.
   Bde. Forward Station... 6
 Messages from the Left and Centre Battalions will go to the Brigade Forward Station. Messages from Right and Reserve Battalions direct to No. 3 Relay Post and thence to Brigade.
 In the event of overland lines being broken, telephone messages will go direct to Cable Head.

(Sheet II)

13. **COMMUNICATIONS.** (Continued)
    (f) Earth Induction Scheme.   1 Amplifier & Power Buzzer. Cable Head
                                  1 Amplifier & Power Buzzer. Bde. Forward Station
                                  1 Power Buzzer with each attacking Battalion.
    Of these three battalion power buzzers, only the power buzzer of the 6th Welsh Regt. may be used for sending messages, the other two being used solely for "S.O.S" messages.
    Calls.   6th Wiltshire Regt.   P B .... A
             9th Welsh Regiment.   P B .... B
             9th Cheshire Regt.   P B C
    Thus, if 9th Welsh Regt., for example, wish to send "S.O.S", they will send "B B B S O S" until a Very Light acknowledgement is obtained from the amplifier.
    Power Buzzer bases will be laid out due N. and S.
    (g) Pigeons.   Distribution of pigeons will be as follows :-
        6th Wilts Regt.   6,   9th Cheshire Regt.   8
        9th Welsh Regt.   6,   9th R.W.Fusiliers.   8
        Brigade Forward Station.   4,   In Reserve   2.

14. **RECONNAISANCE OF CAPTURED AREA.**
    One Officer and 10 men of the 1st Canadian Tunnelling Company have been placed at the disposal of the Division for reconnaisance of enemy dug-outs in the captured area.
    They will be attached to the Reserve Battalion of 58th Brigade for purposes of assembly and will join this Battalion on the afternoon of the 9th inst.

15. **TRACKS.**
    Tracks North of the Canal have been named as under :-
    Track along North Bank of Canal   CANAL WALK.
    Track along North side of BUFFS BANK   BUFFS WALK
    Track which crosses canal between TRIANGULAR
      BLUFF and BUFFS BANK and follows the line
      of OAF AVENUE.   OAF WALK
    Track which crosses just East of IRON BRIDGE
      and runs along IMPERIAL AVENUE   GASPERS WALK
    Track which crosses just West of IRON BRIDGE
      and runs through I.35.central   BATTLE WALK
    Track from PONTOON BRIDGE and runs South of the
      CATERPILLAR and N. of KLEINE ZILLEBEKE   IMP WALK.
    These tracks, where under enemy observation, will be used as little as possible during daylight until "Attack Day"
    Communication with the Front Line by daylight will be carried out along the communication trenches OAF and IMPERIAL AVENUES
    Carrying Parties and working parties moving forward after dark will use all tracks toward the front line for movement forward (In Trenches); communication trenches OAF and IMPERIAL AVENUES will be used as out trenches.
    During the hours of assembly - which will be notified later - all tracks and communication trenches will be used as "IN" trenches.
    Troops coming out of the line on relief on the first night of the assembly will use the tracks as "OUT" trenches.
    From Zero hour onwards all tracks will be used as "IN" trenches the communication trenches OAF and IMPERIAL AVENUES will be used as "OUT" trenches.

16. **RESERVE BRIGADE.**
    (1) 56th Inf. Bde. will assemble on the night previous to "Attack Day" as follows :-
        Brigade H.Q. SPOIL BANK South Side.
        2 Battalions forward in dug-out accomodation between BUFFS BANK and NORFOLK LOCK.
        Remainder of Brigade - BOIS CONFLUENT Area.

(Sheet III)

16. **RESERVE BRIGADE.** (Continued)
    (2) Of the two Forward Battalions, one will be in the area East of PONTOON BRIDGE and will be prepared to replace the Reserve Battalion of 58th Brigade.
    A Liaison Officer from this Battalion will be with the H.Q. of the Reserve Battalion of 58th Brigade.

    One Battalion will be in the area West of the PONTOON Bridge and will be prepared to replace the Reserve Battalion of 57th Brigade.
    (3) The remainder of the Brigade will be prepared to move forward at 15 minutes notice either to replace the two leading Battalions or together with those Battalions to deliver a fresh attack, or relieve the 57th and 58th Brigades.

17. **DISTINGUISHING MARKS.**
    Distinctive Arm Bands laid down in S.S. 135 para XXXII, will be worn by all concerned.

18. **TIMES.**
    In making references to times before and after which operations will take place, the symbols   and   will not be used, but the words plus or minus will be written in full.
    In Referring to times before or after Zero hour, the words "Zero plus   " or "Zero minus   " will be inserted to prevent possible confusion with clock times.

19. **"S.O.S" CALLS.**
    The following will be the "S.O.S" Signals available during operations taking effect from noon Monday 17th September.
    In use.   Rifle Grenade Signal - Parachute - ....
    . Red over Green over Yellow.
    First Change. Rifle Grenade Signal - Parachute - Light changing if necessary from White to Green.
    Second Change. 1½ inch Very Light - Parachute - changing from if necessary White to Red.
    As circumstances permit, this last will also be made into a Rifle Grenade Signal.
    As many as possible of the present S.O.S. Signals will be collected into Reserve Dumps. It must be impressed upon all concerned that the Signal is to be repeated until our Artillery open fire.

20. **SMOKE BARRAGE.**
    In addition to the Smoke Barrage which will be put down on the ZANDVOORDE RIDGE a certain number of Verley Bombs for Stokes Mortars will be carried with the assaulting troops to be used as opportunity offers to blind strong points which may hold up the advance.

21. **GAS.**
    In view of the consistent manner in which the enemy is carrying out gas shell bombardments at night, special instructions will be issued for warning troops who are being moved to forward areas at present, about the necessary precautions to be taken.
    Attention is invited to the instructions for action during Gas Shell Bombardments which were issued under IXth Corps Letter.

22. **STRONG POINTS.**
    82nd Field Coy. R.E. will construct 2 Strong Points on 58th Bde Front at approximately No. 1 at O.6.b.8.2. & No. 2 at P.1.a.6.5.
    Strong Points should be for a garrison of 1 platoon & 2 Vickers Guns.   Garrisons will be detailed beforehand as under :-
    No. 1. 9th Welsh Regt. and 1 or 2 M.G's detailed to move forward to intermediate line when released from barrage.
    No. 2. 9th Cheshire R. and 1 or 2 of the M.G's of those detailed to follow left flank of 9th Cheshire Regt.
    These garrisons will occupy the strong points as soon as reported ready for occupation by R.E. Officer i/c.   82nd Fd. Coy. will also construct a M.G. Post about O.6.c.7.6. This position will be available for Vickers Guns attached to 6th Wiltshire Regt.

9th (S) Bn. Royal Welch Fusiliers.

INSTRUCTIONS FOR THE OFFENSIVE. PART II, ADMINISTRATIVE.

1. **MEDICAL.**
   (a) Aid Posts. Three combined Aid Posts (for two Battalions each) will be constructed as follows :-
      (i) At about I.35.d.60.75. for 9th Cheshire Regt. and Right Battalion of 57th Brigade.
      (ii) At about I.36.c.3.0. for 9th Welch Regt. & 6th Wilts. Regt.
      (iii) At about KLEINE ZILLEBEKE for two left Battalions of 57th Brigade.
   (b) Advanced Dressing Stations.
      (i) NORFOLK BRIDGE, I.33.d.4.5.
      (ii) About the MOUND, O.3.d.6.7.
   (c) Walking Wounded Collecting Post.
      About the MOUND, O.3.d.6.7.
   (d) Main Dressing Stations.
      (i) HOSPICE, LOCRE, for stretcher cases.
      (ii) BREWERY, KEMMEL, for walking wounded.

   Method of evacuation of wounded.
   Stretcher Cases. By hand carriage by Regimental Stretcher Bearers to above mentioned Aid Posts.
   Walking Wounded. Cases will be directed by means of signposts and box lanterns to the Pontoon Crossing at the IRON BRIDGE, and thence to Walking Wounded Collecting Post at the MOUND. They will be removed from there by Light Railway to Main Dressing Station, KEMMEL.

   Marking of Routes for Evacuation.
   (i) Each attacking Battalion will arrange to mark routes from its subsector of the front line to the Regimental Aid Post allotted to it. Boards will be supplied under Brigade arrangements.
   (ii) The A.D.M.S. will mark routes from Aid Posts to Walking Wounded Collecting Station.

2. **SURPLUS PERSONNEL.**
   Surplus Personnel left out of action in accordance with S.S.135 will be as follows :-

   Captain H.L. Williams, M.C.   Second-in-Command.
   Captain D.C.J. Brooks. M.C.   Captain N.L.C. Irwin D.S.O.
   Captain G.L. Kirby.   2/Lieut. A. Wynne.

   The Provost Sergeant.   C.S.M. "D" Company.
   Lewis Gun Instructor. (Bn)   C.S.M. "A" Company.
   Bn. Bombing Instructor.
   "H.Q" Company.
      3 Signallers, 5 Scouts, 2 Orderly Room Staff, 4 Runners.
   Per Company.
      1 Sergt., 1 Cpl., 2 L/Cpls., 1 Lewis Gun Instructor, 4 O.Ranks.
   Per Platoon.
      1 Rifle Grenadier, 2 Lewis Gunners.

   The above withdrawn personnel will be accommodated in the Brigade Transport Lines and will move into these lines by noon, on the 18th inst.

3. **TRANSPORT.**
   The Brigade Transport Officer (Captain H.G. Percival, C/Welsh Regt) will take charge of the Brigade Transport Lines and act as Brigade Staff Officer for Transport.

(Sheet II).

3. **TRANSPORT.** (Continued)
   The Brigade Transport Officer is connected by telephone with Brigade Headquarters.
   The carraige of rations and water will be best achieved by pack mules. By Attack Day, two mule tracks will be completed :-
   i. On the Left via CATERPILLAR TRACK - I.35.b.central - KLEIN ZILLEBEKE - I.36.d.O.8. - IMPERFECT COPSE.
   ii. On the Right via TRANSPORT CORNER - HOLLEBEKE ROAD - along the N. of OAF TRENCH - Railway Embankment at I.36.c.3.3.
   The Transport Officer, 9th R.W.Fus. will reconnoitre (ii)
   Arrangements as to the times at which rations are sent up will be co-ordinated by the B.T.O. in order to avoid congestion. He will inform this Office when rations will be sent up and the information will be sent on to the Units concerned.
   The replenishing of the forward dumps of Ammunition and R.E. material will also be effected by pack mule work. The B.T.O. will be notified by Brigade H.Q. of the amounts required and will arrange accordingly.

4. **SUPPLIES.**
   (a) Supply Railhead, BRULOOZE.
   (b) Refilling Point, BRULOOZE.
   (c) Supplies will be drawn from Railhead in Train wagons and conveyed to Quartermaster's Stores and from Quartermaster's Stores to the troops by 1st Line Transport or Pack Sections.
   (d) In addition to :-
      i. The Iron Rations on the man.
      ii. The current day's rations.
      authority is given for the following rations to be held :-
      iii. One day's Iron Rations for troops in the Front Line System.
         N.B. to be held in reserve in addition to the Iron Rations on the man.
      iv. One day's Barrage Rations consisting of P.M. and biscuits, with tea, sugar and jam for all troops within a possible enemy barrage.
   (e) A day will eventually be fixed and will be notified later for the consumption of the rations in para (d) iv, and balance effected by underdrawing at Railhead. Bacon and cheese will be drawn to supplement this ration and sent forward if possible.
   (f) The rations under (d) iii, will be issued to Units in their Transport Lines, carried up on the night of 18/19, and dumped as follows :-
      9/Welsh Regt.)   Railway Embankment between FUSILIER
      6/Wilts Regt.)   WOOD and CHEQUE WOOD.
      9/Cheshire Regt.)   In the RAVINE on South-Eastern edge
      9/R.W.Fusiliers.)   of FUSILIER WOOD.
      The dumps must be protected from weather and, where possible, from shellfire and camouflaged with earth, grass, etc.
   (g) The rations under (d) iv, will be dumped under Brigade arrangements at Brigade H.Q. I.35.a.90.95.
   (h) Chewing Gum for use during operations will be available.
   (i) There will be a daily issue of Rum to troops in the trenches, and during inclement weather a daily issue of 2 ozs of Pea Soup or two Oxo cubes or other available substitute.
   (j) There will be a daily issue to the Brigade of 350 tins of Solidified Alcohol. These will be issued to Units holding the Front Line. They should be supplemented by "Home Made Tommy's Cookers" under Unit arrangements.

(Sheet III)

5. **WATER.**
    (a) Water is laid on in the Divisional Area as follows :-
       i. Tanks connected to piped water supply etc.
          O.3.b.5.7.   (Tank 105)
          O.9.a.55.10.   (Tank 106)
          O.4.c.3.4.   (Tank 107)
          O.4.a.70.55.   (Tank 108)
          O.4.a.8.7.
       ii. 5 tanks filled by water lorry on each side of the road at
          I.35.a.15.70.
          5 tanks filled by water lorry on each side of the road at
          I.35.a.10.85.
    (b) Additional Tins will be issued to Battalions so as to make
        their total number on charge 300 per Battalion. 100 full tins
        will be dumped under Battalion arrangements together with the
        reserve rations on night of 18/19 as detailed in para 4 (f).
        They will be regarded as a Battalion Reserve and used at the
        discretion of Officers Commanding Battalions.
    (c) Efforts must be made to obtain water in the forward area from
        shallow wells.
    (d) No horse watering places are to be established on roads.
        Arrangements must be made for each Unit to water in its own
        lines, or if this is not possible, tracks must be made across
        the fields from Transport Lines to horse watering places.
        Horses are not to be taken along or across main roads to
        water, unless absolutely unavoidable.
    (e) There is a Divisional Reserve of water in petrol tins at
        Divisional Bomb Store I.34.a.5.2. Empty petrol tins can be
        exchanged for full ones there.
    (f) There will be a small reserve of water in petrol tins at
        Brigade Headquarters.

6. **TRENCH FEET.**
    Whale Oil will be issued to Units and mens' feet will be rubbed with
    it before going into the trenches and as often as possible while
    in the trenches.

7. **REINFORCEMENTS.**
    The IXth Corps Reinforcement Camp BERTHEN will open on Monday.
    O.C. "B" Company will detail 1 Sergt. who will report to 2/Lieut.
    H.W. WHEELER, 7/S. Lancs. Regt, 19th Division Reinforcement Officer
    at 5-0 p.m. on that day, rationed for the 18th inst. After that day,
    he will be rationed under arrangements to be made by the Corps.

8. **PRISONERS OF WAR.**
    (a) A Corps Prisoners Cage will be established at CARRE FARM.
    (b) A Divisional Collecting Station will be established at ST. ELOI.
    (c) The A.P.M., 19th Division will make arrangements to take over
        all prisoners at this Station and escort them to the Corps Station.
    (d) Prisoners with the exception of those enumerated in para (h)
        will be marched to the Divisional Station from the Brigade
        Collecting Station, which will be situated on the track
        skirting the Northern edge of BLUFF'S BANK.
    (e) Escorts should not exceed 10% of the prisoners, should consist
        if possible of lightly wounded men and should use overland tracks
        and not communication trenches.
    (f) The Brigade Collecting Station will be in charge of Captain
        D.C.J. Brooks, 9th R.W.Fus. Each Battalion will detail 4 men
        as a guard to the Collecting Station. The 4 men of the 9th R.W.F
        will be detailed by Sergt. HEWITT. The Officer and men
        detailed for guard will report at Brigade H.Q. at 5-0 p.m. on
        the day before Attack Day, taking rations for 1 day.

(Sheet IV.)

8. **PRISONERS OF WAR.** (Continued.)

(g) After an escort has handed over its prisoners to the Officer i/c Station, the Officer will send such of the escort as are fit back to their Units. He will use men of his own guard as escorts between the Brigade and Divisional Collecting Stations.

(h) A small percentage of Officers, N.C.O's and such privates as are fit and considered intelligent, who are captured, will be detached from the parties of prisoners as they come into Brigade Collecting Stations and escorted with as little delay as possible to Brigade Headquarters at Hill 60 for examination by the Divisional Intelligence Officer in order that any tactical information of importance may be obtained first hand for the Infantry Brigade concerned. After examination by the Divisional Intelligence Officer, prisoners will be marched to the Divisional Collecting Station under escorts of lightly wounded men.

(j) With the exception of Officers and N.C.O's, prisoners will not be searched before arriving at the Corps Cage.

(k) Should a prisoner endeavour to destroy any document, he will be searched by the N.C.O. i/c escort, who will hand over the documents to the A.P.M. at the Divisional Collecting Station or the Corps Intelligence Officer at the Corps Cage. He will obtain a receipt for this.

(l) Weapons and ammunition will be taken from Prisoners on surrendering.

(m) Officers and N.C.O's will be kept separate as far as possible from the men.

(n) One L/Cpl. and ten men will be detailed by Sergt. HEWITT as escort for prisoners from Divisional Collecting Station to Corps Cage. They will report to the A.P.M. at a time and place to be notified later.

9. **BURIAL.**

(a) /Lieut. F. HORTON, 7/N. Lancs. Regt., is appointed Divisional Burial Officer. 9th R.W.Fus. have detailed 1 N.C.O. and 3 men to work under his orders.

(b) The system of burials will be as laid down in "IXth Corps Instructions for Burials" already in possession of Units.

(c) The burial of German dead will be carried out in the same manner as our own, but in separate cemeteries. Effects of German dead will be sent to Divisional Intelligence Officer as quickly as possible and thence to Corps Intelligence Department.

(d) Formations and salvage parties will inform B.B.O. of the location of any bodies awaiting burial, as quickly as possible.

(e) In the event of the Division being relieved in the line before burials are completed, a sufficient party will be detailed to remain behind with the D.B.O. to complete the work under the supervision of the Corps Burials Officer. This party will rejoin the Division under orders from Corps H.Q.

10. **AMMUNITION.**

(a) Divisional Bomb Store   - YORK HOUSE, N.16.c.3.0.
Advanced Div. Bomb Store - near RAVINE WOOD, I.34.a.5.2.
Brigade Reserve Store   - RAILWAY Emb\ᵗ, I.36.c.3.2.
Advanced Bde Dump Right - OPAQUE WOOD, O.6.a.8.6.
Advanced Bde Dump Left - IMPERFECT COPSE, I.36.d.35.10.

(b) The above will be formed of ammunition of every kind. The Brigade Dumps will be marked at night with a shaded red lamp. There will be a storeman at each who will issue to any party on demand. A detailed list of the contents of each dump will be issued later as Appendix I.

(Sheet V.)

11. **SUPPLY OF R.E. MATERIAL.**
    (a) The Main Divisional Dump will be established between BUS HOUSE and ST. ELOI at O.3.a.9.8.
    (b) Advance dumps will be established at DIP DUMP (O.4.b.1.7.) and MOLEN DUMP (I.35.a.3.5.)
    The former will be in charge of the O.C., 33nd Field Coy., R.E. and the latter of the O.C. 94th Field Coy. R.E.
    (c) Trench Dumps will be established in the Front Line system in the same positions as the advanced Brigade Ammunition Dumps.
    Lists of contents will be issued.

12. **VETERINARY ARRANGEMENTS.**
    Sick or wounded horses will be taken to No. 31 Mobile Veterinary Section at LOCRE. M.33.c.8.2. (Sheet 28.)

[signature] Captain & Adjt.,
9th (S) Bn. Royal Welch Fusiliers.

INSTRUCTIONS FOR THE OFFENSIVE, - PART II. (Contd)
------000------

13. ORDNANCE.
   (a) The Ordnance Stores are situated at LOCRE.
   (b) Ordnance Supply during operations will be normal.
   (c) Corps Ordnance Workshops are at LOCRE.

14. SALVAGE.
   (a) Divisional Salvage Coy is located at N.6.c.6.0.
   (b) The system of salvage will be as follows :-
      (i) Brigades will be responsible for salving in their respective
          sectors from present front line forward to final objective,
          all salvage being brought back to Brigade Dumps.
      (ii) The Divisional Salvage Officer will be responsible for clearing
           area from CANAL to present Front Line.
      (iii) The O.C. Salvage Coy will collect from Brigade Dumps by wagon
            and will take all Salvage to the Divisional Dump at O.3.d.6.7.
   (c) The Brigade Salvage Dump will be at I.35.d.3.3. Personnel of the
       Salvage Coy will be in charge and will be ready to load salvage from
       the dump on to ration limbers.
   (d) If it is found that additional Brigade Salvage Dumps would facilitate
       salvage operations, application should be made at once to this Office
       and the new dump will be placed in charge of men of the Salvage
       Coy attached to the Brigade. The site chosen for a dump should
       invariably be on a limber or pack mule track, so that the dump can
       be cleared by returning ration trains.
   (e) All Dumps will be clearly marked by sign-boards.
   (f) The work of salvage is to commence as soon as possible after
       operations start.

PART II ADMINISTRATIVE. APPENDIX I.

Bombs, Etc.

	Main Brigade Store. Railway Embankment. I.36.c.3.3.	Right Adv. Bde. Store, CHEQUE WOOD. O.3.a.8.6.	Left Adv Bde Store IMPERFECT COPSE I.33.d.3.1.
Mills Bombs.	3,500	3,000	3,000
Mills R.G.	1,500	1,500	1,500
Hales R.G.	1,000	500	500
S.A.A.	100,000	50,000	50,000
Very Lights 1"	1,500	1,350	1,350
" "	500	500	500
Smoke Cases.	350	350	350
"P" Bombs.	350	350	350
"S.O.S"	Will be kept at Main Brigade Store.		
Stokes	Dumps are formed at (a) Railway Embankment O.6.a.3.5.		
	(b) The Ravine, I.36.c.8.3.		
	(c) Imperfect Copse, I.36.d.3.1.		

R.E. MATERIAL.

Barbed wire (coils.		200 (x)	135
French wire " 40 yds.		100 (x)	80
Stakes.		300 (x)	300
Sandbags.		1,500	1,500

(x) This includes the R.E. Dump on the Western edge of the
    Railway Embankment.

WAR DIARY
INTELLIGENCE SUMMARY

9th (S) Bn Royal Welch Fusiliers Volume 28
Page 1

Army Form C. 2118

Vol 28

Place	Date	Hour	Summary of Events and Information	Remarks and references to Appendices
	October 1st & 2nd		The Battalion in Brigade Reserve in SPOIL BANK	
	3rd		Relieved 9th Cheshire Regt in Front Line (left Battalion)	
	4th-6th		In Front Line	
	7th		Relieved by 9th Cheshire Regt and proceeded to SPOIL BANK	
	8th		In SPOIL BANK	
	9th		Relieved 9th Cheshire in Front Line	
	10th		In Front Line	
	11th		Relieved by 10th Roy Warwickshire Regt and proceeded to BEGGARS REST CAMP (N 6 d 1.7) Such 28. Total Casualties. 6 OR Killed 22 OR Wounded	
	12th & 13th		In tents at BEGGARS REST CAMP	
	14th		Moved to KEMMEL SHELTERS	
	15th & 16th		Training at KEMMEL SHELTERS	
	17th		Moved to Brigade Reserve at HILL 60 and relieved 8th N Staff Regt	
	18th & 19th		In Brigade Reserve at HILL 60	

M Murdmin
Lt Col

Army Form C. 2118

WAR DIARY
9th Royal Welsh Fusiliers
INTELLIGENCE SUMMARY.

Volume 28
Page 2

(Erase heading not required.)

Place	Date	Hour	Summary of Events and Information	Remarks and references to Appendices
	Oct 23rd		Relieved 9th Cheshire Regt in Front Line	
	24th to 26th		In Front Line	
	27th		Relieved by 10th Kings Own R.L. Regt and proceeded to BEGGARS REST CAMP. Total Casualties 5 OR Killed, 13 OR Wounded	
	28th to 31st		In camp at BEGGARS REST CAMP. Battalion on working parties	

Noel Musselwhite
Lieut-Colonel
Commanding 9th Royal Welsh

Army Form C. 2118.

WAR DIARY
9/(S) Batt Royal Welch Fus Volume 29
INTELLIGENCE SUMMARY.
(Erase heading not required.)

Page 101 29

Place	Date	Hour	Summary of Events and Information	Remarks and references to Appendices
	Nov 1st		In tents at BEGGARS REST CAMP	
	2nd 6th		do	
	7th		Moved to TOURNAI CAMP, VIERSTRAAT.	
	8th		In huts at TOURNAI CAMP	
	9th		Marched to STRAZEELE	
	10th		In billets at STRAZEELE	
	11th		Marched to EBBLINGHEM via HAZEBROUCK	
	12th-28th		Battalion in training in EBBLINGHEM area	
	29th		Ribbon presentation by I.O.C. Division	
			Moved to BLARINGHEM area for training	
	30th		Training in BLARINGHEM area	

JKMos Capt & Adjt
for Lt-Colonel
9th Royal Welch Fus
Commanding 9 Royal Welch Fus

9th (S) Bn. R.W. Fus: Volume 30 Army Form C. 2118.

WAR DIARY
INTELLIGENCE SUMMARY.
(Erase heading not required.)

Page 1

Place	Date	Hour	Summary of Events and Information	Remarks and references to Appendices
Field	Oct 1st		In billets at BLARINGHAM.	9/1 30
	2nd		Move by route march to TILQUES.	
	3rd		In billets at TILQUES. Musketry practice on the Range.	
	4th		Have practice on the Range. Received sudden orders to move back to BLARINGHAM.	
	5th		In billets at BLARINGHAM.	
	6th		Move by route march to ARQUES.	
	7th		Entrain at ARQUES for BEAUMETZ. Detrain here and march to BLAIRVILLE.	
	8th		Move by route march to GOMIECOURT.	
	9th		Move by route march to ETRICOURT.	
	10th		In camp at ETRICOURT. In tents.	
	11th		Move up into the Line and relieve 11th ESSEX Regt: in HINDENBURG LINE, near RIBECOURT.	
	12th		Relieve the 9th SUFFOLK Regt: in outpost to the front line near RIBECOURT. Everyone expecting attack by Germans at any minute.	
	13th		-do-	
	14th		-do-	

9th (S) Bn. R.W.F.
WAR DIARY
or
INTELLIGENCE SUMMARY.

Volume 30 Army Form C. 2118.
Page 2

Place	Date	Hour	Summary of Events and Information	Remarks and references to Appendices
Field	Aug 15		Still repulsing attack.	
	16th		— do —	
	17th			
	18th			
	19th		Relieve 1st ARTISTS RIFLES in the front line in the Right of Brigade Sector. The line was a piece of the old KAISER LINE just in front of MARCOING. Very quiet. Weather bad – snow and frost every night.	
	20th 21st 22nd 23rd 24th			
	25th		Relieved 8th GLOUCESTER Regt: in support in the HINDENBURG LINE.	
	26th 27th		Relieved by 9th WELSH Regt: and move back to camp in HAVRINCOURT WOOD. In tents and tarpaulins well below zero. Considerable sickness among the men.	
	28th		Relieve the 4th SOUTH LANCS: Regt. in RIBECOURT in support to left sub-sector.	
	28th 29th 30th 31st		Relieve 9th CHESHIRE Regt. in left front sub-sector.	

Mm A Miller
Lt Colonel
Comdg 9th (S) Bn. R.W.F.

9th Bn VOLUME 31 5/9
9 RWF
Vol 31

WAR DIARY
or
INTELLIGENCE SUMMARY.

Army Form C. 2118.

(Erase heading not required.)

Place	Date	Hour	Summary of Events and Information	Remarks and references to Appendices
Field	1-1-18		In C.I. Sub Sector, Left Section, in front of RIBECOURT.	
	2-1-18		— do —	
	3-1-18		— do — Casualties 3 men killed & 2 wounded	
	4-1-18		— do —	
	5-1-18		Moved back to Intermediate line (HINDENBURG LINE) in relief of 4th East Lancs.	
	6-1-18		Moved up into Right Sub Sector, Right Section, in relief of 10th Worcester Regt.	
	7-1-18		— do —	
	8-1-18		— do — 1 man killed	
	9-1-18		— do — 1 — wounded	
	10-1-18		— do —	
	11-1-18		— do —	
	12-1-18		Moved back into Support (FORK AVENUE) in relief of 9th Cheshire Regt.	
	13-1-18		— do —	
	14-1-18			
	15-1-18		Left into Right Sub Sector, Right Section in relief of 9th Cheshire Regt.	
	16-1-18		— do —	
	17-1-18		— do —	
	18-1-18		Relieved by 4th East Lancs and moved back by Light Railway from	
	19-1-18		THESCAULT to GRAZING CAMP.	
	20-1-18		GRAZING CAMP. — do —	

9th R.W. Fus   VOLUME 31 (contd)   Army Form C. 2118.

WAR DIARY
or
INTELLIGENCE SUMMARY.

(Erase heading not required.)

Place	Date	Hour	Summary of Events and Information	Remarks and references to Appendices
Field	21-1-18		GRAZING CAMP.	
	22-1-18		– do –	
	23-1-18		– do –	
	24-1-18		Move up from GRAZING CAMP by bus, to TRESCAULT and relieve 4th South Lancs in Right Sub Sector, Right Sector.	
	25-1-18		– do –	
	26-1-18		– do –	
	27-1-18		– do –	
	28-1-18		Move back by light Railway from TRESCAULT, to GRAZING CAMP after being relieved by 4th East Lancs. Regt.	
	29-1-18		GRAZING CAMP	
	30-1-18		– do –	
	31-1-18		– do –	

[signature]
Lieut-Colonel
Commanding 9th Royal Welch Fus.

WAR DIARY
INTELLIGENCE SUMMARY.

9th Royal Welch Fusiliers

Volume 32
Page 1

Place	Date	Hour	Summary of Events and Information	Remarks and references to Appendices
	Feb 1st 1918		Moved from GRAZING CAMP (near YTRES) and relieved 6th Wiltshire Regt. at Front Line COULLIET SECTOR. Right Subsector Right Group	
	2nd-4th		In Front Line	
	5th		Relieved by 9th Cheshire Regt and proceeded to EASTWOOD CAMP in HAVRINCOURT WOOD	
	6th		Moved to WESTWOOD CAMP in HAVRINCOURT WOOD	
	7th		In WESTWOOD CAMP	
	8th		Relieved 7th N Lancashire Regt in Front Line COULLIET SECTOR. Left Subsector Right Group	
	9th-11th		In Front Line. 2 Other Ranks wounded	
	12th		Relieved by 9th Cheshire Regt and proceeded to WESTWOOD CAMP	
	13th		In Huts in WESTWOOD CAMP	
	14th		Marched to VALLULART CAMP near YTRES	
	15th		Marched to CAMP "B" near ROCQUIGNY	
	16th-22nd		In Camp "B" near ROCQUIGNY Training	
	23rd		Moved to MERRIER CAMP near HAPLINCOURT	
	24th-28th		In Huts in HERRICK CAMP Training	

AW.J. Mure
Commanding 9th R.W.F.

Vol 33

19th Division.

58th Infantry Brigade

WAR DIARY

9th BATTALION ROYAL WELCH FUSILIERS MARCH 1918

Report on Operations attached.

Army Form C. 2118.

WAR DIARY
or
INTELLIGENCE SUMMARY.

(Erase heading not required.)

1st Royal Irish Fusiliers Volume 33
Page 1

17
5/19

Instructions regarding War Diaries and Intelligence Summaries are contained in F. S. Regs., Part II. and the Staff Manual respectively. Title pages will be prepared in manuscript.

Place	Date	Hour	Summary of Events and Information	Remarks and references to Appendices
	March 1st to 29th		The Battalion was in HERRICK CAMP, between HAPLINCOURT and BERTINCOURT in training for the German offensive.	
			See attached narrative	
	30th		Entrained at DOULLENS and detrained	
	31st		then marched by lorries to WAKEFIELD HUTS between LOCRE and DRANOUTRE	

W M Kirkpatrick
Lieut Col
Commanding 9th R.I.F.

D. D. & L., London, E.C.
(A701) Wt. W4771/M2031 750,000 5/17 Sch. 52 Forms/C2118/14

9th (S) Bn Royal Welch Fusiliers.

Narrative of Events from 20th March 1918 to 29th March 1918.

20th March The Battalion was in HERRICK CAMP between HAPLINCOURT and BERTINCOURT. The enemy barrage opened about 5-0 a.m. on the Front Line. At 7-0 a.m. the Transport Lines just west of BERTINCOURT were heavily shelled and several men and mules hit. Several direct hits were registered on the Quartermaster's Stores resulting in a loss of most of the Stores.

The Battalion "stood to" at 5-0 a.m. and awaited orders until about 11-30 a.m. when a move was made to assembly positions in GAIKA COPSE, West of VELU WOOD.

The neighbourhood of this position was somewhat heavily shelled during the morning and early afternoon.

At 4-30 p.m. orders were received to move up and dig a new line on the BEAUMETZ - HERMIES Ridge.

The 9th. Welsh Regt: dug on the Right and the 9th. R.W.F. on the Left and the 6th. Wiltshire Regt: in Support. This line was partially dug by 9-30 p.m. when orders were received to rest the men as much as possible as another move was impending.

At 10-30 p.m. orders were received to move back behind the crest on which trenches had been dug and await further orders for a move.

22nd March. At 12-30 a.m. on the 22nd: orders were received to move to the Cross Roads at I.28.b.6.3. (Map Sheet 57c N.W.).

This move was completed by 4-0 a.m. and the Battalion was accomodated in a hut Camp at this point.

At 9-30 a.m. orders were received to move forward and dig a new line covering the two ridges in I.10 and I.11. about 500 yards South West of the village of MORCHIES. The 6th. Wiltshire Regt: digging a line down the road running due South from MORCHIES to the BEETROOT FACTORY in I.17.d.

This line was dug in without trouble by 1-0 p.m. and Battalion H.Q. established in the same road at I.17.a.5.7. Three Companies were in the front line and one in Support. The Wilts: H.Q. were established in the same place.

A Battalion of Cheshires in the 35th. Division were dug in 200 yards behind the line taken up by this Battalion and their Battalion H.Q. were in position at the same point as ours. Touch was maintained on the Right with the 6th. Wiltshire Regt: but no connection could be secured with any troops on the Left flank.

Two Companies of the 9th. Welsh Regt: were at, about 2-30 p.m., thrown in on the Left flank to endeavour to get into touch with any troops who might be in this neighbourhood.

At about 3-30 p.m. the enemy could be seen massing in large numbers on the high ground between VAULX and MORCHIES.

It appeared at this time that some of our troops were in positions North and West of MORCHIES and the 1st. Leicesters subsequently withdrew through our lines. The enemy developed a heavy attack about 3-30 p.m. along the whole of the front occupied by this Battalion which was beaten off at all points with much loss to him.

Cavalry could be seen on the high ground before mentioned in support of this attack.

A counter attack with a large number of tanks was started by us at about 5-0 p.m. which was supported by two Coys: of the 9th. Welsh Regt:. These Coys: failed to materialise but one Coy: of the Cheshire Regt: (35th. Division) ultimately supported the tanks.

The enemy was driven back over the line of the MORCHIES VAULX Road by this counter-attack and could be seen fleeing up the high ground North of this Road.

Many tanks however were knocked out and at dusk the enemy again crossed the line of this Road.

A Battalion of Royal West Kents and a Battalion of the

(Sheet 3).

22nd. March.
(contd:)

Queens West Surrey Regt of the 41st. Division came up after dark and the line was reorganised as follows :-

The R.W.Kents relieved the two Companies of the 9th. Welsh Regt and the left Coy: of the 9th. R.W.Fus: with four Companies, their line running approximately from I.9. Central to I.10.Central.

Three Coys: of the 9th. R.W.Fus: from I.10.Central to I.11.b.6.3. (one of these Coys: having relieved the left Coy: of the 6th. Wiltshire Regt:).

The 4th. Coy: of the 9th. R.W.Fus: in Support in I.10.d.

The 6th. Wiltshire Regt: line ran from I.11.b.6.3. to the BEETROOT FACTORY in I.17.d.

The Queens relieved the Cheshire Battalion previously mentioned and the Cheshire Battalion dug a new line from the BEETROOT FACTORY in I.17.d. to Battalion H.Q. at I.17.a.5.7.

Another Brigade of the 41st. Division were to continue the Left flank of the R.W.Kents but this Brigade appears to have lost its way in the dark, at any rate the Left of the R.W.Kents was reported during the night to be in the air.

During the night of the 2½/23rd March 6 prisoners and one Machine Gun were captured by the 9th. R.W.F. by patrols.

23rd. March.

Consolidation was continued during the night 22/23rd and the early morning of the 23rd.

At 7-0 a.m. on the 23rd: the enemy opened a heavy bombardment on the 6th. Wilts: front and the troops in front of them were seen coming back although no attack actually developed on the 6th. Wiltshire Regt.

During the whole of the morning of the 23rd. the enemy could be seen massing on the VAULX MORCHIES high ground and moving in a S.W. direction. The whole area was very heavily shelled, particularly Battalion H.Q., and no connection was possible either with Companies or Brigade except by runner or pigeon after about noon.

At about noon reports were received that the right flank of the 6th. Wiltshire Regt: was in the air.

This news with various other information and a request for Artillery support was sent off by pigeon.

Orders were received about noon by runner from Brigade that the line would be withdrawn after dark to the Green Line West of BEUGNY.

A conference of the 5 Commanding Officers was arranged and it was decided to endeavour to support the Right flank by throwing out two Companies of the Cheshire Battalion to make a line of Posts from the BEETROOT FACTORY in a S.W direction.

This was done without opposition in the first place but it subsequently appeared that the enemy were working round the flank of these posts. At 3-15 p.m. orders were received from the 58th. Brigade to withdraw in small groups to a line round East and N.E. of BEUGNY.

The 41st. Division had received no orders to withdraw and it was obvious that we could not withdraw without involving them. The 5 Commanding Officers again conferred and orders were sent to all Companies to withdraw at once.

The shelling by this time had become most intense on Battalion H.Q. and it subsequently transpired that no runner got through to Coys: with this message.

Various attempts were made with Battalion H.Q. Staff to form a defensive flank but all these attempts were completely wiped out by the enemy barrage.

The remaining two Coys: of the Cheshire Battalion were also practically wiped out by the same barrage.

The Battalion H.Q. of the 6th. Wiltshire Regt:, 9th. R.W.Fus: and the Cheshire Battalion came away at 5-0 p.m. after it became obvious that Companies were endeavouring to withdraw, but very few managed to get through the barrage and undoubtly many Officers, N.C.O's and men were captured in the Battalion H.Q. Dug-out.

By 5-0 p.m. the enemy had worked up the BAPAUME - COEMER

(Sheet 3.)

23rd. March. CAMBRAI Road practically to BEUGNY and it appeared from his Machine Gun fire that he was established on the high ground in I.10.a.

Accurate information as to times, etc: cannot be given as escape seemed so impossible that all papers, etc: were burned before leaving Battalion H.Q. at 5-0 p.m.

The Green Line was reached at about 6-30 p.m. and all available troops were reorganised

The 9th. R.W.Fus: were then about 80 strong with 9 Officers.

A line was consolidated behind the Green Line in I.29.a by the Battalion. No further attacks took place that night.

24th. March. Next morning, 24th., an attack was delivered on the 9th. Cheshire and 9th. Welsh Regts: who were holding the Green Line in I.30.d. This attack was driven off.

At 11.0 a.m. orders were received that if a withdrawal was forced by the enemy this would take place to the Red Line East of BAPAUME and troops would withdraw fighting.

At about 2-30 p.m. the troops on the Right of this Division gave way and it was decided to withdraw the Welsh Regt: covered by the 9th. R.W.Fus and South Wales Borderers who had come up in Support. The enemy pressed forward so quickly that it was considered necessary to counter attack on to the high ground N.E. of FREMICOURT. This was carried out and the retirement carried out in an orderly manner to the Red Line,which was reached at 6-30 p.m.

The troops were again organised on the Red Line and the position on this line was as follows :-

The remainder of the 58th. Brigade were in the Brickyard in H.28.c., one Battalion of the 56th. Brigade (9th. Cheshires) was on the Right and subsequently one Battalion of the Worcesters were on the Left, extending from the BAPAUME - CAMBRAI Road to the Road and Railway junction in H.28.a.

At about 10-0 p.m. the 9th. Cheshire Regt: reported that they had had orders to withdraw and at the same time orders were received by the 57th. Brigade Units on the Left to withdraw. It was therefore decided to withdraw all Units to the West of BAPAUME in H.31.d. This withdrawal was carried out without opposition and a fresh position was taken up on the Road running through H.31.a. and c. to the BAPAUME - ALBERT Road at which point a junction was effected with the 56th. Brigade. The Line was held with the 6th. Wiltshire Regt: on the Left, the 9th. R.W.Fus: in the Centre and the 9th. Welsh on the Right. Position was taken up at about 11-30 p.m.

A draft of 60 men from the Depot met the Battalion on this Road bringing the strength of 80 rifles. (approximately).

25th. March. At 7-0 a.m. on the 25th.it became apparent that the enemy were approaching from the South East and heavy Machine Gun fire and sniping started from this direction.

At 9-0 a.m. the Shropshire Light Infantry withdrew 500 yards to a trench on the Right leaving the Right flank of the Welsh in the air. This flank was withdrawn to conform.

At 9-50 a.m. it would seem that the troops on the Left were being pushed back on GREVILLERS.

At this time the 58th. Brigade were holding the high ground in G.36.d. with the 56th. Brigade running in a S.W. direction from this point and the 57th. Brigade running in a N.E. direction to the East of GREVILLERS.

By 10-30 a.m. the 57th. Brigade had come back on GREVILLERS and as a dangerous salient was then formed the 58th. Brigade withdrew to a line running along the edge of LOUPART WOOD through a previously organised line held by the 9th. Cheshires and some troops of the 58th. Brigade who had been sent back to cover the retirement on a line running roughly along the Sunken Road in G.35.b. and d.

The line to the East of LOUPART WOOD was not given up until 1-3 0 p.m. when the enemy had attacked several times and been beaten off, and only then because both the Right and Left flanks were in the air.

The Brigade then retired through the 51st. Division and took up a position in G.36.c. on a line running N.E. from the Quarry in that square. This line was reached by 4-0 p.m.

(Sheet 4.)

25th. March. (contd).	The Brigade at this juncture was 30 strong with 4 Officers. The 9th. R.W.Fus. was 8 strong with one Officer.
	At 5-0 p.m. the 51st. Division were again pushed out and our troops retired on PUISIEUX where they were again reorganised and placed in a position of defence on the Southern outskirts of this village.
	Neither on the Right or Left were they at this point in touch with anyone. This position was occupied by 7-0 p.m.
	At 10-30 p.m. orders were received to withdraw to HEBUTERNE
26th. March.	This withdrawal was complete by 2-0 a.m. 26th. inst and the 58th. Brigade was billeted in the village with outposts thrown out on the Eastern and Southern outskirts.
	The 58th. Brigade was at this juncture organised into a composite Battalion. The 9th. R.W.F. at this time consisted of about 90 men who had been collected at various times and were reorganised under 3 Officers into 3 platoons.
	At 10-0 a.m. on the 26th. reports were received that the enemy were on the Southern outskirts of the village and orders were received by the composite Battalion to withdraw to the N.W. outskirts of the village and there take up a defensive position. The 57th. Brigade were in touch on the Left and the 56th. Brigade were in Reserve. There was no contact with any troops on the Right.
	At 11-0 a.m. patrols were pushed through the village. These patrols met with resistance on the Southern edge of the village. Fluctuating fighting took place in the village which was untimately retaken by us at 5-0 p.m., and a Machine Gun captured.
	At 10-0 p.m. an Anzac Division relieved the 58th. Brigade who withdrew to billets in BAYENCOURT, placing outposts round the village.
27th. March. 28th. March.	The 27th. was spent in the outpost positions round BAYENCOURT and on the 28th. the Division was relieved and marched to FAMECHON where it remained until early morning of the 30th. on which day it marched to DOULLENS and CANDAS and entrained for the Second Army area.

The casualties of the 9th. R.W.Fus: during the period were :-

OFFICERS.	Killed.	3.
	Wounded.	5
Wounded & Missing.		3.
	Missing.	3.
	Total.	14

OTHER RANKS.

(Killed, Wounded and Missing) 446.
The greater part of whom were missing.

Lieut-Colonel,
Commanding 9th. (S) Bn. Royal Welch Fusiliers

1-4-18.

58th Brigade.
19th Division.

1/9th BATTALION

ROYAL WELCH FUSILIERS

APRIL 1918.

WAR DIARY
or
INTELLIGENCE SUMMARY.

Army Form C. 2118.

9th Royal Welsh Fusiliers Volume 34
Page 1

Vol 34

Place	Date 1918	Hour	Summary of Events and Information	Remarks and references to Appendices
	Apl 1st 2nd		Billeted in Wakefield Huts near LOCRE	
			Moved to Stankhill Huts, NEUVE EGLISE on Stankhill Huts	
	4/4/18		The Battalion relieved the 2nd Bn. located in the Centre Subsector, NYSCHAETE Sector	
	5th		In Centre Sub sector	
	6th 7th 8th 9th		See attached narrative	
			Battalion remained in same place and reorganised itself with a view of re-equipping	
	21st		Battalion moved to PENTON Camp, PROVEN area	
	22nd 23rd 24th 25th 26th 27th		In Penton Camp	
	28th		At 6-o am Battalion moved to ne.... ... near BUSSEBOOM in same position near BUSSEBOOM	
			At 9-0 pm Battalion proceeded to dig and occupy position at LA CLYTTE – VLAMERTINGHE Line from H 33 a 9 6, L I 2 a 6 y (sheet 28)	
	29th		In same line	
	30th		Battalion relieved the 1st Bn. ... ... in sup... position H 36 a 8 6, L I 25 a 0.15 and an outpost line at INGOBRIDGE	

H Lloyd Williams

9th. (S) Bn. Royal Welch Fusiliers.

Narrative of events from 10-4-18 to 19-4-18.

10th. The Battalion was in the line in front of GREENWOOD and OOSTAVERNE. Two Companies ("A" & "D") holding a series of Posts in the front line and a series of Posts in the Support line, and two Companies ("B" & "C") holding a series of Posts which formed the Reserve line.

Battalion Headquarters was at ONRAET FARM.

The enemy barrage was put down at 5-30 a.m. although no attack appears to have been made until 9-0 or 10-0 a.m. At 12-0 noon information was received that the front line posts had been overwhelmed. The barrage was exceedingly heavy and accurate especially on the Left in RAVINE WOOD and all the posts in this wood were ultimately blown in with very heavy casualties, leaving a gap through with the enemy commenced to come.

This necessated the withdrawal of the Posts in ROSE WOOD which took place about 3-0 p.m. at the same time touch was lost on the Right with the 6th. Wiltshire Regt:, and the Right Company also withdrew to the Reserve Line.

By 4-0 p.m. all Companies were occupying the Reserve Line.

This was maintained intact until about 7-0 p.m. when the Right Companies found the enemy behind them in OOSTAVERNE WOOD, presumably owing to the fact that the 6th. Wilts: on the Right had been unable to maintain their Reserve Line.

The Right Company ("D") was surrounded and fought till the last, only about 20 getting away.

At 9-0 p.m. a patrol from the left reserve Company ("B") reported that "C" Coy: in the Reserve line, near GOUDEZEUNE FARM (O.15.b.) were not in position.

Upon instructions from the G.O.C. "B" Coy: were then handed over to the 9th. Division (who were on the left) and were ordered to dig in on the line of the DAMMSTRASSE.

Battalion Headquarters moving at the same time to PARMA DUMP (N.12.d.) This move was completed by 11-0 p.m., but by 11-30 p.m. Battalion H.Q. was shelled out of the neighbourhood of PARMA DUMP and took up position in N.10.b., parties being sent out to collect remnants of the Battalion.

11th. At 6-0 a.m. "C" Coy: who, it then appeared, had not left the reserve line near GOUDEZEUNE FARM until 3-30 a.m. and had then found that there was no one on either of their flanks withdrew.

What remained of the Battalion (less "B" Coy:) were on the 11th. collected in TOURNAI CAMP (N.10.b.8.4.)

12th. "B" Coy: was relieved by the 9th. Division on the morning of the 12th. and came down to TOURNAI CAMP. The Battalion moved on the evening of this day to DE ZON CAMP (near SCHERPENBURG).

13th. At 10-0 a.m. on the 13th. orders were received to move at once to assembly position in N.13.b. and N.14.a. (Map 28 S.W.)

This move was completed by 12-0 noon. At 2-30 p.m. orders were received to reconnoitre the line (held by the South African Brigade) from MAEDELSTEDE FARM (N.24.c.8.4.) to SPANBROEKMOLEN (N.30.c.2.8.). This was done and the line taken over from part of the 4th. Bn. S.A.I. and from the 2nd. Bn. S.A.I.

Three Companies being in the front line and one in Support.

Battalion H.Q. being at N.29.c.8.4. (near REGENTS DUG-OUTS).

14th & 15th. This line was held until the night of the 15/16th. (Battalion H.Q. having moved on the 15th. to trenches in N.17.d.8.1.) when the line was taken over by one Company of the 7th. West Yorks.

This meant that one Coy: (130 strong) relieved a whole Battalion (400 strong) in a most critical point in the line.

The Battalion withdrew to trenches in N.23.c. and d.

16th. On this day the 7th. West Yorks were attacked and came off the Ridge. When this occured "A" - "B" & "C" Coys: were sent up to form a line running from LAGACHE FARM (N.23.d.2.2.) to N.29.b.2.2. and "D" Coy: was sent in Support to old trenches in N.29.a and

(Sheet 2).

16th. Battalion H.Q. moved to FARRAIL FARM (N.28.c.7.5.), in conjunction with the H.Q. of the 5th. Welsh and 6th. Wilts:-

17th. & 18th. This line was held until taken over by the French on the night of the 18/19th.

19th. On the 19th. the Battalion moved by route march to a field on the main road between RENINGHELST and ABEELE.

[signature]
Major
for O.C. 9 R.W.F.

Volume 35"
S/19
Page 1. Army Form C. 2118.

9th Bn Royal Welch Fusiliers

WAR DIARY or INTELLIGENCE SUMMARY.

(Erase heading not required.)

Vol 35

Place	Date 1918	Hour	Summary of Events and Information	Remarks and references to Appendices
TRENCHES	MAY 1		Battalion in line (G.H.Q.1.Line) from H.36.b.5.6. to I.25.a.05.15, and in outpost line on IRONBRIDGE (SHEET 28SW)	
	2nd		Post gradually pushed forward S. of Canal and in p.m. until by night J.g. continuous line I.19.b.25 had been formed from H.36.b.6.6. - IRONBRIDGE Opposite our front line being two advanced about 1000x, and in close touch with the enemy	
			Enemy attack at 4-15 am. Enemy attack at RIDGEWOOD & som Bunaries beaten. attack fell on KEMMEL at 4-15 am. G.H.Q.I. Line. Left Coy a IRONBRIDGE no right companies G.H.Q.1. Line. relieved by a Coy of WELCH Reg.t En route for Coy respec. G.H.Q.I. Line around SWAN CHATEAU.	
			Batn having but hot line a G.H.Q.1. Line from Canal to H.36.b.6.6.	
	9th	10"	Batn relieved by 1/4 K.S.L.I., 37th Bde and proceeds a relief by train to Bivouacs W. of ST JAN-TER-BIEZEN.	
	10th	11"	Day spent in part cleaning up	
	13th	1"	Bn proceeds by march route to bivouacs near HERZEELE	

Army Form C. 2118.

Page 11

WAR DIARY
9th Bn Royal Welch Fusiliers
INTELLIGENCE SUMMARY.
(Erase heading not required.)

Place	Date	Hour	Summary of Events and Information	Remarks and references to Appendices
HERZEELE	May 13th			
	14th		Training and Reorganization	
	15th			
	16th			
	17th		Proceeded by march route to REXPOEDE STATION and left by train at 11.32 pm	
	18th		In train	
	19th		Detrained at COULOS and marched to CHEPY	
	20th		Parades and training	
	21st		" " "	
	22nd		" " "	
	23rd		GENERAL GOURAUD, commanding 4th French army, inspected the Battalion at work.	
	24th		Training	
	25th		"	
	26th		"	
	27th		"	
	28th		Received orders to move away at an hour's notice. Training draught moved off at 9 p.m.	
	29th		Battalion moved in the morning to CHAMPLAT.	
	30th			
	31st		as per attached Summary	

F.J. Webb Major
Commanding 9th Bn Royal Welch Fus.

9th (S) Bn Royal Welch Fusiliers.

NARRATIVE OF OPERATIONS.

Tuesday
28th May.   The Battalion embussed at CHEPY, debussed at CHAUMUZY at 3-30 a.m. 29th May.

29th May.   Marched to billets in BLIGNY.
3-0 a.m. Battalion moved up to fill up a gap and establish an outpost line which should take in FAVEROLLES and COEMY. The Battalion was responsible for both these flanks. Touch on the right was obtained with the 154th French Division and fragments of the 25th British Division, on the left with the 57th Infantry Brigade (Glosters). During the day, Officers patrols were sent forward with a view to advancing the line and making good the SAVIGNY - PRIN line, but the enemy was found to be strongly established in these places. The line forward of FAVEROLLES and COEMY however was maintained until 9-0 a.m.

30th May.   In the meantime the enemy endeavoured to push forward patrols, most of which were caught by our men and some prisoners taken. By 3-30 a.m. on the 30th the troops on the right had been compelled to withdraw, every endeavour was made to re-establish connection but by 9-0 a.m. it became necessary to withdraw on to the COEMY - TRAMERY Line in accordance with orders previously issued.

By this time the enemy having attacked from the direction of LHERY the troops on our left were driven in. The Battalion was now, with the 9th WELSH Regt:, very much in the air in the valley of the River ARDRE. By 11-0 a.m. orders were received for a withdrawal to the POILLY - BOIS D'AULNEY Line but by this time the Battalion was engaged in a hand to hand conflict with the enemy who had come round on both flanks.

The portion that was extracted took up a position on the POILLY - BOIS D'AULNEY Line and, later, amalgamated with the 9th Cheshire Regt who were holding a line immediately North West of SARCY.

They were later withdrawn into a reserve position along the road running East from CHAMBRECY and there formed into a composite Company.

1st June.   On Saturday, 1st June when the troops on the left had made a tactical withdrawal this Composite Company was pushed forward to secure the MONTAINE de BLIGNY, and occupied a line of outposts on the Western slopes of this hill.

6th June   This was the position until the morning of the 6th June when the enemy under cover of a barrage endeavoured to drive in our position but without success.

The Battalion was relieved that night by troops of a Composite Brigade of the 50th Division and came into Reserve in the BOIS de COURTON.

Major,
Commanding 9th (S) Bn Royal Welch Fusiliers

WAR DIARY
or INTELLIGENCE SUMMARY.

Army Form C. 2118.

9th (S) Bn Royal Welch Fus.

Volume 36
Page 1

Place	Date	Hour	Summary of Events and Information	Remarks and references to Appendices
CHAMBRECY	June 1st		On Saturday 1st June when the troops on the left had made a backward movement, the Composite Company was pushed forward to secure the montaine de BLIGNY and occupied a line of outposts on the western slopes of the hill. This was the position until the morning of the 6th June when the enemy made some strong manoeuvres to drive in our position but without avail. The Battalion was relieved fortnightly by troops of composite Brigade of the 50th Division and came into Reserve in the Bois de COURTON.	
	7th & 8th		Battalion remained in Bois de COURTON. Divisional Reserve.	
	12th		Battalion moved to Brigade Reserve at CHAMUZY.	
	13th & 14th		In Brigade Reserve at CHAMUZY.	
	15th		Relieved by 2nd Italian Division and moved to bivouac at HAUTVILLERS WOOD.	
	19th		In HAUTVILLERS WOOD.	
	20th		Battalion moved to CRAMANT.	
	21st		Moved by motor buses to BROUSSY-le-GRAND.	
	22nd		In training. Draft of 327 Other Ranks arrived.	
	23rd to 29th		Battalion in training at BROUSSY-le-GRAND. 2 Officers (Lieuts. TO GRIFFITH and O.C. MARSTON) joined Battalion on 28th.	
	30th		Battalion moved by march route to HUSSIMONT Logging Area.	

H Lloyd Williams
Lieut Colonel
Commanding 9th (S) Bn R.W.F.

WAR DIARY
or
INTELLIGENCE SUMMARY

Army Form C. 2118.

9th (S) Bn R.W.F. or Welch Rgt Volume 37/19 Page 1.

Place	Date	Hour	Summary of Events and Information	Remarks and references to Appendices
HAUSSIMONT	July 1	8.30 pm	Battalion entrained at HAUSSIMONT	
HAPPE	3	4.30 am	Battalion detrained at ANVIN, and proceeded by route march to WAVRANS, arriving at 9.30 am	
"	4	10 am	Battalion inspected by Lieut Col W.B. GARNONS WILLIAMS, arriving at HAPPE 11.0 pm	
"	5		Company Training Day. R.S.M. received	
"	6		Company Training. Following awards were announced:— Military Cross — 2/Lieut D.J. JONES.	
			Sergt T. JONES D.C.M.	
			114837 Sergt G. [illegible]	
			[illegible]	
	7		[illegible]	
			[illegible]	
			Company Training. [illegible]	
	8		[illegible]	
			Whole battalion went to 300 [illegible]	
	9		[illegible]	
	10		[illegible]	
	11		[illegible]	
	12		[illegible]	
	13		[illegible]	
	14		[illegible]	
	15		Company Training Classes as above	

Army Form C. 2118.

WAR DIARY or INTELLIGENCE SUMMARY.

9th (S) Bn Royal Welch Fusiliers.   Volume 37.   Page 2.

(Erase heading not required.)

Place	Date	Hour	Summary of Events and Information	Remarks and references to Appendices
LIBBY LEAFRE (SHEET 36 ...)	July 16.		Company Training, two Companies firing on range.	
	17		Battalion paraded for Reorganization parade, following officers warned:- 2Lt Armitage, 2Lt W.D. Richds 2Lt N.S. Cox. 2Lt H.G. Jager.	
	18		Battalion Firing on Ranges. W.Q. LOZINGHEM. Brevet Sgt E.E. Jones, DCM appointed a/CSM "C" Coy.	
	19		Company Training. Sgt G. ELLIS DCM. appointed Provost Sgt.	
	20		Range and Route march.	
	21		Divine Service.	
	22		Company Training.	
	23		Company Training.	
	24		Company Training. Lt Col Salt assumed command of the Battalion Capt R. Page (from 4th Worcestershire Regt) acted as Adjutant.	
	25		Battalion Training remaining. Company W.Q. LOZINGHEM.	
	26		Company Training.	
	27		Company Training.	
	28		Divine Service.	
	29		Company Training.	
	30		Company Training.	
	31		Battalion inspected at No.33 Range by the Bde/ Commander Major General 25 Division R. Gen. During the month representatives parties attended the following Schools: "Branch attack" "Reconnaissance" "Hunter Rifle" in BETHUNE - BEURY	

DWJ Salt Lieut Col.
Commanding 9th(S) Bn Royal Welch Fusiliers.

WAR DIARY
or INTELLIGENCE SUMMARY.

Army Form C. 2118.

Volume 36
9th (S)B" Royal Sufflk of Suffers. Page 2

Place	Date	Hour	Summary of Events and Information	Remarks and references to Appendices
Lampus-Abb	August 1		Company Training. Lieut Col M. Morgan N.C. in my reported his arrival & taken over the Strength & Estoal. irwin and to B Coy	
"	2		Company Training	
"	3		Company Training. 3rd reinf there arrived = Officer in Surfolls Haus J Somaster Matrix 115 Prints	
"	4		4 mint Service Training other arrival & other reinforcement to Court	
"	5		Company Training. Strength parade. passed to Coln in the from the Bayan.	
"	6	12N	Battalion moved by road East. V.3 c. Italy and 7.47 at H.Q. Royal Suffolk Battalion in Bivouac.	Sheet 28 28 B
Ciscomes	7		In the morning Company Training. At 10 pm warnings orders were received for to Coy to hold Thatcher in redinate to move to be Empress Position at GORDEN and Support Lines respectively. Coy by six Italian to the Position respectively.	Mop A. (Sheet 20A)
"	8		Company Training. Two casualties from shell-fire at night.	
"	9		Company Training	
"	10		Visit of MM Dickin LXIII Corps Comn. She battalion worked by Pt Railway to time I the road between C3.C. 7.4 and X Road Burbure, & clear approaches the Report issued by Kent and Support to relieve of WEICHRECHT by HQ Suffolks that	

Army Form C. 2118.

WAR DIARY
or
INTELLIGENCE SUMMARY.

9th (S) Bn Royal Welsh Fusiliers

(Erase heading not required.)

Instructions regarding War Diaries and Intelligence Summaries are contained in F. S. Regs., Part II. and the Staff Manual respectively. Title pages will be prepared in manuscript.

Place	Date	Hour	Summary of Events and Information	Remarks and references to Appendices
HINGES	12th		Support in HINGES	
"	13th			
"	14th		Relieved 9th IMBICH in front line. Line B entrance @ 33.d. & N.6.a. & B BRIDGES on	
TRENCHES	15th		EDINBURGH LINES.	
"	16th		front line	
"	17th			
"	18th		Bn relieved by 2nd WILTS REGT and moved into Brigade Reserve in CHOCQUES. Being SHROPSHIRE LINE	
CHOCQUES	19th		Inspection parade and baths.	
"	20th		Company Training and ranges.	
"	21st		Company training	
"	22nd		Company training	
"	23rd	(2.30)	Bn relieved 4th R. WARWICKSHIRE REGT in B. BATTLE ZONE. were attacked and relieved	WEST SUSSEX
TRENCHES	24th		along Canal Bank, London BRIDGE and were support along front B Canal & other Half way to Hd Qrs.	
"	25th		Bn in support	
"	26th			
"	27th	Night	Bn relieved 4th NORFOLK in Trenches, Coys Coys on front, & 2 in Support Coy "A" at G.27.d.25.75.	
"	28th		Newly enemy retiring. Line advanced of ZELOBES	
"	29th		Line pushed further forward 6. R.I.C. @ B19 7th R.W.F. 70.30 Capt N.L. HARRIS M.C. & 2nd Lt. S. ROBERTS and 2 men killed	
"	30th		Line pushed further forward 22.230 ins B Loc A Bn 9th R.W. REGT, 8th R. LANC,	
"	31st		Bn relieved by 2nd 7th WILTSHIRE REGT, and moved to HINGES	

H.J. Williams Major
Comdg 9th R.W.F.

Army Form C. 2118.

WAR DIARY
9th (S) Bn Royal Welch Fus
INTELLIGENCE SUMMARY.
(Erase heading not required.)

Volume 39
Page 1

Place	Date	Hour	Summary of Events and Information	Remarks and references to Appendices
Battalion in Brigade Reserve Headquarters in HALFWAY HOUSE	1918 Sept 1st		Took up reserve position near River LAWE	
do	2nd 3rd		Battalion under orders of 57th Brigade. Relieved on night of 5th and came into Divisional Reserve at ESSARS.	
	4th & 5th		Resting at ESSARS.	
	6th & 9th 10th		Relieved 10th Bn Royal Warwickshire Regt in Right Subsector of Left Brigade Sector (Front Line)	
	13th		CURZON POST bombarded fiercely with Gas Shells. "C" Company suffered somewhat	
	18th		Relieved in Front Line by 9th Bn Welch Regt and came into Line of Retention behind RICHEBOURG-ST VAAST	
	22nd		Relieved by 9th Bn Cheshire Regt and returned to Divisional Reserve in ESSARS	
	28th		Relieved 8th Bn Gloucestershire Regt in Right Subsector of Right Brigade Sector	
	30th		'A' & 'D' Companies under a light barrage took part in an operation and successfully advanced 600, taking 10 prisoners and 1 machine gun. Our casualties were 3 Officers wounded (1 of whom died of wounds) 11 Other Ranks Killed and 38 Other Ranks Wounded	

Lloyd Williams
Major
Commanding 9 Royal Welch Fus.

Army Form C. 2118.

9th Bn Royal Welch Fusiliers   Volume 40
                                 Page 1

WAR DIARY
INTELLIGENCE SUMMARY.
(Erase heading not required.)

Vol 4

Place	Date	Hour	Summary of Events and Information	Remarks and references to Appendices
In the line	1-10-18		In the line RICHEBOURG ST VAAST Sector.	
"	2-10-18		Relieved by a Batt. of the 4th Division and proceeded to LE-TOURET Station on the Rue-de-BOIS where the Battalion entrained to BURBURE arriving there about 08.30 hours on the 3rd	
"	3-10-18		The Battalion moved to SACHIN by march Route	
"	4-10-18		Entrained at PERNES at 20.46 and detrained at SAULTY at 06.00 hours on the 5th inst.	
"	5-10-18		Marched from the station to SOMBRIN.	
"	6-10-18		Battalion training at SOMBRIN.	
"	7-10-18		Battalion entrained at BARLY at 15.45 hours and arrived at GOMMECOURT at 23.00 hours	
"	8-10-18		In Bivouacs at GOMMECOURT. moved to CANTAING.	
"	9-10-18		In trench near CANTAING.	
"	10-10-18		Moved to CAMBRAI.	
"	11-10-18		at CAMBRAI.	

Army Form C. 2118.

WAR DIARY
or
INTELLIGENCE SUMMARY.
(Erase heading not required.)

Instructions regarding War Diaries and Intelligence Summaries are contained in F. S. Regs., Part II. and the Staff Manual respectively. Title pages will be prepared in manuscript.

Place	Date	Hour	Summary of Events and Information	Remarks and references to Appendices
La Wieue	12.10.18		Moved to CAGNONCLES.	
"	13.10.18		Batt Training at CAGNONCLES	
"	14.10.18		do	
"	15.10.18		do	
"	16.10.18		Moved to RIEUX.	
"	17.10.18		Batt training RIEUX.	
"	18.10.18		The Batt moved into assembly positions near ST AUBERT and MONTRECOURT. Steen in assembly positions.	
"	19.10.18			
"	20.10.18		The Batt attacked at 02.00 hrs. The object of the attack being to capture the High Ground E of the RIVER·SELLE. All objectives were gained. 6 guns were considered and taken.	
"	21.10.18		Still in line.	
"	22.10.18		do	
"	23.10.18		do	
"	23/24		The Batt was relieved by a Battalion of the 61st Division 2/7 R.W.Regt and marched to RIEUX. Total Casualties for the operations 1 officer killed 2 officers Wounded 19 O.R Killed 61 O.R Wounded	

Army Form C. 2118.

WAR DIARY
or
INTELLIGENCE SUMMARY.
(Erase heading not required.)

Instructions regarding War Diaries and Intelligence Summaries are contained in F. S. Regs., Part II. and the Staff Manual respectively. Title pages will be prepared in manuscript.

III

Place	Date	Hour	Summary of Events and Information	Remarks and references to Appendices
On the Ticket	24-10-18 to 31-10-18		at RIEUX training	

Nr J MacAhun
Lieut Colonel, Commdg
9th (S) Batt Royal Welch Fusiliers

Army Form C. 2118.

WAR DIARY

9th (S) Batt Royal Welch Fusiliers
INTELLIGENCE SUMMARY.

Page 1

(Erase heading not required.)

Instructions regarding War Diaries and Intelligence Summaries are contained in F. S. Regs., Part II. and the Staff Manual respectively. Title pages will be prepared in manuscript.

Place	Date	Hour	Summary of Events and Information	Remarks and references to Appendices
In the Field	1-11-18		The Battalion moved by March Route to HAUSSY. arriving about 11.00. and later at 20.00 hours moved on to Billets at SOMMAING.	
"	2-11-18		Battalion preparing for an attack; making up of S.A.A. Grenades etc.	
"	3/4		The Battalion moved into assembly position. Account of operations attached covering period to the 8-11-18 inclusive	1

Army Form C. 2118.

Page 11

WAR DIARY
or
INTELLIGENCE SUMMARY.
(Erase heading not required.)

Place	Date	Hour	Summary of Events and Information	Remarks and references to Appendices
In the Field	9-11-18		The Battalion moved by March Route to the ETH and BRY. area and were accommodated in Billets at ETH.	
	10-11-18		At ETH. Cleaning up and Kit Inspections. The following awards announced in Routine Orders "Military Cross" 7/2 Lt H.S. Pickard 7/2 Lt G.D. Roberts	
		13.30	C.S.M Thomas J.A. D.C.M 32554 Sgt Brey J.A.	
	11-11-18		Still at ETH. Three Coys training one Coy Salvaging. Batt. received news that Hostilities would cease from 11.00 hrs. Coy were at of 8.45 hours.	
	12-11-18		Still at ETH. Three Coys training One Coy Salvaging. Following awards announced in Routine Orders. Bar to Military Medal 36334 Sgt W.H. Pickersgill. Military Medal 24436 Sgt C. Waite L8834 Pte Wikes J.	
	13-11-18		Still at ETH. Training and Salvaging.	

Army Form C. 2118.

WAR DIARY
or
INTELLIGENCE SUMMARY.
(Erase heading not required.)

Page 111

Instructions regarding War Diaries and Intelligence Summaries are contained in F. S. Regs., Part II. and the Staff Manual respectively. Title pages will be prepared in manuscript.

Place	Date	Hour	Summary of Events and Information	Remarks and references to Appendices
In the Field	15/11/18		The Battalion moved by march route to BERMERAIN	
"	16/11/18		The Battalion moved by march route to AVESNES-LES-AUBERT	
"	17/11/18		Cleaning up of Billets and equipment. Church Parade.	
"	18/11/18		Training	
"	19/11/18		Training	
"	20/11/18		Training	
"	21/11/18		Training	
"	22/11/18		Training	
"	23/11/18		The Battalion was inspected by the G.O.C. Church Parade.	
"	24/11/18		The Battalion moved by march route to Billets in CAMBRAI.	
"	25/11/18			

D. D. & L. London, E.C.
(A801) Wt. W1771/M2931 750,000 5/17 Sch. 82 Forms/C2118/24

WAR DIARY
or
INTELLIGENCE SUMMARY.

Army Form C. 2118.

Page 4

Place	Date	Hour	Summary of Events and Information	Remarks and references to Appendices
In the Field	27.11.18		CAMBRAI. Training	
"	28.11.18		Training	
"	29.11.18		The Battalion moved by Bus to the CANDAS area and Billeted at CANAPLES.	
"	30.11.18		Cleaning up and improvement of Billets	

Off Com. Capt Conway
9th (S) Batt Royal Welsh Fus

SHORT ACCOUNT OF OPERATION UNDERTAKEN BY THE
9th (S) Bn Royal Welch Fusiliers
from Nov: 3rd to Novr: 9th 1918.

Sheets
51.N.E. & 51.N.W.
1/20,000.

Night of 3rd/4th Novr: 1918.

The Battalion assembled in L.30.a. being in Support to the Wilts. and Welsh Regiments. The assembly was completed by 20.30 hours, no trouble being experienced in this part of the Operation in spite of complete darkness and much rain.

Battalion Headquarters assembled at L.30.central. Orders were received before the assembly was complete that as the enemy had withdrawn a further move would have to be made forward that night. Accordingly at 23.00 hours (an hour fixed in consultation with the Wilts and Welsh) a move forward to the area L.21.a, c and d was commenced. This movement was completed by approximately 01.00 hours and Battalion H.Q. were by then established in the FARM de WULT (L.20.b.9.9.) This move was difficult owing to the darkness of the night but fortunately very little enemy shelling interfered with it.

4th Novr:. At 06.00 hours the barrage commenced and a move forward was made to the area L.16.a. and c. Battalion Headquarters moved to the Copse at L.16.c.3.5. where telegraphic communication was established direct with Brigade H.Q. at the FARM de WULT. The hostile reply to our barrage was feeble except in certain places, such as the FARM de WULT which was quite heavily shelled for about half hour after Zero.
The principal shelling appeared to be air burst of gas shell which caused a good deal of coughing and some sickness, as the valleys very soon became full of gas, but no casualties. The morning was misty early but quite fine later on.
At about 12.00 hours orders were received to move the Battalion into the area of squares L.12.a. and c.
This move was completed without difficulty by 13.00 hours and Battalion H.Q. established at L.11.d.5.4. where there were evident signs that the enemy had hastily evacuated, leaving half consumed meals behind them.
Touch was obtained with the H.Q. of the 9th Welsh, 2nd Wilts and the 9th Cheshires. Orders were received at about 15.00 hours that the Welsh and Wilts would attack under a barrage starting at 16.30 hours and that the Battalion would occupy the GREEN Line in G.2.d. and G.9.a. and c. at Zero plus 5. This was carried out to time in spite of the fact that there were only two bridges over the PETIT AUNELLE which was a deep stream running between high banks some 10 yards wide.
The Country in this area was wooded and full of steep valleys with small streams through them and would, had the enemy meant to fight seriously, have been most difficult and costly to capture.

5th Novr:. At 11.00 hours verbal orders were received that the Welsh and Wilts had reached the line of the road running through G.5.a. and G.11.a. and were endeavouring to make the line of the road through G.12.a. and b. and that the Battalion was to pass through them on this line and push forward as far as possible without limit.
Three objectives were chosen to be taken successively as follows :-
  1. The line of the road through H.7.a. and c.
  2. The high ground in H.8.a.
  3. The high ground in H.9.a.
The Battalion was in position behind the road running through G.5.c. and G.11.a. by 13.00 hours. Battalion Headquarters being established in MAISON BLANCHE L.6.c.2.2. which had previously been connected by wire to the H.Q. of the 9th Welsh in BRY.

Two sections of field guns were placed at my disposal for this operation and 8 Machine Guns.

(Sheet 2).

5th Novr: (contd)
Only one liaison Officer for the former arrived (he belonged to one section only) and as it appeared that his guns were nearly 3,000 yards away and he had no means of communication to them & as he did not report until 13.00 hours the guns were of no use. The Machine Gun Gunner failed to report at all.

The first objective was taken with only spasmotic opposition from the enemy Machine Gun fire with very few casualties. The Second objective was taken by 15;30 hours but on passing over the crest very heavy opposition was encountered from a larger number of machine Guns skillfully placed and the progress of the attack was arrested.

It was by this time getting quite dark and had been raining uninteruptedly for approximately 12 hours and the going was exceedingly heavy and the troops very tired.
Touch was obtained with troops on both flanks. The West Yorks (11 Division) on the left and the N.Staffs on the right.
The points of touch being approximately H.2.c.0.9 and H.8.a.5.0.

The village of MEAURAIN was found by a patrol to be clear of the enemy but inhabited by a large number of civilians. Battalion H.Q. was accordingly established at H.1.c.5.5. and it was decided that in view of the darkness and strength of the enemy machine gun fire to attempt after dark to take the 3rd objective by means of strong patrols.

The enemies reply to our barrage was quite feeble until 15.30 hours when it became more intense.
Two patrols went out one on the left and one on the right and in each case they reached a point 200 yards short of their objective but failed to quite get on top of the High ground in H.9.a. It was accordingly decided they should be withdrawn and a fresh attack opened under a barrage at 06.00 hours on the 6th inst. with the object of taking the village of BETTRECHIES and forcing the passing of the river HOGNEAU and if possible capturing the High ground in H.5.c.

6th Novr:
This attack was successful in capturing the village of BETTRECHIES and in two cases patrols were actually pushed across the river but these were driven back by the weight of the enemy machine gun fire from the East bank.
By 09.00 hours a line was established running from H.3.b.2.2. where touch was maintained with the 11th Division through H.3.a.4.8, - H.3.d.4.5. - H.3.d.4.4. to H.10.a.2.8. and thence in a S.W. direction along the line of the road running through H.9.b. and H.9.d. to H.9.d.2.6. where touch was obtained with the N.Staffs.

This line was held by two Companies with one Company in close Support at H.9.b.0.2. and one Company in Reserve at H.2.d.8.2., there was in addition one Company of the 2nd Bn Wilts at H.3.c.3.9. and Battalion H.Q. were at H.9.a.8.9.
No artillery materialised for this attack and the barrage was so thin and feeble that it was practically impossible to say where it was, one or two guns shot consistently very short all the way through.

Eight machine guns were allotted to the Battalion which were used as follows:. 3 to cover the left flank from the Sunken Road at H.2.c.8.8. (it was not at this period known that the 11th Division on the left were attacking) Two to follow up the forward infantry and take up position on the High ground in H.9.a. and Three to remain in reserve under the hands of the Battalion Commander.
Subsequently 12 more machine guns turned up and were used to keep the BOIS DANGAME and squares B.27.c. and d under indirect fire throughout the operation.
The enemy replied fairly heavily with his guns and very heavily with his machine guns but on the whole slight opposition was met with on the West side of the HOGNEAU.

(Sheet 3.)

Attempts were made all day to push forward patrols over the stream but without success.

The village of BETTRECHIES which was full of civilian inhabitants was exceedingly heavily shelled from 10.00 to 17.00 hours, as many as between 2 & 3 thousand 5'.9' & 4'.5's. shells landing in the village, obviously from a due North direction between these hours.

In the circumstances the casualties were not heavy.

7th Nov: Orders were received at 15.00 hours (approx) on the 6th that the 57th Brigade would at 06.00 hours on the 7th attack and take the Spur in H.10.c. and then the line of the road through H.10.a and b. The 9th R.W.Fus: were ordered to co-operate with rifle and machine gun fire throughout the operation on the BOIS DANGADE and to push out patrols to take the high ground in H.5.c. and get down to the line of the river beyond this if possible if the enemy defence showed signs of weakening. At 08.00 hours when the barrage lifted it became apparent that the enemy had withdrawn, and patrols and subsequently two Companies were sent forward to occupy the high ground and take the village of BELLIGNIES.

This line was established by approximately 11.00 hours having encountered brisk enemy shelling on the high ground West of BELLIGNIES and Battalion Headquarters were established at H.10.c.7.4.

The line then held ran approximate from H.5.a.8.4. where touch was established with the West Yorks (11 Division) to H.11.b.4.4., while the 57th Brigade on the right were going forward. This line was held with two Companies, two Companies remaining in cellars in BETTRECHIES.

At 15.00 hours orders were received to extend the right to H.12.d.6.7. and these two Companies were thrown into prolong the line to this point.

The troops at this period were sopped to the skin and tired out having come approximately 14 miles since the 3rd Novr: consolidated no less than 3 different lines and had practically no hot food during the whole period.

8th Novr: During the morning of th 8th Novr: owing to the advance of the 57th Brigade it became necessary to extend our flank EASTWARDS and by 11.00 hours the two Westermost Companies were removed and disposed One round the Marble works in I.2.c. and one in HON HERGIES.

From these patrols were sent out which reached and reconnoitred HERGNIES and MIOLOT - FOLLET and found no trace of the enemy.

Subsequently as the 11th Division on the left came up into the line Companies were withdrawn and billeted in HOUDAIN. This movement being complete by 23.00 hours.

The Casualties during the period were as follows.

	O/O Killed	Wdd.	O.R Killed	O.R
24 hours ending 12.00 hours 4th				6
5th				14
6th			3	21
7th	1	(at duty)	5	10
Total	1		8	51

Army Form C. 2118.

WAR DIARY

9th (S) Batt Royal Welch Fusiliers

INTELLIGENCE SUMMARY.

(Erase heading not required.)

Instructions regarding War Diaries and Intelligence Summaries are contained in F. S. Regs. Part II. and the Staff Manual respectively. Title pages will be prepared in manuscript.

Place	Date	Hour	Summary of Events and Information	Remarks and references to Appendices
CANAPLES	1-12-15		Church Parade Inspection	
"	2-12-15		Training: Classes of Junior N.C.O's	
"	3-12-15		do	
"	4-12-15		do	
"	5-12-15		Training, Lewis Gun Classes commenced	
"	6-12-15		"	
"	7-12-15		Training; Batt Baths at FIEFFES	
"	8-12-15		Church Parade; Inspections	
"	9-12-15		Training; Officers Riding School commenced	
"	10-12-15		Training	
"	11-12-15		"	
"	12-12-15		The Battalion moved into Billets at BERTEAUCOURT moved off at 11.25 hours	
BERTEAUCOURT	13-12-15		Cleaning up and arranging billets	
"	14-12-15		Training	
"	15-12-15		Church Parades Inspections	

Army Form C. 2118.

WAR DIARY
or
INTELLIGENCE SUMMARY.
(Erase heading not required.)

Instructions regarding War Diaries and Intelligence Summaries are contained in F. S. Regs., Part II. and the Staff Manual respectively. Title pages will be prepared in manuscript.

Place	Date	Hour	Summary of Events and Information	Remarks and references to Appendices
BERTEAUCOURT	16/12/18		Training.	
"	14/12/18		Training	
"	18/12/18		Training	
"	19/12/18		Training	
"	20/12/18		Commanding Officers Inspection of Coys. full marching order	
"	21/12/18		Training	
"	22/12/18		Church Parades. Inspections	
"	23/12/18		Training	
"	24/12/18		Training. 19644 C.S.M. JONES awarded French Medaille Militaire	

Army Form C. 2118.

WAR DIARY
or
INTELLIGENCE SUMMARY.
(Erase heading not required.)

Instructions regarding War Diaries and Intelligence Summaries are contained in F. S. Regs., Part II. and the Staff Manual respectively. Title pages will be prepared in manuscript.

Place	Date	Hour	Summary of Events and Information	Remarks and references to Appendices
BERTEAUCOURT	15/12/18		Church Parade. X mas festivities.	
	26/12/18		Route March.	
	27/12/18		Training	
	28/12/18		Commanding Officers Inspection of Coy. "in full marching order"	
	29/12/18		Church Parades, Inspections	
	30/12/18		Batt. Ceremonial Parade.	
	31/12/18		Battalion Baths. BERTEAUCOURT. In addition to the training being carried out, & have Education daily has been carried out, also lectures on different subjects. Games have been carried out each afternoon, football, Rugby, Cross Country Runs, etc.	H Explosions Major Connery 9/4 (S) Batt TD at 11th at Week. training.

Army Form C. 2118.

WAR DIARY
9th (S) Batt Royal Welch Fusiliers
INTELLIGENCE SUMMARY. SHEET I.

(Erase heading not required.)

Instructions regarding War Diaries and Intelligence Summaries are contained in F. S. Regs., Part II. and the Staff Manual respectively. Title pages will be prepared in manuscript.

Vol. 4

Place	Date	Hour	Summary of Events and Information	Remarks and references to Appendices
BERTEAUCOURT	1-1-19		Training	
"	2-1-19		" Rugby match in the afternoon. Batt officers v. Battalion.	
"	3-1-19		" Football match in the afternoon Batt. v. 9th Welch Regt.	
"	4-1-19		" Rugby match in the afternoon. Batt officers v. officers 9th Welch Regt.	
"	5-1-19		Church Parade.	
"	6-1-19		Training.	
"	7-1-19		" afternoon Batt Cross Country Run, about four miles	
"	8-1-19		"	
"	9-1-19		Ceremonial Parade: Training	
"	10-1-19		Batt allotted the Baths. BERTEAUCOURT.	
"	11-1-19		Training.	
"	12-1-19		Church Parade.	

Army Form C. 2118.

WAR DIARY
or
INTELLIGENCE SUMMARY.   SHEET II

(Erase heading not required.)

Instructions regarding War Diaries and Intelligence Summaries are contained in F. S. Regs., Part II. and the Staff Manual respectively. Title pages will be prepared in manuscript.

Place	Date	Hour	Summary of Events and Information	Remarks and references to Appendices
BERTEAUCOURT	13-1-19		Training	
"	14-1-19		"	
"	15-1-19		Practice Parade. ceremonial for Presentation of Colours (Brigade Parade)	
"	16-1-19		Training	
"	17-1-19		Practice Parade. ceremonial for Presentation of Colours. (Brigade Parade)	
"	18-1-19		Training	
"	19-1-19		Church Parade.	
"	20-1-19		Practice Parade Ceremonial for Presentation of Colours (Brigade Parade)	
"	21-1-19		Battn Route march. 2½ hours.	
"	22-1-19		Ceremonial Parade. Presentation of Colours by the Divisional Commander to this Battn and the 9th Welch Regt.	
"	23-1-19		Baths. BERTEAUCOURT.	
"	24-1-19		Training	
"	25-1-19		Training	
"	26-1-19		Church Parades.	

Army Form C. 2118.

WAR DIARY
or
INTELLIGENCE SUMMARY.
(Erase heading not required.)

SHEET III

Instructions regarding War Diaries and Intelligence Summaries are contained in F. S. Regs., Part II. and the Staff Manual respectively. Title pages will be prepared in manuscript.

Place	Date	Hour	Summary of Events and Information	Remarks and references to Appendices
BERTEAUCOURT	27-1-19.		Training.	
"	28-1-19.		Batt Route March. 2½ hours.	
"	29-1-19.		Training.	
"	30-1-19.		"	
"	31-1-19.		"	
			The training carried out by the Batt has consisted of Steady Drill, Musketry, Preliminary, and firing on Range, Physical training, Bayonet training, Extended order drill, and Route marches. Instruction classes for both Senior and Junior N.C.Os have been carried on. Lewis Gun classes and training for Lewis Gunners has been carried out. The training of Signallers has been carried on. Athletic training has consisted of Football, Rugby, Boxing & cross Country Runs. 1 hour Education has been carried out daily	

H L Williams Major Commdg.
9th (S) Batt Royal Welch Fusiliers

Army Form C. 2118

WAR DIARY
9th (S) Batt. Royal Welch Fusiliers
INTELLIGENCE SUMMARY

Instructions regarding War Diaries and Intelligence Summaries are contained in F.S. Regs., Part II. and the Staff Manual respectively. Title Pages will be prepared in manuscript.

(Erase heading not required.)

74

Place	Date	Hour	Summary of Events and Information	Remarks and references to Appendices
BERTEAUCOURT	1.2.19		Training 2 hours partly Education than N.C.O's class. Various fatigues.	
"	2.2.19		Church Parade.	
"	3.2.19		Training & Education as for 1/2/19.	
"	4.2.19		" " " "	
"	5.2.19		" " " "	Outdoor recreation consisted of organised snowball fights, bombing raids with snowballs etc.
"	6.2.19		" " " "	
"	7.2.19		" " " "	
"	8.2.19		" " " "	
"	9.2.19		Church Parade. Afternoon Organised Boxing Competition in Aeroplane Hangar.	
"	10.2.19		Training & Education etc. as for 1/2/19.	During this period outdoor organised games were impossible owing to weather conditions.
"	11.2.19		" " " "	
"	12.2.19		" " " "	"
"	13.2.19		" " " "	
"	14.2.19		" " " "	"
"	15.2.19		" " " "	
"	16.2.19		Church Parade.	
"	17.2.19		Training & Education as for 1/2/19. Companies amalgamated	No I 15 Officers 1920 OR
"	18.2.19		Batt. Roll Call 09.00 hours. Training etc as on 17/1/19. Less education	No II 14 " 1640 OR
"	19.2.19		"	crowd owing to saturation in numbers due to dispersed
"	20.2.19		"	Scratch Football matches between Coys

1875 Wt. W593/826   A.D.S.S./Forms/C. 2118.

WAR DIARY
9th (S) Batt Royal Welsh Fusiliers
INTELLIGENCE SUMMARY

Army Form C. 2118

SHEET II

(Erase heading not required.)

Instructions regarding War Diaries and Intelligence Summaries are contained in F.S. Regs., Part II. and the Staff Manual respectively. Title Pages will be prepared in manuscript.

Place	Date	Hour	Summary of Events and Information	Remarks and references to Appendices
BERTEAUCOURT	24.2.19		Roll Call parade 0900 hours, then dismissed to various fatigues.	
"	25.2.19		"	
"	23.2.19		Batt moved by train from BERTEAUCOURT to Camp at VILLERS L'HOPITAL.	
VILLERS L'HOPITAL	24.2.19		Roll Call Parade & Inspection. meanwhile various fatigues.	
"	25.2.19		— " —	
"	26.2.19		— " —	
"	27.2.19		— " —	
"	28.2.19		Draft of 2 Officers & 93 O.R. retained at CANDAS (NORD) for DUNKIRK to join 26th Batt R.W.F. 59th Division.	
			The Training of the Battn has consisted of Steady Drill, Musketry (firing on Range), Elementary Q. & B.T. & Route March. Instruction Classes for Junior N.C.Os. have been carried on until 15th Feb. Lewis Gun Classes training Lewis Gunners have been carried on until the same date. The signallers have constant practice in all branches of training. Athletic training has been interfered with considerably by the weather, whenever possible games have been organised.	

Signed L M Jones Lieut & Adjt
9th (S) Batt Royal Welsh Fusiliers

9th (S) Bn Royal Welch Fusiliers

Army Form C. 2118.

WAR DIARY
or
INTELLIGENCE SUMMARY.

(Erase heading not required.)

Sheet II.
Vol 4 5

Place	Date	Hour	Summary of Events and Information	Remarks and references to Appendices
Villers Hopital	1-3-19		Extracts from XVII Corps Routine orders of 25-2-19. The Army Commander has awarded the "Military Medal" to the undermentioned N.C.O's in connection with the forthcoming Peace Despatch. 23669 Sgt Reece W. G. 10912 " Penlington B.	Cased
"	2-3-19		Church Parades	
"	3-3-19		Cleaning up and sorting of stores preparing to reduction of Batt to Cadre.	
"	"			
"	"			
"	"			
"	18-3-19		Decorations. Chevalier Star of Roumania. Capt & A/Adjt W. R. Rogt attached 9th R.W.F. "Croix de Richie Militaire" 2nd Class. 13102 Sgt Roberts J.	

9th (S) Batt Royal Welch Fusiliers
WAR DIARY
or
INTELLIGENCE SUMMARY.

Army Form C. 2118.

Sheet II

Place	Date	Hour	Summary of Events and Information	Remarks and references to Appendices
Williard Hospital	19-3-19 to 31-3-19		Clearing up and sorting of stores preparatory to reduction of Batt. to "cadre".	
"			During the month drafts of returning men have been sent to the 26th Bn Royal Welch Fusiliers stationed at Dunkirk. The Batt. is now practically reduced to "cadre".	
Nurses' Hospital 31-3-19				

H.J. Williams Major Commdg
9th (S) Bn Royal Welch Fusiliers

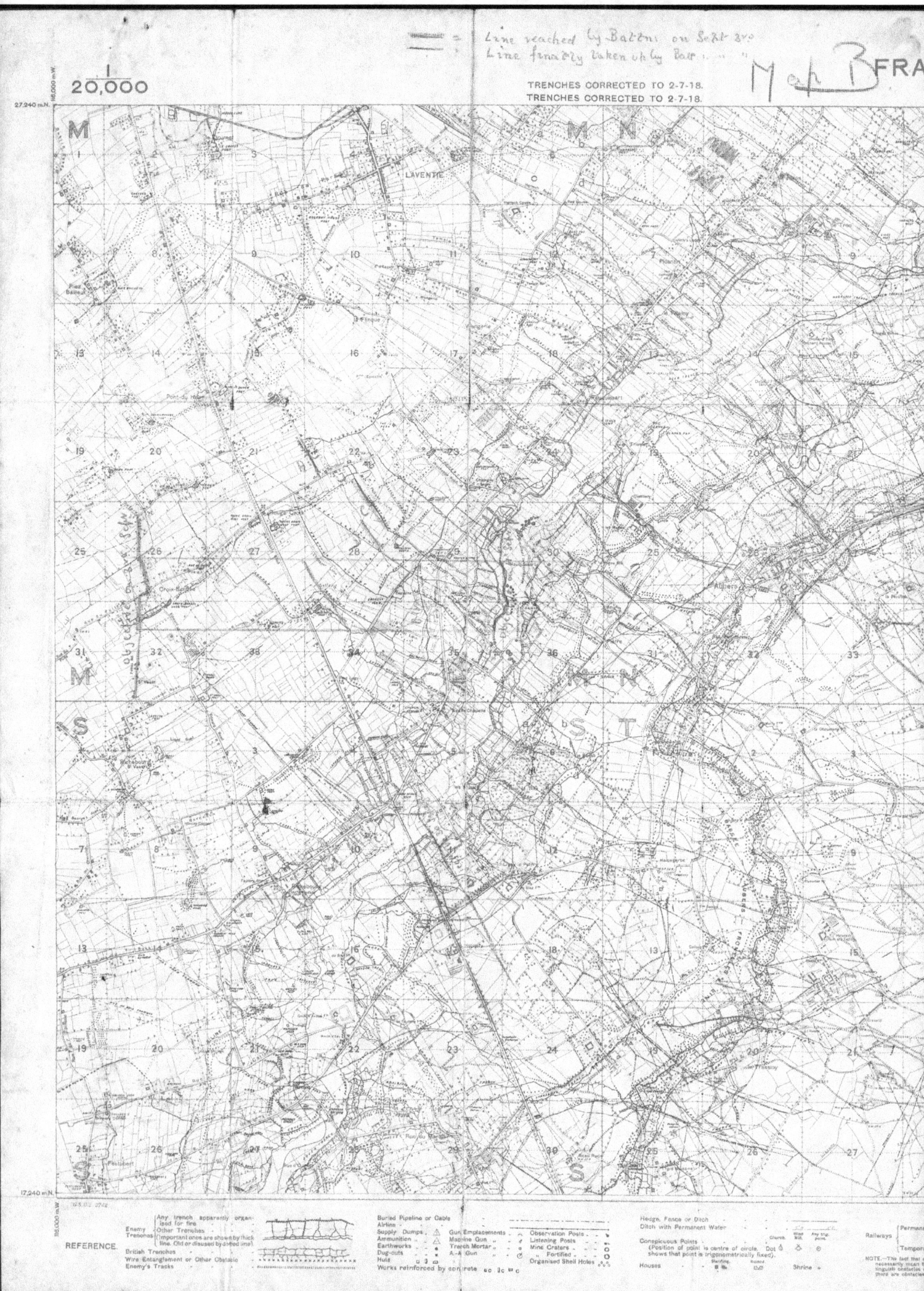

Nacelle	Ferry.
Orme	Elm.
Orphelinat	Orphanage.
Oseraies	Osier-beds.
Ouvrage	Fort.
Ouvrages hydrauliques	Water works.
Papeterie	Paper-mill.
Parc	Park, yard.
,, aérostatique	Aviation ground.
,, à charbon	Coal yard.
,, à pétrole	Petrol store.
Passage à niveau P.N.	Level-crossing.
Passerelle, Pss^{lle}	Foot-bridge.
Pépinière	Nursery-garden.
Peuplier	Poplar tree.
Phare	Light-house.
Pilier, Pil^r	Post.
Plaine d'exercice	Drill ground.
Pompe	Pump.
Ponceau	Culvert.
Pont	Bridge.
,, levis	Drawbridge.
Poste de garde- Station de côte	Coast-guard station.
Poteau P^{eu}	Post.
Poterie	Pottery.
Poudrière, Poud^{re} Magasin à poudre	Powder magazine.
Prise d'eau	Water supply.
Puits	Pit-head, Shaft, Well.
,, artesien	Artesian well.
,, d'épuisage ,, ventilateur ,, de sondage	Ventilating shaft. Boring.
Quai	Quay, Platform.
,, aux bestiaux	Cattle platform.
,, aux marchandises	Goods platform.
Raccordement	Junction.
Raffinerie	Refinery.
,, de sucre	Sugar refinery.
Râperie	Beet-root factory.

Remblai	Embankment.
Remise (des Machines) (aux)	Engine-shed.
Réservoir, Rés^r	Reservoir.
Route cavalière	Bridle road.
Rubanerie Ruine	Ribbon Factory.
Ruines En ruine Ruiné - o	Ruin.
Sablière	Sand-pit.
Sablonnière, Sablon^{re}	
Sapin	Fir tree.
Saule	Willow tree.
Saunerie	Salt-works.
Scierie, Sc^{ie}	Saw-mill.
Sondage	Boring.
Source	Spring.
Sucrerie, Suc^{rie}	Sugar factory.
Tannerie	Tannery.
Tir à la cible	Rifle range.
Tissage	Weaving mill.
Tôlerie	Rolling mill.
Tombeau	Tomb.
Tour	Tower.
Tourbière	Peat-bog, Peat-bed.
Tourelle	Small tower.
Tuilerie	Tile works.
Usine à gaz	Gas works.
,, d'électricité	Electricity works.
,, métallurgique	Metal works.
,, à agglomérés	Briquette factory.
Verrerie, Verr^{ie}	Glass works.
Viaduc	Viaduct
Vivier	Fish Pond.
Voie de chargement ,, ,, déchargement ,, ,, d'évitement ,, ,, formation ,, ,, manœuvre	Siding.
Zinguerie	Zinc works.

INSTRUCTIONS AS TO THE USE OF THE SQUARES.

1. The large rectangles on the map, lettered M, N, S, etc., are divided into squares of 1,000 yards side, which are numbered 1, 2, 3, etc. Each of these squares is sub-divided into four minor squares of 500 yards side. These minor squares are considered as lettered a, b, c, d. (See Square No. 6 in each rectangle.) A point may thus be described as lying within Square R.6, M.5.b, etc.

2. To locate a point within a small square, consider the side divided into tenths, and define the point by taking as many tenths from W. to E. along Southern side, and so many from S. to N. along Western side; the S.W. corner always being taken as origin, and the distance along the Southern side being always given by the first figure. Thus the point X would be 63; i.e., 6 divisions East and 3 divisions North from origin.

3. When more accurate definition is wanted (on the 1 : 20,000 or 1 : 10,000 scales) use exactly the same method, but divide side into 100 parts and use four figures instead of two. Thus 0047 denotes 00 parts East and 47 parts North of origin (see point X). Point Y is 6599.

4. Use 6 but not 10; use either two or four figures; do not use fractions (½, ¼, etc.).

On squared maps all bearings should be given with reference to the vertical grid lines, which are parallel to the East and West edges of the sheet. Bearings should always be reckoned clockwise from 0° to 360°.

Grid bearings are less than compass bearings, the difference being called the deviation of the compass. To find out what this deviation is, take a compass bearing to a distant point, and measure on the map the grid bearing to this point. The difference between the two bearings is the deviation of that compass from Grid North. To obtain the grid bearing of any point this deviation must be subtracted from the compass bearing (adding 360° to the latter if necessary).

On this sheet the mean deviation of a normal compass is 11° 41′, but to obtain accurate results the exact deviation of each compass should be tested as described above, and this test should be repeated in each locality.

TABLE FOR CONVERTING METRES TO FEET.

Mtrs.	0	1	2	3	4	5	6	7	8	9
0	0	3·3	6·6	9·8	13·1	16·4	19·7	23·0	26·2	29·5
10	32·8	36·1	39·4	42·6	45·9	49·2	52·5	55·8	59·0	62·3
20	65·6	68·9	72·2	75·4	78·7	82·0	85·3	88·6	91·8	95·1
30	98·4	101·7	105·0	108·2	111·5	114·8	118·1	121·4	124·6	127·9
40	131·2	134·5	137·8	141·0	144·3	147·6	150·9	154·1	157·4	160·7
50	164·0	167·3	170·6	173·8	177·1	180·4	183·7	187·0	190·2	193·5
60	196·8	200·1	203·4	206·6	209·9	213·2	216·5	219·8	223·0	226·3
70	229·6	232·9	236·2	239·4	242·7	246·0	249·3	252·6	255·8	259·1
80	262·4	265·7	269·0	272·2	275·5	278·8	282·1	285·4	288·6	291·9
90	295·2	298·5	301·8	305·0	308·3	311·6	314·9	318·1	321·4	324·7
100	328·0	331·3	334·6	337·8	341·1	344·4	347·7	351·0	354·2	357·5

TRENCH MAP.
FRANCE.
SHEET 36 S.W.
EDITION 11 A

INDEX TO ADJOINING SHEETS

SCALE 1/20,000.

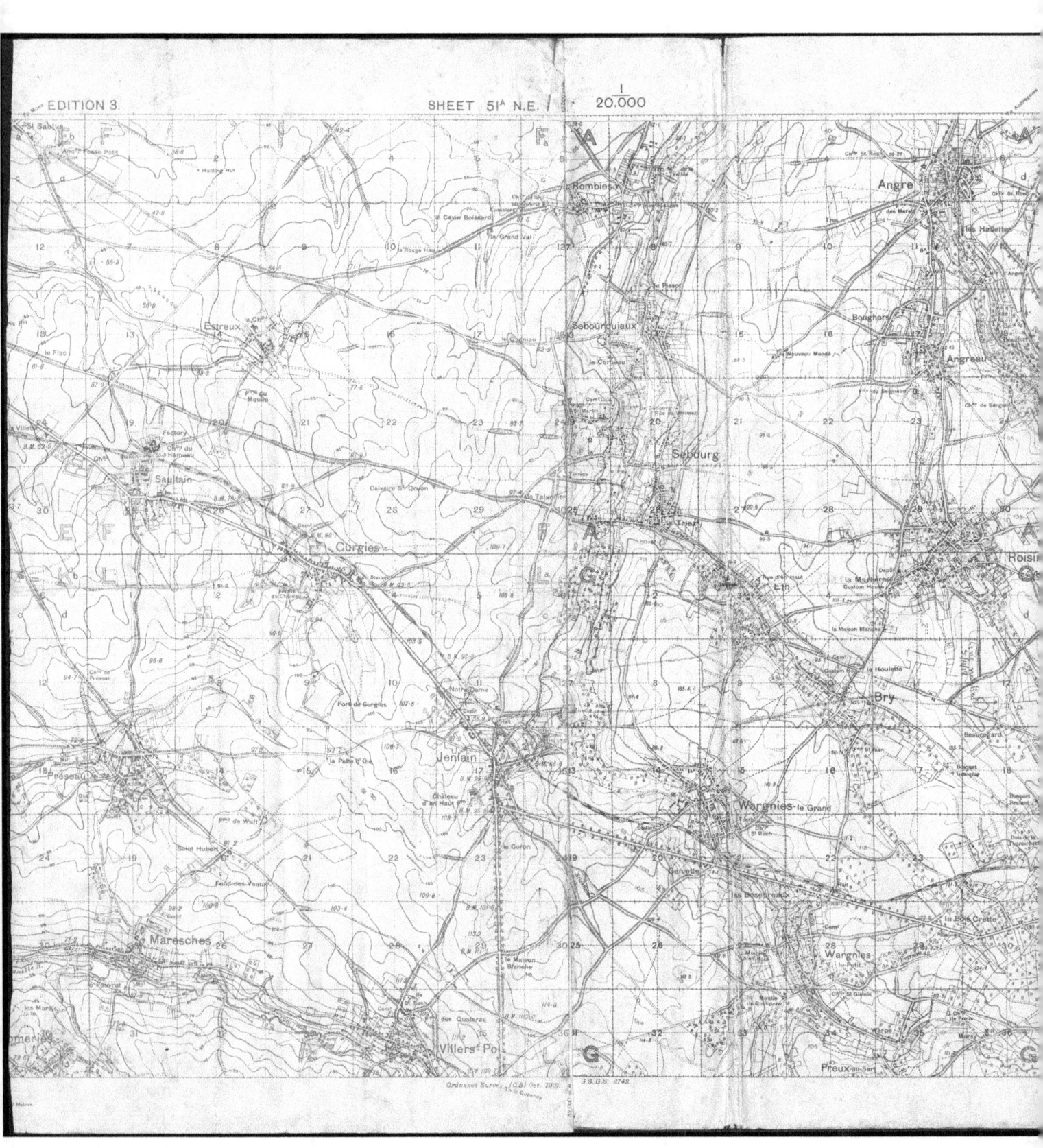

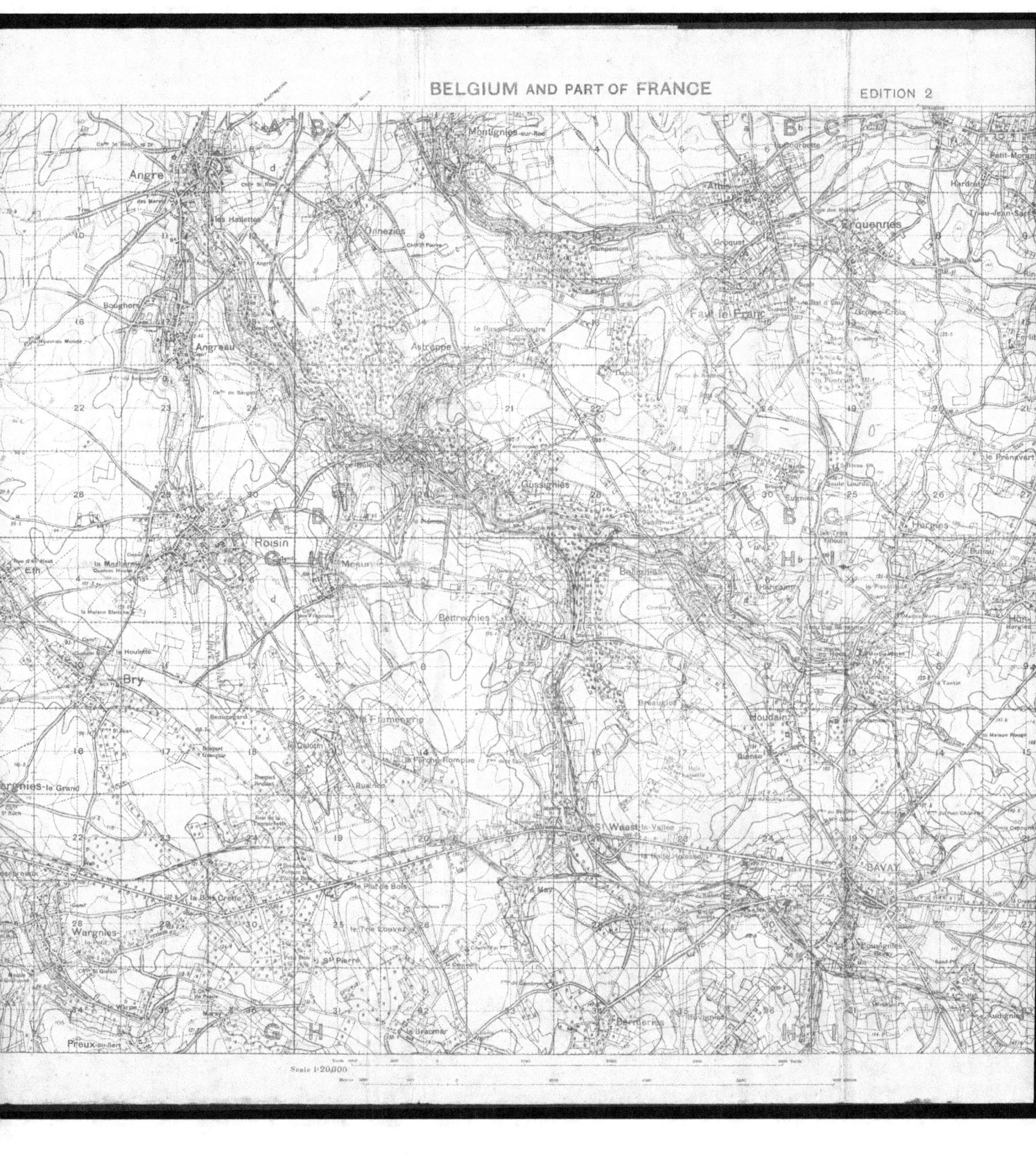

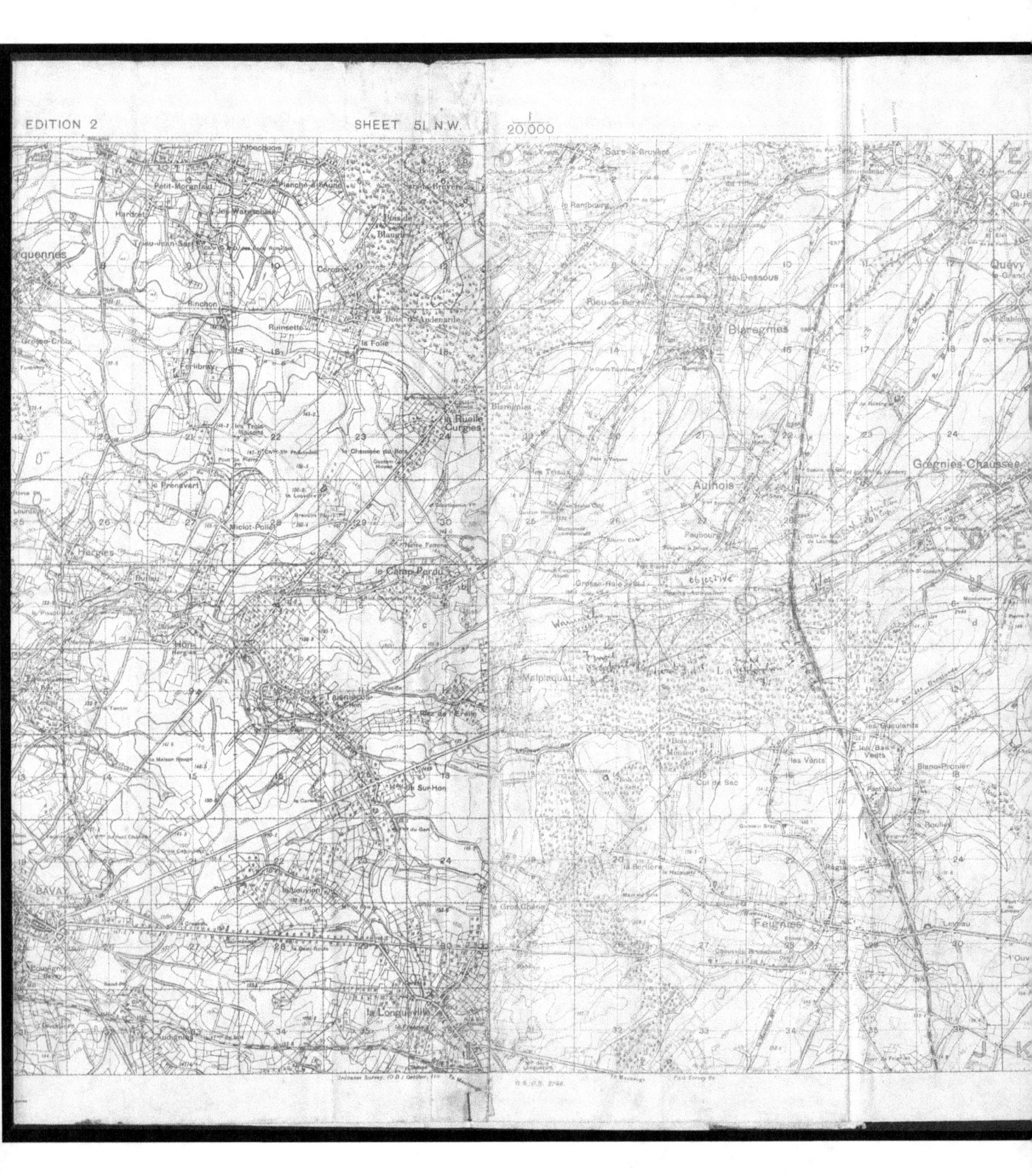

www.ingramcontent.com/pod-product-compliance
Lightning Source LLC
Chambersburg PA
CBHW080831010526
44112CB00015B/2490